Ready to Test

SKILLS & STRATEGIES

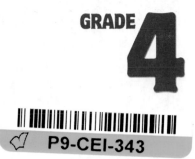

P9-CEI-343

AMERICAN EDUCATION PUBLISHING™

An imprint of Carson-Dellosa Publishing
Greensboro, NC

American Education Publishing™
An imprint of Carson-Dellosa Publishing LLC
P.O. Box 35665
Greensboro, NC 27425 USA

Printed in the USA • All rights reserved.   ISBN 978-1-60996-536-5

01-363117784

Table of Contents

Language Arts
Reading

Language Arts
Language

Math

Chapter 6: Concepts

Chapter 7: Computation

Chapter 8: Geometry

Chapter 9: Measurement

Chapter 10: Applications

Letter to Parents

Dear Parents and Guardians:

The *Ready to Test* series will prepare your child for standardized tests by providing him or her with test-taking tips and strategies for success. The sample questions and tests in this book will allow your child to gain familiarity with standardized tests, making him or her more comfortable on test day and, therefore, more likely to do well.

You can help your child with this important part of learning. Allow your child to become familiar with the testing strategies presented in this book. If your child gets stuck at any point when completing the book, encourage him or her to think of those tips to help determine what to do.

Time your child to help him or her learn time management when taking tests. On average, a lesson page in this book should take about 10 minutes to complete. A Practice Test should take about 45–60 minutes to complete. Keep in mind, however, that the goal is not how fast your child can complete each page. Instead, the goal is to provide practice and strategies for success on test day.

Below are some additional suggestions that will help your child make the most of *Ready to Test*:

- Provide a quiet place to work.
- Go over the work with your child.
- Tell your child he or she is doing a good job.
- Remind him or her to use the tips that are included throughout the book.

By preparing your child with test-taking tips and strategies, *Ready to Test* can help take the fear out of standardized tests and help your child achieve the best scores possible.

Introduction

About the Common Core State Standards

The Common Core State Standards Initiative is a state-led effort developed in collaboration with teachers, school administrators, and experts to provide a clear and consistent framework to prepare children for college and the workforce. The standards are based on the most effective models from states across the country. They provide teachers and parents with a common understanding of what students are expected to learn. Consistent standards will provide appropriate benchmarks for all students, regardless of where they live.

The Common Core State Standards provide a consistent, clear understanding of what students are expected to learn, so teachers and parents know how to help them. The standards are designed to be relevant to the real world, reflecting the knowledge and skills that children need for success in college and their future careers. With students fully prepared for the future, our communities and our country will be best positioned to compete successfully in the global economy.

These standards define the knowledge and skills students should have within their education so that they will graduate high school able to succeed in college and in workforce training programs. The standards:

- are aligned with college and work expectations.

- are clear, understandable, and consistent.

- include rigorous content and application of knowledge through high-order skills.

- build upon strengths and lessons of current state standards.

- are informed by other top-performing countries, so that all students are prepared to succeed in our global economy and society.

- are evidence-based.

Common Core Standards: Language Arts

The Language Arts standards focus on five key areas. Students who are proficient in these areas are able to demonstrate independence, build strong content knowledge, comprehend as well as critique, respond to the varying demands of the task, value evidence, use technology strategically and effectively, and understand other perspectives and cultures.

Reading

The Common Core Standards establish increasing complexity in what students must be able to read, so that all students are ready for the demands of college- and career-level reading. The standards also require the progressive development of reading comprehension, so that students are able to gain more from what they read.

Writing

The ability to write logical arguments based on substantive claims, sound reasoning, and relevant evidence is a cornerstone of the writing standards. Research is emphasized throughout the standards but most prominently in the writing strand, since a written analysis and presentation of findings is often critical.

Speaking and Listening

The standards require that students gain, evaluate, and present increasingly complex information, ideas, and evidence through listening and speaking, as well as through media.

Language

The standards expect that students will grow their vocabularies through a mix of conversations, direct instruction, and reading. The standards will help students determine word meanings, appreciate the nuances of words, and steadily expand their vocabulary of words and phrases.

Media and Technology

Skills related to media use are integrated throughout the standards, just as media and technology are integrated in school curriculum for life in the 21st century.

Common Core Standards: Math

The mathematically proficient student must be able to:

Make sense of problems and persevere in solving them. Mathematically proficient students start by thinking about the meaning of a problem and deciding upon the best way to find the solution. They think the problem through while solving it, and they continually ask themselves, "Does this make sense?"

Reason abstractly and quantitatively. Mathematically proficient students make sense of quantities and their relationships in problem situations. Quantitative reasoning entails an understanding of the problem at hand; paying attention to the units involved; considering the meaning of quantities, not just how to compute them; and knowing and using different properties of operations and objects.

Construct viable arguments and critique the reasoning of others. Mathematically proficient students understand and use stated assumptions, definitions, and previously established results in constructing arguments. Students at all grades can listen or read the arguments of others, decide whether they make sense, and ask useful questions to clarify or improve the arguments.

Model with mathematics. Mathematically proficient students can apply the math they've learned to solve problems arising in everyday life.

Use appropriate tools strategically. Mathematically proficient students consider the available tools when solving a mathematical problem and make appropriate decisions about when each of these tools might be helpful.

Attend to precision. Mathematically proficient students try to communicate precisely to others and in their own reasoning. They state the meaning of the symbols they choose. They calculate accurately and express answers efficiently.

Look for and make use of structure. Mathematically proficient students look closely to discern a pattern or structure. Students can also step back for an overview and shift perspective.

Look for and express regularity in repeated reasoning. Mathematically proficient students look for patterns and shortcuts. As they work to solve a problem, students continue to keep the big picture in mind while attending to the details. They continually evaluate whether or not their results make logical sense.

To learn more about the Common Core State Standards, visit corestandards.org.

Synonyms

Directions: Read each item. Choose the word that means the same, or about the same, as the underlined word.

Example

a fast <u>vehicle</u>

(A) runner

(B) animal

(C) car

(D) computer

Answer: C

1. attend a <u>conference</u>

(A) party

(B) game

(C) meeting

(D) race

2. a <u>beautiful</u> painting

(F) pretty

(G) interesting

(H) colorful

(J) light

3. <u>repair</u> the car

(A) clean

(B) drive

(C) fix

(D) sell

4. a <u>thin</u> slice

(F) short

(G) skinny

(H) long

(J) wide

5. To <u>rush</u> through your homework is to _____.

(A) relax

(B) slow

(C) finish

(D) hurry

6. <u>Raw</u> vegetables are _____.

(F) uncooked

(G) green

(H) smelly

(J) young

7. A <u>dim</u> light bulb is _____.

(A) dull

(B) bright

(C) unintelligent

(D) new

8. To walk <u>quickly</u> is to walk _____.

(F) confidently

(G) carefully

(H) rapidly

(J) happily

Not sure about the right answer?

Try each answer choice in place of the underlined word. Choose the one that makes the most sense.

Name _____   Date _____

Synonyms

Directions: Read each item. Choose the word that means the same, or about the same, as the underlined word.

1. a <u>venomous</u> snake

- (A) vicious
- (B) poisonous
- (C) sharp
- (D) huge

2. <u>encourage</u> friends

- (F) fascinate
- (G) worry
- (H) cheer up
- (J) disappoint

3. a <u>mature</u> person

- (A) grown-up
- (B) dying
- (C) new
- (D) green

4. The teacher was <u>irritated</u>.

- (F) excited
- (G) helpful
- (H) annoyed
- (J) boring

5. His pants were <u>baggy</u>.

- (A) loose
- (B) brown
- (C) too small
- (D) made of cotton

6. He was the first <u>conductor</u> of the train.

- (F) driver
- (G) janitor
- (H) owner
- (J) rider

7. Sharon was <u>elated</u> when she won.

- (A) grim
- (B) joyful
- (C) outside
- (D) unpleasant

Are you having trouble with a question?

First, eliminate any choices you know are wrong. Then, select your answer from the remaining choices.

Chapter 1: Vocabulary

Antonyms

Directions: Read each item. Choose the word that means the opposite of the underlined word.

Example

recall information

- (A) forget
- (B) remember
- (C) write
- (D) find

Answer: (A)

---

1. refuse an offer
- (A) deny
- (B) reply
- (C) change
- (D) accept

2. a messy room
- (F) strange
- (G) old
- (H) untidy
- (J) neat

3. a bent branch
- (A) broken
- (B) straight
- (C) curved
- (D) sharp

4. a strong personality
- (F) powerful
- (G) weak
- (H) annoying
- (J) unusual

5. a rough board
- (A) large
- (B) heavy
- (C) smooth
- (D) long

6. a docile animal
- (F) vicious
- (G) gentle
- (H) shy
- (J) active

7. an active child
- (A) immobile
- (B) exhausted
- (C) bored
- (D) thrilled

8. left promptly
- (F) late
- (G) recently
- (H) quietly
- (J) slowly

9. Shauna visits us often.
- (A) never
- (B) weekly
- (C) sometimes
- (D) always

Name _____ Date _____

Antonyms

Directions: Read each item. Choose the word that means the opposite of the underlined word.

1. Sachiko was <u>disappointed</u> when it rained.

- Ⓐ saddened
- Ⓑ pleased
- Ⓒ relieved
- Ⓓ entertained

2. The car was <u>fast</u>.

- Ⓕ shallow
- Ⓖ sluggish
- Ⓗ speedy
- Ⓙ rabbit

3. The dog's fur felt <u>silky</u>.

- Ⓐ soft
- Ⓑ smooth
- Ⓒ rough
- Ⓓ dirty

4. Banana slugs are <u>moist</u> to the touch.

- Ⓕ dry
- Ⓖ slimy
- Ⓗ rough
- Ⓙ rubbery

5. What time will the plane <u>arrive</u>?

- Ⓐ depart
- Ⓑ land
- Ⓒ call
- Ⓓ glide

6. The story is about a <u>foolish</u> frog.

- Ⓕ funny
- Ⓖ young
- Ⓗ mean
- Ⓙ wise

7. The sun seemed to <u>disappear</u>.

- Ⓐ exit
- Ⓑ brighten
- Ⓒ appear
- Ⓓ rise

If you are not sure which answer is correct, take your best guess.

Don't forget to eliminate some of the answer choices first, if you can!

Multiple-Meaning Words

Directions: Choose the answer in which the underlined word is used in the same way as it is in the box.

Example

Please ☐file☐ these papers.

(A) The counselor pulled out her file on the Jones family.

(B) Sally used a file to smooth her fingernails.

(C) I put the file cards in order.

(D) Ms. Greenbaum asked her secretary to file the reports on water safety.

Answer: D

---

1. I used a ☐lemon☐ to make lemonade.

(A) The color of the baby's room is lemon.

(B) That car was a lemon.

(C) This cleaner has a lovely lemon scent.

(D) Rachel bought a lemon at the store.

2. She could never reach the right ☐note☐ on the piano.

(F) Please make a note of this change.

(G) I wrote a note so you will not forget.

(H) The musical note he asked us to play was C.

(J) Note the large size of the buildings.

3. Aaron scored two ☐goals☐ in yesterday's game.

(A) What are your goals for the summer?

(B) One of my goals is to learn how to play the piano.

(C) The Lions need three more goals to win the game.

(D) Mario is going to set some goals for the school year.

4. Liam asked for a ☐second☐ helping of lasagna.

(F) Brianna was the second person in line at the theater.

(G) I'll be ready in a second.

(H) One second is equal to $\frac{1}{60}$ of a minute.

(J) Let me know the second you hear the news.

5. Did you notice the ☐spot☐ on your shirt?

(A) Miyako tried to spot the owl in the tree.

(B) Omar wanted to find a spot near the front of the room.

(C) I could spot you a mile away!

(D) The red paint made a small spot on the floor.

> If a question is too difficult, skip it and come back to it later if you have time.

Multiple-Meaning Words

Directions: Read the two sentences. Choose the word that fits best in both sentences.

1. Will you _____ me the new painting you made?
   My parents are going to dinner and a _____ for their anniversary.

   (A) display
   (B) show
   (C) movie
   (D) sell

2. The walls need another _____ of paint.
   Myla just got a new winter _____.

   (F) jacket
   (G) layer
   (H) hat
   (I) coat

3. Do you feel _____?
   We get our water from a _____.

   (A) well
   (B) good
   (C) pipe
   (D) sick

4. Mrs. Johnson said Carrie was a _____ student.
   The light from the headlights was _____.

   (F) noisy
   (G) red
   (H) bright
   (J) hard-working

5. The surface of the car was _____.
   Mr. Abed gave a _____ speech.

   (A) dirty
   (B) shiny
   (C) painted
   (D) dull

6. Aunt Harriet showed me her _____ ring.
   Let's meet at the baseball _____ at 2:00.

   (F) beautiful
   (G) diamond
   (H) field
   (J) ruby

7. Set the package _____ to the side.
   We had the day _____.

   (A) over
   (B) off
   (C) apart
   (D) away

8. Bess put a clean _____ on the bed.
   Jason washed the cookie _____ after he finished baking.

   (F) pillow
   (G) tray
   (H) sheet
   (J) cover

Words in Context

Directions: Read the paragraph. Choose the word that fits best in each numbered blank.

Examples

In-line skating might be the fastest-growing _____ **(A)** in America. Typical _____ **(B)** follow roads, sidewalks, or bike paths. This sport is relatively new, but it is already enjoyed by people young and old.

A. (A) thing

    (B) people

    (C) town

    (D) sport

B. (F) skaters

    (G) vehicles

    (H) hikers

    (J) results

Answer: D

Answer: F

> Read the passage once. Then, carefully read each sentence with a blank. Use the meaning of the sentence to find the answer.

Glass is an amazing substance. Made by heating sand with a few other simple chemicals, glass is both _____ **(1)** and beautiful. In the _____ **(2)**, you drink your juice in a glass. At your school, you may _____ **(3)** the building through a glass door. The lights inside the school are made of glass, as is the _____ **(4)** of the computer you will use. If you go to gym class, the basketball backboard might even be made of glass. Your family may have pieces of glass as decorations around the house, and if you go to a _____ **(5)**, you might see _____ **(6)** glass from hundreds of years ago.

1. (A) ugly

    (B) useful

    (C) cloudy

    (D) thin

2. (F) evening

    (G) time

    (H) morning

    (J) mood

3. (A) open

    (B) see

    (C) like

    (D) enter

4: (F) inside

    (G) keyboard

    (H) screen

    (J) mouse

5. (A) aquarium

    (B) bus stop

    (C) gas station

    (D) museum

6. (F) new

    (G) antique

    (H) full

    (J) broken

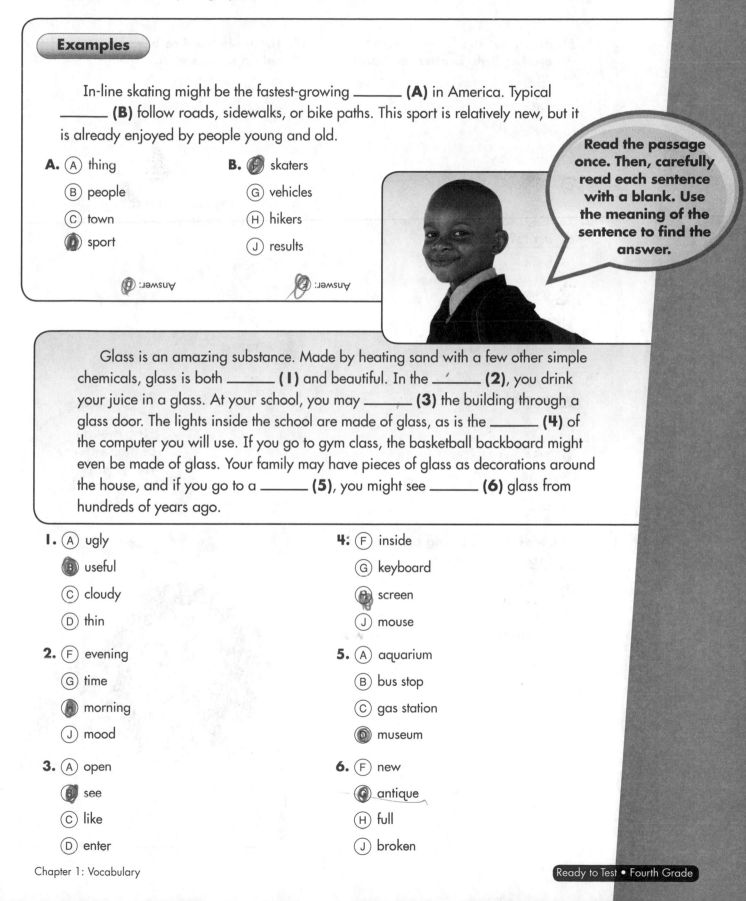

Words in Context

Directions: Find the answer choice that means the same thing as the underlined word.

1. Madison put the <u>fragile</u> vase where her little brother couldn't reach it.

(A) rare

(B) beautiful

(C) brand-new

(D) delicate

2. Is the information in your report <u>accurate</u>?

(F) interesting

(G) correct

(H) incorrect

(J) confusing

3. Everyone received an equal <u>portion</u> of the pie.

(A) share

(B) slice

(C) weight

(D) size

4. The leaf was floating on the <u>surface</u> of the water.

(F) underneath

(G) back

(H) bottom

(J) top

5. The mole tried to <u>burrow</u> under the soil in the garden.

(A) run

(B) hide

(C) dig

(D) sleep

6. Mr. D'Angelo wanted to <u>request</u> that the band play his favorite song.

(F) guess

(G) ask for

(H) pretend

(J) believe

The meaning of the sentence will give you a clue about which answer to choose.

Word Study

Directions: Read each item, and mark the best answer.

Example

Which of these words probably comes from the <u>Latin</u> word *circuitus*, meaning *a going around*?

- (A) circus
- (B) circuit
- (C) cirrus
- (D) circa

Answer: (B)

---

1. Which of these words probably comes from the Greek word *logos*, meaning *word or speech*?

- (A) locate
- (B) logo
- (C) lodge
- (D) log

2. Which of these words probably comes from the French word *ravager*, meaning *to uproot*?

- (F) ravage
- (G) ravel
- (H) rave
- (J) ravine

3. The Greek root *graph* means *to write*. Which of the following words means *a book written about a person's life*?

- (A) paragraph
- (B) autograph
- (C) geography
- (D) biography

4. The Latin root *ped* means *foot*. Which of the following words means *an insect with many feet*?

- (F) pedal
- (G) centipede
- (H) pedestrian
- (J) petal

5. The owner had to _____ the puppy for chewing the shoes. Which word means *to speak harshly*?

- (A) scold
- (B) pursue
- (C) alert
- (D) inspire

6. José _____ his report to include a section on bugs. Which word means he *changed it by adding something*?

- (F) wrote
- (G) amended
- (H) erased
- (J) corrected

Mark the correct answer as soon as you find it!

Word Study

Directions: Choose the answer that best defines the underlined part of the words.

1. **wonder<u>ful</u>**   **mouth<u>ful</u>**
   - Ⓐ to be doing
   - Ⓑ full of
   - Ⓒ outside
   - Ⓓ underneath

2. **<u>mis</u>take**   **<u>mis</u>lead**
   - Ⓕ correctly
   - Ⓖ before
   - Ⓗ to do after
   - Ⓙ wrongly

3. **<u>over</u>charge**   **<u>over</u>cook**
   - Ⓐ too much
   - Ⓑ too little
   - Ⓒ under
   - Ⓓ against

4. **<u>re</u>live**   **<u>re</u>check**
   - Ⓕ many
   - Ⓖ to do before
   - Ⓗ partly
   - Ⓙ to do again

5. **<u>bi</u>cycle**   **<u>bi</u>monthly**
   - Ⓐ one
   - Ⓑ many
   - Ⓒ two
   - Ⓓ three

6. **notice<u>able</u>**   **understand<u>able</u>**
   - Ⓕ made of
   - Ⓖ full of
   - Ⓗ able to be
   - Ⓙ more than

7. **<u>non</u>fiction**   **<u>non</u>sense**
   - Ⓐ true
   - Ⓑ empty
   - Ⓒ humorous
   - Ⓓ not

8. **<u>trans</u>portation**   **<u>trans</u>fer**
   - Ⓕ across
   - Ⓖ above
   - Ⓗ under
   - Ⓙ round

Sample Test 1: Vocabulary

Directions: Choose the word that means the same, or about the same, as the underlined word.

Example

calm <u>ocean</u>

- (A) water
- (B) sea
- (C) lake
- (D) body

Answer: (B)

1. a <u>high</u> fence
- (A) tall
- (B) happy
- (C) long
- (D) wide

2. <u>paste</u> the paper
- (F) fold
- (G) attach
- (H) patch
- (J) glue

3. <u>fix</u> the car
- (A) polish
- (B) repair
- (C) sell
- (D) buy

4. a <u>chilly</u> day
- (F) long
- (G) frozen
- (H) cold
- (J) unpleasant

5. If something is moving <u>swiftly</u>, it is moving
- (A) slowly.
- (B) smoothly.
- (C) quickly.
- (D) on the land.

6. <u>Shallow</u> means
- (F) not intelligent.
- (G) deep.
- (H) not deep.
- (J) able to swim.

7. To <u>remain</u> is to
- (A) stay.
- (B) leave early.
- (C) go to the middle.
- (D) do over again.

8. That store was the <u>nearest</u>.
- (F) the most distant
- (G) the biggest
- (H) the best
- (J) the closest

GO

Name _____ Date _____

Sample Test 1: Vocabulary

Directions: Choose the meaning for each underlined word.

9. The wings of the butterfly were <u>fluttering</u> in the breeze.

(A) waving

(B) colorful

(C) lovely

(D) flashing

10. Gazelles and impalas are <u>prey</u> to the cheetah.

(F) food

(G) friends

(H) similar

(J) predators

11. David gave his sister a <u>smirk</u>.

(A) friendly smile

(B) scar

(C) smug expression

(D) face mask

12. We were <u>exhausted</u> after running.

(F) very tired

(G) refreshed

(H) excited

(J) wide awake

Directions: Choose the antonym for the underlined word.

13. a <u>valuable</u> painting

(A) strange

(B) expensive

(C) worthless

(D) humorous

14. a <u>loose</u> tie

(F) tight

(G) lost

(H) plain

(J) ill-fitting

15. a <u>narrow</u> ledge

(A) thin

(B) cement

(C) skinny

(D) wide

16. We <u>always</u> use this road to go to school.

(F) never

(G) sometimes

(H) usually

(J) frequently

17. The workers want to <u>unpack</u> the trunk.

(A) carry

(B) pack

(C) remove

(D) move

18. Ahmad was <u>awake</u> most of the night.

(F) up

(G) asleep

(H) restless

(J) watching TV

GO

Sample Test 1: Vocabulary

Directions: Read the two sentences. Choose the word that best fits the blanks in both sentences.

19. The sun _____ at 5:45.
A _____ grew beside the steps.

- (A) appeared
- (B) rose
- (C) flower
- (D) set

20. It's not safe to _____ a boat.
This _____ is too heavy to move.

- (F) sink
- (G) stone
- (H) push
- (J) rock

21. What _____ will you be on vacation?
I enjoy eating _____.

- (A) days
- (B) fruit
- (C) weeks
- (D) dates

22. Follow the deer tracks.

In which sentence does *tracks* mean the same thing as in the sentence above?

- (F) The train moved swiftly on the tracks.
- (G) Gerald tracks satellites for the government.
- (H) The dog made tracks in the snow.
- (J) Never stop your car on the train tracks.

23. Hand me the plant with the tiny pink flowers.

In which sentence does *plant* mean the same thing as in the sentence above?

- (A) The electric plant was a busy place to work.
- (B) Plant those bushes here.
- (C) They used Joe as a plant to spy on the kids.
- (D) I gave Mom a plant for Mother's Day.

Directions: Choose the answer that best defines the underlined part of the words.

24. mother<u>less</u>   pain<u>less</u>

- (F) with
- (G) like
- (H) more
- (J) without

25. <u>magn</u>ify   <u>magn</u>ificent

- (A) magnetic
- (B) great
- (C) smaller
- (D) open

GO

Sample Test 1: Vocabulary

Directions: Read each item, and mark the best answer.

26. Which of these words probably comes from the Latin word *lampein*, meaning *to shine*?

- (F) lampoon
- (G) lament
- (H) lamp
- (J) lamprey

27. Which of these words probably comes from the Middle English word *ose*, meaning *juice*?

- (A) ooze
- (B) worst
- (C) wowser
- (D) wound

28. _____ Mom had forgotten the can opener.
Which of these words means that it was *unlucky*?

- (F) Fortunately
- (G) Mournfully
- (H) Excitedly
- (J) Unfortunately

29. Anton _____ around the room.
Which of these words means that he *walked in a bragging manner*?

- (A) tiptoed
- (B) strutted
- (C) ran
- (D) skipped

Directions: Read the paragraph. Choose the word that fits best in each numbered blank.

Lindsay is becoming _____ (30). People know about her art and her athletics. She is _____ (31) in the music department for her skills. I'm really _____ (32) of what she's done.

30. (F) famous
- (G) released
- (H) exhausted
- (J) fragile

31. (A) disliked
- (B) prepared
- (C) respected
- (D) always

32. (F) confused
- (G) rejected
- (H) lessened
- (J) proud

STOP

Main Idea

Directions: Read each passage. Answer the questions that follow.

Example

Mario walked back and forth at the end of the pool. He had been practicing his starts for months, and today he would have a chance to show off what he had learned. Just then, Dave walked into the building. Mario felt a lump in his throat. Dave was the one person he would have a hard time beating.

What is the main idea of the story?

(A) Mario has been practicing jumping into the pool.

(B) Mario is nervous about beating Dave in the swimming race.

(C) Dave is just as good at swimming as Mario.

(D) Mario is a good swimmer.

Answer: (B)

Skim the passage again after you have read it. Then, read the questions. You don't have to reread the story to answer each question.

Thousands of immigrants arrived each day at Ellis Island in New York. This was one of the reception centers set up by the United States government. The immigrants arrived with high hopes. Many had a great deal to offer the United States. However, not all those who came through Ellis Island were allowed to stay in this country.

Immigrants had forms to fill out, questions to answer, and medical exams to face. They waited for many hours in the Great Hall to hear their names called. Many had spent months in poor conditions on ships to come to the United States to make a better life. They had spent their savings to make the trip. Even after this, some were turned away.

1. What is the main idea of paragraph 1?

(A) Thousands of immigrants arrived each day at Ellis Island.

(B) Many immigrants were not allowed to stay in the United States.

(C) Immigrants to the United States arrived at Ellis Island in New York.

(D) Many immigrants arrived in the United States at Ellis Island, but not all were allowed to stay.

2. What is the main idea of paragraph 2?

(F) Many immigrants had to go through a lot to get into the United States, and some did not make it.

(G) Immigrants had to stand in long lines.

(H) Many immigrants were poor.

(J) Immigrants stood in the Great Hall waiting for their names to be called.

Main Idea

Directions: Read the passage. Choose the best answer to the questions that follow.

Ryder's grandpa is coming to visit for a week. Ryder is really excited because he and his grandpa have always had a great time together. He's also nervous, though, because his grandpa had a stroke a few months ago. Ryder's mom said Grandpa moves a little more slowly than he used to. "No problem," Ryder thinks, "we'll still have fun."

On the day of Grandpa's arrival, Ryder is up early. He is too excited to sleep. Finally, it is time to go to the airport. Grandpa walks off the plane using a cane. Mom never mentioned that to Ryder. What about their long walks down to the creek? Ryder gives his grandpa a really big hug. Grandpa seems older and frailer than he did during his last visit. Ryder feels a bit sad as he thinks about all the things he and Grandpa used to do together.

Ryder is quiet on the way home. Then, he starts to think of all kinds of new things that he and his grandfather can do together, like build model airplanes, watch movies, put together his train set, and organize his baseball card collection.

"This is going to be a great visit, Grandpa," Ryder says. Grandpa turns around, grins, and squeezes Ryder's hand.

"That's just what I was thinking!" he said.

1. What is the main idea of paragraph 2?

(A) Ryder's grandpa is using a cane.

(B) Ryder is worried that this visit will be different because of Grandpa's stroke.

(C) Ryder and Grandpa plan on putting together Ryder's train set.

(D) Ryder wakes up early on the day of Grandpa's arrival.

2. What is the main idea of paragraph 3?

(F) Ryder is quiet in the car.

(G) Ryder wishes his grandpa were younger.

(H) Ryder asks his grandpa to go to the movies with him.

(J) Ryder thinks of new things he and Grandpa can do together.

3. How does Ryder feel about his grandpa's visit?

(A) exhilarated

(B) anxious

(C) optimistic

(D) depressed

4. What is the turning point in the story?

(F) Ryder sees his grandpa using a cane.

(G) Ryder's grandpa arrives.

(H) Ryder thinks of lots of new things he can do with his grandpa.

(J) Grandpa looks very happy.

Recalling Details/Sequencing

Directions: Read the passage. Choose the best answer to the questions that follow.

Example

A medal was given to Mrs. Garcia for bravery. While going shopping, Mrs. Garcia had seen a house on fire. She could hear someone screaming, so Mrs. Garcia rushed into the house. A minute later, she came out carrying a young boy.

> Read the question and all the answer choices. Once you have decided on the correct answer, ask yourself, "Does this really answer the question being asked?"

How did Mrs. Garcia know there was someone inside the house?

Ⓐ She knew the boy was always at home.

Ⓑ Someone told her.

Ⓒ She saw him.

Ⓓ She could hear him screaming.

Answer: Ⓓ

People around the world use energy every day, and some forms of energy are being used up very quickly. Luckily, resources like energy from the sun, energy from ocean waves, and hydroelectric power do not get used up completely. These resources last and last. They are called *renewable resources*. Hydropower is a renewable resource that is very common. The beginning of the word, *hydro*, refers to water. Hydropower is power that comes from water.

What makes hydropower work? A dam, which looks like a tall cement wall built across a body of water, raises the level of water in an area by blocking it. This causes the water to fall over the side of the dam. The falling water pushes against a machine called a *turbine*. The force of the falling water makes the blades inside spin. A machine called a *generator* captures the power from the spinning turbines. This makes electrical energy and sends out electricity to people who need it.

1. Resources that last a long time are called

Ⓐ hydropower.

Ⓑ energy.

Ⓒ fossil fuels.

Ⓓ renewable resources.

2. What happens after the water falls over the side of the dam?

Ⓕ The dam blocks the water in.

Ⓖ The force makes the blades spin.

Ⓗ The water pushes against the turbine.

Ⓙ A generator captures the power.

Recalling Details/Sequencing

Directions: Read the passage. Choose the best answer to the questions that follow.

Abigail Adams was the wife of one American president and the mother of another. When she was a girl, she had no idea she would grow up to hold such an important position in American history.

Abigail Smith was born in 1744. Although women were not given much schooling in those days, Abigail was allowed to study and read as much as she liked.

Abigail met and married John Adams in 1764. They moved to a farm that John owned in Braintree, Massachusetts. Then, trouble started with the British. John and Abigail sided with the colonists during the Revolutionary War. After helping to write the Declaration of Independence, John played an important part in helping to start the new nation. He always had Abigail to advise him.

Abigail was one of the earliest Americans to support women's rights. When John was working on the Declaration of Independence, she urged him to add a phrase to say that all men and women were equal. During the war, Abigail's letters were John's main way of finding out about the fighting and the location of British ships. After the war was over, she and John were the first people to live in the White House. John depended on Abigail's wisdom and ideas his whole life.

1. What made Abigail's early life unusual?

(A) She ran a farm.

(B) She advised her husband.

(C) She was allowed to read and study as much as she wanted.

(D) She was born in 1744.

2. Which of the following shows the correct order of events?

(F) Abigail and John moved into the White House. The war began.

(G) Abigail's son became president. Abigail studied and read a lot.

(H) John and Abigail moved to a farm. John and Abigail got married.

(J) The war ended. Abigail and John moved into the White House.

3. Why were Abigail's wartime letters important?

(A) They helped her husband feel better.

(B) They reported information about the war.

(C) They told John Adams about his business.

(D) They were well written.

4. Which of the following statements is not true?

(F) Abigail and John were married when she was only 20 years old.

(G) Abigail was an important advisor to her husband.

(H) Abigail began to support women's rights after the signing of the Declaration of Independence.

(J) John and Abigail moved to a farm before the war began.

Determining Meaning Using Content

LANGUAGE ARTS

27

Directions: Read the passage. Choose the best answer to the questions that follow.

> **How much do you know about snakes? Read these snake facts and find out.**
>
> - A snake skeleton has <u>numerous</u> ribs. A large snake may have as many as 400 pairs!
> - Most snakes have <u>poor</u> eyesight. They <u>track</u> other animals by sensing their body heat.
> - Snakes can't blink. They sleep with their eyes open.
> - Although all snakes have teeth, very few of them—only the <u>venomous</u> ones—have fangs.
> - Many snakes are very <u>docile</u> and unlikely to bite people.
> - Pet snakes recognize their owners by smell. They flick their tongues in the air to <u>detect</u> smells.

1. *Numerous* means about the same as _____.

- (A) number
- (B) many
- (C) few
- (D) special

2. In this passage, *poor* means the opposite of _____.

- (F) rich
- (G) good
- (H) happy
- (J) broke

3. What does *track* mean as it is used in this passage?

- (A) the rails on which a train moves
- (B) a sport that includes running, jumping, and throwing
- (C) to follow the footprints of
- (D) to find and follow

4. What does the word *venomous* mean as it is used in this passage?

- (F) vicious
- (G) sharp
- (H) poisonous
- (J) huge

5. Which word means the opposite of *docile*?

- (A) vicious
- (B) shy
- (C) gentle
- (D) active

6. Which word means the same as *detect*?

- (F) enjoy
- (G) arrest
- (H) find
- (J) hide

Determining Meaning Using Content

Directions: Read the passage. Choose the best answer to the questions that follow.

California is a state <u>teeming</u> with life. Not only is it one of the most populous states, it is also one of the country's major farming states. Despite the lack of water in California, farmers have managed to make it a very fertile area.

Fruits, including grapes, grow well in California. California supplies the <u>majority</u> of the grapes in the United States. Many are sold fresh, but they are also turned into raisins, juice, and wine.

In the winter, cuttings from <u>mature</u> grape plants are buried to make new plants. Growers are careful to take special care of the grapevines until they are old enough to <u>produce</u> grapes. Grapes are harvested in the summer and fall. The bunches are carefully cut by hand. This work requires a lot of <u>labor</u>. Many migrant workers are brought into the state from other areas, including Central America. The money that migrant workers earn is very <u>useful</u> to their families, who may live in far less abundant regions.

1. What does the word *teeming* mean as it is used in this passage?

(A) full of

(B) without

(C) nearby

(D) looking for

2. Which word means the opposite of *useful*?

(F) helpful

(G) new

(H) used

(J) useless

3. What does the word *majority* mean as it is used in this passage?

(A) none

(B) few

(C) most

(D) several

4. Which word means the same as *mature*?

(F) young

(G) grown-up

(H) newborn

(J) rotten

5. What does the word *produce* mean as it is used in this passage?

(A) use

(B) fruits and vegetables

(C) destroy

(D) make

6. What does the word *labor* mean as it is used in this passage?

(F) work

(G) time

(H) thought

(J) machines

Making Inferences

Directions: Read the passage. Choose the best answer to the questions that follow.

Example

Sometimes, we see sand dunes near the water. These sand dunes do not always stay in the same place. The wind blows them along. Some sand dunes move only a few feet each year. Others move more than 200 feet in a year.

Sand dunes move the most

(A) near the water.

(B) where it is coldest.

(C) where it is windiest.

(D) where there are a lot of people.

Answer: C

After you read the story, think about why things happened and about what might happen after the story ends.

It's as black as ink out here in the pasture, and I'm exhausted. But even if I were in my bed, I don't think I'd be sleeping tonight.

Last summer for my birthday, my parents gave me my dream horse. Her name is Goldie. She is a beautiful palomino. I love to watch her gallop around the pasture. She looks so carefree when she runs. I hope I'll see her run that way again.

Yesterday, after I fed her, I forgot to close the door to the feed shed. She got into the grain and ate and ate and ate, which is very unhealthy for a horse. The veterinarian said I have to watch her like a hawk tonight to be sure she doesn't get colic—a very bad stomachache. He also said I should keep her moving, so I have walked her around and around the pasture until I feel like we're on a merry-go-round.

Now, the sun is finally beginning to peek over the horizon, and Goldie seems content. I think she's going to be as good as new.

1. What will the narrator most likely do the next time she feeds the horse?

(A) She will feed the horse too much.

(B) She will make sure she closes the feed shed door.

(C) She will give the horse plenty of water.

(D) She will leave the feed shed door open.

2. How much experience do you think the narrator has with horses?

(F) She's probably owned many horses before.

(G) This is probably her first horse. She doesn't have a lot of experience.

(H) She's probably owned a horse before this, but not many.

(J) I can't tell from the story.

Making Inferences

Directions: Read the passage. Choose the best answer to the questions that follow.

The North Star is one of the most famous stars. Its star name is *Polaris*. It is often called the *North Star* because it shines almost directly over the North Pole. If you are at the North Pole, the North Star is overhead. As you travel farther south, the star seems lower in the sky. Only people in the Northern Hemisphere can see the North Star.

Because the North Star is always in the same spot in the sky, it has been used for years to give direction to people at night. Sailors used the North Star to navigate through the oceans.

Polaris, like all stars, is always moving. Thousands of years from now, another star will be the North Star. Vega was the North Star thousands of years before it moved out of position and Polaris took its place.

1. The North Star might be one of the most famous stars because _____.

(A) it is near the North Pole

(B) it is always moving

(C) it is always in the same spot in the sky

(D) it is difficult to find in the sky

2. Another star will someday get to be the North Star because _____.

(F) stars are always moving

(G) there are many stars in the sky

(H) Earth will turn to the South Pole

(J) scientists rename it every 50 years

3. The name *Polaris* most likely comes from which name?

(A) polecat

(B) polar bear

(C) Poland

(D) North Pole

4. Only people in the _____ Hemisphere see the North Star.

(F) Eastern

(G) Western

(H) Northern

(J) Southern

Fact and Opinion

Directions: Read the passage. Choose the best answer to the questions that follow.

Example

The *Hindenburg* was an airship that was 804 feet (245 m) long. Airships are much more interesting than boats. Airships fly in the sky. In 1937, the *Hindenburg* was starting to land but blew up, killing and injuring many people.

Which states an opinion?

Ⓐ Airships fly in the sky.

Ⓑ The *Hindenburg* blew up, killing and injuring many people.

Ⓒ The *Hindenburg* was an airship that was 804 feet (245 m) long.

Ⓓ Airships are much more interesting than boats.

Answer: D

During the 1770s, America worked to gain independence from the British. Many struggles happened as a result.

The British passed a law in 1765 that required legal papers and other items to have a tax stamp. It was called the *Stamp Act*. Colonists were forced to pay a fee for the stamp. Secret groups began to work against the requirement of the tax stamp. The law was finally taken away in 1766.

In 1767, the British passed the Townshend Acts. These acts forced people to pay fees for many items, such as tea, paper, glass, lead, and paint. This wasn't fair.

Colonists were furious. On December 16, 1773, they tossed 342 chests of tea over the sides of ships in Boston Harbor. This was later called the *Boston Tea Party*. Colonists had shown that they would not accept these laws.

I. Which of the following sentences from the story states an opinion?

Ⓐ The British passed a law in 1765 that required legal papers and other items to have a tax stamp.

Ⓑ The law was finally taken away in 1766.

Ⓒ This was later called the *Boston Tea Party*.

Ⓓ This wasn't fair.

2. What caused the colonists to throw 342 chests of tea into Boston Harbor?

Ⓕ They were angry about the Townshend Acts.

Ⓖ They wanted to make a big pot of tea.

Ⓗ The tea was bad.

Ⓙ They were angry because of the Stamp Act.

Name _____ Date _____

Fact and Opinion

Directions: Read the passages. Choose the best answer to the questions that follow.

Bloodhounds are dogs that have a very good sense of smell. They are used by the police to track down people. Bloodhounds have wrinkled faces and long, floppy ears. Most bloodhounds are black and tan.

1. Which of the following is an opinion?

Ⓐ Bloodhounds have long ears.

Ⓑ Bloodhounds are used by the police.

Ⓒ Bloodhounds are good dogs to have around.

Ⓓ Bloodhounds have a special sense of smell.

2. Which of the following is a fact?

Ⓕ Bloodhounds have adorable floppy ears.

Ⓖ Bloodhounds are better police dogs than German shepherds.

Ⓗ Bloodhounds make the best pets.

Ⓙ Bloodhounds have wrinkled faces.

Chandra was eating her lunch when she heard a desperate meow. She ran to the backyard to see what was wrong. Her white kitten, Chloe, was up on a branch and couldn't get down. Chandra looked around the yard. She saw a ladder leaning against the shed. *It's too dangerous for me to use that ladder alone*, thought Chandra.

3. Which of the following is an opinion?

Ⓐ The kitten's meow sounded desperate.

Ⓑ Chandra was eating lunch.

Ⓒ The ladder was leaning against the shed.

Ⓓ Chloe is a white kitten.

4. In the space below, write a fact from the selection.

_____

_____

_____

Facts are pieces of information you can prove. **Opinions** are what people think about things. To see if something is a fact, think about whether or not you could prove it.

Story Elements

Directions: Read the passage. Choose the best answer to the questions that follow.

Example

Maggie and Isabel went to the park on Saturday. They both headed for the slides, but they couldn't decide who should go first. Isabel said she should because she was older. Maggie said she should because Isabel always got to. Just then, Brett came over and said, "Why don't you each get on one slide and start down at the same time?"

And that's just what they did.

What is the turning point of this story?

(A) Maggie and Isabel argue over the slide.

(B) Brett comes up with a solution.

(C) The girls go down the slides at the same time.

(D) The girls immediately head for the slides.

Answer: (B)

Joel's hockey team had been playing well all season, and this was their chance to win the tournament. He was their best player.

He glanced around at his teammates. "Guys," he said, "let's skate really hard and show them how great we are!"

The teammates cheered and started to walk out to the ice. Joel turned around to grab his helmet, but it wasn't there. He looked under the benches and in the lockers, but his helmet wasn't anywhere. He sat down and felt his throat get tight. If he didn't have a helmet, he couldn't play.

Just then, there was a knock on the door. Joel's mom peeked her head around the locker room door. "Thank goodness," she said. "Looks like I got here just in time."

1. This story takes place in

(A) a locker room.

(B) an ice center lobby.

(C) a sporting goods store.

(D) an outdoor playing field.

2. Why does Joel become upset?

(F) He can't find his hockey helmet.

(G) He missed his game.

(H) His mom will miss the game.

(J) His coach is counting on him.

3. Joel's mom resolves the conflict by

(A) taking him out for pizza.

(B) finding his hockey stick.

(C) playing for him.

(D) bringing him his helmet.

Story Elements

Directions: Read the passage. Choose the best answer to the questions that follow.

"All right, boys, it's time for bed," said Mrs. Lopez from outside the tent. There was a moment of silence and then some muffled giggles. "You're not fooling me," she added. "I know you're still up. And you're all going to be grumpy and tired tomorrow if you don't get some sleep. Good night, boys!"

Luke, Tomas, and Markus laughed and snuggled further into their sleeping bags. The three boys kept talking for a few more minutes, but before long they drifted off to sleep.

A sudden clap of thunder woke them in the middle of the night. Rain was drumming on the tent, and flashes of lightning lit the sky. Luke, Tomas, and Markus were sitting straight up in their sleeping bags when Mrs. Lopez ducked inside their tent. She was dripping wet and looked worried.

"Let's go, guys," she said, motioning to the boys. "Grab your jackets, and put on your boots. We need to evacuate."

"What's wrong, Mom? What's going on?" asked Tomas.

"The ranger is worried about a flash flood," said Mrs. Lopez. "You know that stream we crossed today when we were hiking? It fills up quickly in big storms. It's not safe for us to stay here. We need to get to higher ground."

Mrs. Lopez unzipped the tent, and she and the three boys ran for the car as lightning zigzagged across the sky.

1. Which of the following shows the correct sequence of events in the story?

(A) The stream floods. Mrs. Lopez tells the boys to go to sleep.

(B) The boys go to sleep. The thunder wakes them up.

(C) Mrs. Lopez comes inside the tent dripping wet. She tells the boys to go to sleep.

(D) The boys run for the car. A clap of thunder wakes them up.

2. What is the setting for this story?

(F) a backyard

(G) a cabin in the woods

(H) a tent in a campground

(J) an RV

3. What is the main conflict in the story?

(A) Mrs. Lopez wants the boys to go to sleep.

(B) Mrs. Lopez disagrees with the park ranger.

(C) Tomas wants to go home, but the other boys do not want to.

(D) The campsite may be in danger of flooding, and they need to evacuate.

4. From whose point of view is the story told?

(F) Mrs. Lopez's point of view

(G) the narrator's point of view

(H) the park ranger's point of view

(J) Tomas's point of view

Fiction

Directions: Read the passage. Choose the best answer to the questions that follow.

Example

Bobby saw Dad lying on the sofa. He looked peaceful with his eyes closed and his hands resting on his stomach. Bobby took his roller skates and quietly left the room. A few minutes later, Bobby's mother asked where Bobby was. His dad said that Bobby had gone skating.

How did Bobby's dad know where he was?

(A) He has ESP.

(B) He had set up a video camera to watch Bobby.

(C) He wasn't really asleep on the couch.

(D) Bobby left a note for him.

Answer: (C)

Austin went zooming to the park to meet his buddies for an afternoon of hoops. It would have been a perfect day, but he had to bring his little brother, Carter, along.

"Wait for me, Austin," whined Carter.

Austin walked Carter over to a nearby tree, handed him his lunch, and said, "Sit here and eat. Don't move until I come back and get you." Austin ran off to meet his friends.

As Carter began eating, he heard the pitter-patter of rain falling around him. When Carter saw lightning, he ran for shelter. Suddenly a loud crack of lightning sounded. Looking behind him, Carter saw the top of the tree come crashing down right where he had been sitting. Austin saw it, too, from the other side of the park.

"Carter!" Austin yelled as he ran. At the moment the lightning struck, Austin thought, "I know he can be a pain, but he's still my brother!"

1. What is the main conflict in this story?

(A) Austin has to drag his brother along to the park.

(B) There is a lightning storm.

(C) The tree crashes down.

(D) Austin thinks Carter is hurt.

2. What is Austin going to the park to play?

(F) baseball

(G) tennis

(H) basketball

(J) soccer

Name _____   Date _____

Fiction

Directions: Read the passage. Choose the best answer to the questions that follow.

When we first climbed into the car and strapped on our safety belts, I wasn't very nervous. I was sitting right next to my big brother, and he had done this many times before. As we started to climb the hill, however, I could feel my heart jump into my throat.

"Jonah?" I asked nervously. "Is this supposed to be so noisy?"

"Sure, Ari," Jonah answered. "It always does that."

A minute later, we were going so fast down the hill that I didn't have time to think. With a twist, a loop, and a bunch of fast turns, everyone on board screamed in delight. No wonder this was one of the most popular rides in the park. By the time the car pulled into the station and we got off the ride, I was ready to do it again!

1. Which of the following is a characteristic of fiction?

(A) It provides facts.

(B) It tells a story.

(C) It is real and true.

(D) It informs the reader.

2. Which of the following best describes the setting of this story?

(F) a car ride to school

(G) a train ride

(H) a ride on a roller coaster

(J) a trip to the grocery store

3. Why do you think Ari is nervous?

(A) He doesn't like roller coasters.

(B) He doesn't trust his brother.

(C) His brother is trying to scare him.

(D) He's never been on a roller coaster before.

4. At what point in the story did you realize where it was taking place? What words or phrases helped you figure out the setting?

_____

_____

_____

_____

_____

_____

_____

_____

_____

Chapter 2: Reading Comprehension

Fiction

Directions: Read the passage. Choose the best answer to the questions that follow.

"Cassie, you don't realize how grateful we are! We were afraid we wouldn't be able to get a babysitter. Here's a list of instructions. Bye, Bart," Mr. and Mrs. Bradford both said as they left.

Cassie read the note. She was supposed to feed Bart spaghetti, give him a bath, put on his pajamas, play a game with him, and then put him to bed.

But it wasn't that simple. When Bart didn't want to eat his spaghetti, he dumped it on her head. When she tried to give him a bath, he dumped the whole bottle of bubble bath in the tub. And when they tried to play a game, Bart threw blocks all over his room.

Just as Cassie was starting to relax after getting Bart in bed and cleaning up his messes, the Bradfords came home.

"The house looks great!" said Mrs. Bradford. "By the way, we'd like to know if you can come back again tomorrow."

1. What is the main problem in this story?

(A) Bart is misbehaving.

(B) Cassie has to clean up a mess.

(C) The Bradfords have gone out to dinner.

(D) Cassie does not want to babysit again.

2. What do you think Cassie will do if the Bradfords ask her to babysit again?

(F) She will do it.

(G) She will find a way to get out of it.

(H) She will volunteer eagerly.

(J) She will offer to do it only if she doesn't have to feed Bart.

3. What did Bart do with his spaghetti?

(A) He threw it in the tub.

(B) He ate it.

(C) He dumped it on Cassie's head.

(D) He threw it around his room.

If you have enough time, review both questions and answers. You might see something you missed!

Name _____   Date _____

Fiction

Directions: Read the passage. Choose the best answer to the questions that follow.

"Hurray!" cried Meghan. "Today is the day we're going to Waterland!" It was a hot July day, and Meghan's mom was taking her to cool off on the water slides. Meghan's new friend, Natasha, was going, too.

Just then, Meghan's mom came out of her bedroom. She did not look very happy. "What's the matter, Mom? Are you afraid to get wet?" Meghan teased. "I'll bet you'll melt, just like the Wicked Witch of the West!"

Mrs. Millett didn't laugh at the joke. Instead, she told the kids that she wasn't feeling well. She was too tired to drive to the water park.

Meghan and Natasha were disappointed. "My mom has chronic fatigue syndrome," Meghan explained. "Her illness makes her really tired. She's still a great mom."

"Thank you, dear," said Mrs. Millett. "I'm too tired to drive, but I have an idea. You can make your own waterland, and I'll rest in the lawn chair."

Meghan and Natasha set up three different sprinklers. They dragged the play slide over to the wading pool and aimed the sprinkler on the slide. Meghan and Natasha got soaking wet. Mrs. Millett sat in a lawn chair and rested. The kids played all day.

"Thank you for being so understanding," Meghan's mom said. "Now I feel better, but I'm really hot! There's only one cure for that." She stood under the sprinkler with all her clothes on. She was drenched from head to toe.

Meghan laughed and said, "Now you have chronic wet syndrome." Mrs. Millett rewarded her daughter with a big, wet hug. It turned out to be a wonderful day after all, in the backyard waterland.

Read carefully. Make sure you know all the characters and the main events. Skim or read again if necessary.

Fiction

Directions: Answer the questions about the story on page 38.

1. Which sentence best tells the main idea of the story?

(A) Meghan's mom has chronic fatigue syndrome.

(B) Natasha and Meghan miss out on Waterland, but they make their own water park and have fun anyway.

(C) Natasha and Meghan cannot go to Waterland.

(D) Sprinklers make a great backyard water park.

2. Which of the following happened after the kids dragged the slide over to the pool?

(F) Natasha arrived at Meghan's house.

(G) Meghan and Natasha set up three sprinklers.

(H) Meghan's mom stood in the sprinkler with her clothes on.

(J) Meghan's mom was too tired to drive.

3. How do you think Mrs. Millett feels about not being able to take the kids to Waterland?

(A) She's glad that she won't have to spend her whole day with kids.

(B) She feels sorry for herself and is glad she got out of it.

(C) She's disappointed that she can't take them.

(D) She's hurt and confused.

4. Why didn't Meghan and Natasha go to Waterland?

(F) They were too late.

(G) They wanted to play in the sprinklers instead.

(H) It was too hot outside.

(J) Mrs. Millett was too tired to drive them.

5. What is the turning point of this story?

(A) Meghan's mom feels better and gets wet in the sprinkler.

(B) Meghan and Natasha can't go to Waterland.

(C) Meghan's mom gives her a wet hug.

(D) Natasha arrives at the house early.

6. Why did the author write this story?

(F) to explain

(G) to persuade

(H) to entertain and inform

(J) to understand

Fiction

Directions: Read the passage. Choose the best answer to the questions that follow.

"Are you sure you're going to be all right at home alone?" Chun's mother asked. "Yes, Mom," Chun replied, trying not to roll her eyes. "I'm old enough to stay here alone for three hours."

Chun's mom and dad were going to a barbecue that afternoon. Since kids weren't invited, Chun was staying home alone. It was the first time her parents had left her home by herself. Chun was a little nervous, but she was sure she could handle it.

"Let me give you a last-minute quiz to make sure," her dad said. Chun's father was a teacher, and he was always giving her little tests. "What happens if somebody calls and asks for your mom or me?"

"I tell them that you are busy and can't come to the phone right now," Chun said. "Then, I take a message."

"What if there is a knock on the door?" asked her dad.

"I don't answer it, because I can't let anyone in anyway."

"Okay, here's a tough one." Her father looked very serious. "What if you hear ghosts in the closets?"

"Dad!" Chun giggled. "Our house isn't haunted. I'll be fine. Look, I have the phone number for the house where you'll be, so I can call if I need to. I've got the numbers for the police, the fire department, and the poison control center. I won't turn on the stove or leave the house. And, I'll double lock the doors behind you when you leave."

Chun's parents were satisfied. They hugged her good-bye and left for the afternoon. Chun sat for a few minutes and enjoyed the quiet of the empty house. Then, she went to the kitchen to find herself a snack. She opened the cupboard door. She jumped back, startled. There was a ghost in the cupboard! Chun laughed and laughed. Her dad had taped up a picture of a ghost. It said, "BOO! We love you!"

Fiction

Directions: Answer the questions about the story on page 40.

1. **Which answer shows the best summary of this story?**

   (A) Chun is staying home by herself for the first time and must remember all the important safety rules.

   (B) Chun cannot go to the barbecue with her mom and dad.

   (C) Chun's parents play a trick on her by hiding a paper ghost in the cupboard.

   (D) Chun enjoys a peaceful afternoon at home alone.

2. **What should Chun do if someone knocks at the door?**

   (F) She should answer it.

   (G) She should call her dad.

   (H) She should not answer it and not let anyone in.

   (J) She should see who it is before letting the person in.

3. **What do you think Chun will do if she spills drain cleaner and the dog accidentally licks some up?**

   (A) She will call her friend Sam to tell him.

   (B) She will call the fire department.

   (C) She will do nothing.

   (D) She will call the poison control center and then her parents.

4. **Because kids are not invited to the barbecue**

   (F) they won't have any fun.

   (G) Chun's parents will not go.

   (H) Chun must stay home alone.

   (J) Chun will not get any dinner.

5. **Who are the main characters in this story?**

   (A) Chun, her mom, and her dad

   (B) Chun and her friend Sam

   (C) Chun, her dad, and the dog

   (D) Chun and her dad

6. **What is the main reason Chun's dad keeps asking her questions?**

   (F) He wants to make sure she knows all the emergency phone numbers.

   (G) He wants to make sure she will be safe while they are gone.

   (H) He likes giving her quizzes.

   (J) He played a trick on her.

Look for the Who? What? Where? When? Why? and How? of the story.

Fiction

Directions: Read the passage. Then, answer the questions below.

In my family, we don't celebrate birthdays—at least not like most families. My friends say I have an "un-birthday."

The tradition started with my grandmother. She and my grandfather grew up in Poland. They escaped before World War II and made their way to America. When they got here, they were so grateful that they decided to share what they had with others. On their birthdays, they gave each other just one small gift. Then, they each bought a gift for someone who needed it more than they did.

As the years passed and the family grew, the tradition continued. On my last birthday, I got a backpack for school. We had a little party with cake, balloons, friends, and family. Then, we headed off for the Lionel School—a nearby school for kids who have disabilities. I picked this school because my friend has a sister who goes there.

When we walked in with our arms full of gifts, the kids were really excited. Even though we gave them little things, like sticker books and puzzles, all the presents were wrapped and had bows.

I gave Maggie, my friend's sister, a floppy stuffed animal. Maggie can't talk, but she hugged her stuffed animal and smiled, so I knew she was happy.

I don't get as much stuff as some of my friends, but it's okay. Seeing Maggie and the others receive their gifts was a lot better than getting a bunch of presents myself!

1. How do you think the narrator feels about this unusual family tradition?

_____

_____

_____

2. How does the narrator know that Maggie liked her gift?

_____

_____

_____

3. Why does the narrator call this family tradition an "un-birthday"?

_____

_____

_____

_____

4. Would the narrator agree with the saying "It is better to give than to receive"? Explain your answer.

_____

_____

_____

_____

_____

Nonfiction

Directions: Read the passage. Choose the best answer to the questions that follow.

Example

Can you picture a coin so big that you can hardly carry it? The country of Sweden had such a coin more than 200 years ago. It was 2 feet long and 1 foot wide. The coin weighed 31 pounds.

How long was the coin?

Ⓐ 2 feet

Ⓑ 1 foot

Ⓒ 31 feet

Ⓓ 3 feet

Answer: (A)

Fossils are most often found in sedimentary rock. Suppose that a plant or animal died millions of years ago near a lake or an ocean. The mud and sand would cover it. Over many years, the mud and sand would harden and form sedimentary rock.

Two kinds of fossils found in sedimentary rock are cast and mold. A mold fossil is a rock with an empty space left after the creature caught in the sediment wore away.

The cast fossil looks like a mold fossil that has been filled. Solid matter from the ground fills the empty space.

Now, imagine that a dinosaur stepped into soft ground and made a footprint. The footprint would not form a cast or mold fossil, because no part of the dinosaur's body was left behind. If the footprint hardened into rock and a scientist found it millions of years later, he or she would be looking at a trace fossil—the remains of the animal's track, but not its actual body.

---

1. Why does a cast fossil look like a filled mold?

Ⓐ The animal leaves a footprint in the dirt.

Ⓑ Scientists fill the empty space with plaster after they find it.

Ⓒ Solid matter from the ground fills the empty space left by the animal.

Ⓓ The fossil was found in sedimentary rock.

2. In what kind of rock are most fossils found?

Ⓕ sedimentary

Ⓖ metamorphic

Ⓗ cast

Ⓙ mold

Name _____   Date _____

Nonfiction

Directions: Read the passage. Choose the best answer to the questions that follow.

Have you ever wondered how the Great Lakes came to be? The same elements came together to create Lake Superior, Lake Michigan, Lake Huron, Lake Erie, and Lake Ontario.

Thousands of years ago, glaciers—huge masses of slowly moving ice—covered Earth. More and more snow fell. Temperatures grew colder. Glaciers grew larger and larger. The movement of glaciers pulled up huge amounts of soil and rocks. These were shoved ahead and to the sides of the glaciers.

Warming temperatures caused the glaciers to melt. The glaciers had taken up space, and so did the soil and rocks that were pulled up and shoved along by the glaciers. When the glaciers melted, they left behind huge holes.

Water from the melting glaciers and rain filled these holes—and turned them into the Great Lakes!

Read carefully. Make sure you look at all the answer choices before you choose the one you think is correct.

1. What is the best title for this passage?

(A) "Glaciers and Lakes"

(B) "Glaciers Take Up Space"

(C) "Melting Glaciers"

(D) "How the Great Lakes Came to Be"

2. What caused the glaciers to grow larger?

(F) They pulled up huge amounts of soil and rocks.

(G) More snow fell and temperatures got colder.

(H) Temperatures grew warmer.

(J) Melting water fell on them.

3. Where did the water that filled up the glacier holes come from?

(A) Native Americans filled up the holes to use them as lakes.

(B) It rained a lot.

(C) Nearby rivers flowed into the holes.

(D) It came from the melting glaciers and rain.

Nonfiction

Directions: Read the passage. Then, answer each question that follows.

Have you ever seen someone send a code for SOS? Maybe you've seen an old movie showing a ship about to sink. Perhaps someone on the ship was tapping wildly on a device. That person was using the telegraph to send for help.

Samuel Morse invented the telegraph. He also invented the electronic alphabet called *Morse code*. The code was a set of dots and dashes that stood for each number and letter of the alphabet.

In 1832, Morse was sailing back to the United States from Europe. During the trip, he came up with the idea of an electronic telegraph. It would help people communicate across great distances. They could be in contact with each other from ship to shore. He was eager to make his invention as quickly as possible.

By 1835, Morse had made his first telegraph. However, it was only a trial version. In 1844, he built a telegraph line. It went from Baltimore to Washington, D.C. The telegraph line was like a telephone today. It carried Morse code messages from one person to another.

Morse kept working to make his telegraph better. In 1849, the government gave him a patent. This gave him the right to make his invention. Within a few years, there were 23,000 miles of telegraph wire. People could now communicate across great distances.

As a result of Morse's invention, trains ran more safely. Conductors could warn about dangers or problems and ask for help. People in businesses could communicate more easily. This made it easier to sell their goods and services. Morse had changed communication forever.

Circle any words you don't understand, and come back to them later.
Remember, the context (the words surrounding tricky words) can help you figure out their meanings.

Nonfiction

Directions: Use the passage on page 45 to help you answer the questions below.

1. What is the main idea of this passage?

_____

_____

_____

_____

_____

2. Give three details from the passage that helped you answer question 1.

_____

_____

_____

_____

_____

_____

_____

_____

_____

3. What type of writing is this passage?

Ⓐ fiction

Ⓑ poetry

Ⓒ nonfiction

Ⓓ fable

4. What was the author's purpose for writing this passage?

Ⓕ to entertain the reader

Ⓖ to alarm the reader

Ⓗ to inform the reader

Ⓙ to challenge the reader

5. Which of the following was a result of Morse's invention?

Ⓐ The government could give out more patents.

Ⓑ Trains ran more safely.

Ⓒ People could travel from Baltimore to Washington, D.C., more quickly.

Ⓓ People talked on the phone more often.

6. Which of the following is not true?

Ⓕ Morse Code is made of dots and dashes.

Ⓖ The telegraph is still the most common way for people to communicate over long distances today.

Ⓗ Samuel Morse invented the telegraph in just a few years.

Ⓙ The invention of the telegraph and Morse code improved communication.

Nonfiction

Directions: Read the passage. Choose the best answer to the questions that follow.

Both rainforests and kelp forests are important to our ecology because they keep animals safe by providing homes. Rainforests keep land animals safe, while kelp forests keep sea creatures safe.

Like rainforests, kelp forests are home to many types of animals. Crab, eel, lobster, and seahorses are just a few of the creatures that live in sea kelp. In California alone, kelp forests are home to more than 770 animal species. A sandy ocean bottom can be a home for some creatures, but a kelp forest provides a home for thousands more. The animals can live on the many kinds of kelp surfaces, such as rocky or leafy ones.

Like a rainforest, a kelp forest has layers. There are three main layers in a kelp forest. The canopy is at the top, and the floor is at the bottom.

Different sea creatures and plants make use of different kelp forest levels. Herring and mackerel like to swim through the canopy, as do blue-rayed limpets. Sea slugs and snails feast on sea mats they find in the canopy.

Sea urchins look for food in the middle layer. Red seaweeds are often found in this layer of kelp as well, though they might be found at other levels, too.

Sea anemones, crabs, and lobsters live on the floor level. Older blue-rayed limpets feast here, too.

Like a rain forest, a kelp forest is a complete habitat for many sea creatures. It keeps them safe from predators and people. Like rainforests, we must protect kelp forests from pollution and destruction.

After you read, try to summarize the main points of the story in your head. Understanding the main points will help you remember the details.

Nonfiction

Directions: Use the passage on page 47 to help you answer the questions below.

1. Which sentence below best describes the main idea of this passage?

(A) A kelp forest has three levels.

(B) Like rainforests, kelp forests help our ecology by providing homes for many animals.

(C) Many seas creatures live in kelp forests and rainforests.

(D) Kelp forests are like rainforests.

2. Which of the following sea creatures live on the kelp floor?

(F) crabs

(G) herring

(H) mackerel

(J) sea urchins

3. Which of the following is a logical conclusion to make after reading this passage?

(A) Many of the animals in the kelp forests are enemies because they have to compete for food.

(B) Kelp forests are dangerous places to visit.

(C) Kelp forests provide many different kinds of food for sea creatures.

(D) Kelp forests have not been studied very much by scientists.

4. Why is a kelp forest a great home for so many animals?

(F) A kelp forest has many layers in which many different kinds of animals can live safely.

(G) It is extremely large and can hold lots of animals.

(H) The animals have been driven out of other parts of the ocean.

(J) There is no other place for all the sea creatures to live.

5. Which sentence below is most likely to be a topic sentence for this passage?

(A) In California alone, kelp forests are home to more than 770 animal species.

(B) Like a rainforest, a kelp forest has layers.

(C) Both rainforests and kelp forests are important as animal homes.

(D) Like rainforests, kelp forests should be protected.

6. How are rainforests and kelp forests different?

(F) Rainforests have animals, and kelp forests don't.

(G) Rainforests are on land, and kelp forests are in the sea.

(H) Kelp forests have many layers, and rainforests don't.

(J) Rainforests are very important to our ecology, while kelp forests don't really affect it.

Nonfiction

Directions: Read the passage. Choose the best answer to the questions that follow.

Many people believe that Alexander Graham Bell's greatest and most important personal goal was to invent the telephone, but this was not the case. Bell, who was born in 1847, called himself *a teacher of the deaf.*

Bell's father was a well-known speech teacher. Bell also taught speech. He used what he had learned from his father to teach at a school for the deaf in England.

Bell went with his family to Canada in 1870. After two years, he opened a school for the deaf in Massachusetts.

The idea for the telephone came to Bell in 1874. At the same time Bell was experimenting with the telephone, he was working on equipment to help the deaf.

It was 1876 before Bell uttered the first sentence over the telephone, the well-known words: "Mr. Watson, come here; I want you." (Watson was Bell's assistant.) Bell received a patent for the telephone in the same year.

Hundreds of cases were filed against Bell in court. Many people claimed they had already thought of the telephone. But Bell did not lose his patent. He remains on record as its inventor.

The telephone was not Bell's only invention. He received 18 patents for other works and another 12 for work he had done with partners. Fourteen of the patents were for the telephone and telegraph. Others were for inventions such as the photophone, phonograph, and for different types of airplanes.

In 1888, Bell helped found the National Geographic Society. In 1890, he also began the Alexander Graham Bell Association for the Deaf. Bell passed away in August of 1922. Alexander Graham Bell is remembered as a man of many accomplishments.

Pay close attention to the first sentences of each paragraph. They should tell you what you will read about in the rest of the paragraph.

Name _____   Date _____

Nonfiction

Directions: Use the passage on page 49 to help you answer the questions below.

1. What is the main idea of this passage?

- (A) Alexander Graham Bell wanted to prove that he could think of many inventions.
- (B) Alexander Graham Bell invented the telephone.
- (C) Alexander Graham Bell was a man of many achievements.
- (D) Alexander Graham Bell received 30 patents in his lifetime.

2. Which of the following did Bell also invent?

- (F) the automobile
- (G) the light bulb
- (H) the television
- (J) the phonograph

3. Which of the following subjects can you infer interested Bell more than others?

- (A) electricity
- (B) sound
- (C) light
- (D) water

4. Which of the following is not a fact about Alexander Graham Bell?

- (F) Bell passed away in August of 1922.
- (G) The telephone was not Bell's only invention.
- (H) Bell's father was a well-known speech teacher.
- (J) Alexander Bell was a great man.

5. Which sentence below is the concluding sentence of this passage?

- (A) Bell passed away in August of 1922.
- (B) The telephone was not Bell's only invention.
- (C) In 1890, he also began the Alexander Graham Bell Association for the Deaf.
- (D) Alexander Graham Bell is remembered as a man of many accomplishments.

6. What was the author's purpose in writing this article?

- (F) to inform
- (G) to entertain
- (H) to persuade
- (J) to understand

Identifying Literature Genres

Directions: Read the passage. Choose the best answer to the questions that follow.

In 1908, Jacqueline Cochran was born to a poor family in Florida. Like many girls at the time, she went to work at an early age. When she was just eight years old, she started work in a cotton mill. As she made cloth, she dreamed about becoming a pilot. She wanted to fly one of the planes that had been recently invented.

Jacqueline got her wish in the 1930s. At this time, only a few daring young men flew these new planes. There were very few women pilots. That did not stop Jacqueline. She took flying lessons and became a pilot. She began to enter famous races. In 1938, she won first prize in a contest to fly across the United States.

At the beginning of World War II, Jacqueline trained women in England as pilots. She later came back to the United States and trained American women, too. In 1945, she was given the Distinguished Service Medal. It is one of America's highest honors.

When jet planes were invented, Jacqueline learned to fly them, too. She was the first woman to fly faster than the speed of sound. She also set many other records, including flying higher than anyone had before her.

Jacqueline was a pioneer in new technology. She helped to make air travel one of our most important means of transportation.

1. This passage is which genre, or type of literature?

(A) fiction

(B) poetry

(C) biography

(D) fable

2. What clues in the passage helped you decided what genre it is?

_____

_____

_____

_____

A **genre** is a type of literature. Some examples of genres include:

- A **biography**, which is a story that gives details about a real person's life.

- A **fable**, which is a story that teaches a moral, or lesson. It often has animal characters.

- A **poem**, which is a short piece of writing set up in lines. It often has a rhythm and words that rhyme.

Name _____ Date _____

Identifying Literature Genres

Directions: Read the passage. Choose the best answer to the questions that follow.

> One warm summer day, a fox was walking along when he noticed a bunch of grapes on a vine above him. Cool, juicy grapes would taste so good. The more he thought about it, the more the fox wanted those grapes. He tried standing on his tiptoes. He tried jumping high in the air. He tried getting a running start before he jumped. But no matter what he tried, the fox could not reach the grapes. As he angrily walked away, the fox muttered, "They were probably sour anyway!"
>
> **Moral:** A person (or fox) sometimes pretends that he or she does not want something that cannot be had.

1. This passage is which genre, or type of literature?

Ⓐ poetry

Ⓑ biography

Ⓒ nonfiction

Ⓓ fable

2. What clues in the passage helped you decided what genre it is?

_____

_____

_____

_____

Directions: Read the passage. Choose the best answer to the questions that follow.

> My backpack's so heavy
> It must weigh a ton.
> With thousands of books—
> My work's never done.
>
> My arms are so sore
> I can't lift a pen.
> My breath is so short
> I need oxygen.
>
> When I stoop over,
> It makes me fall down.
> I think I'll just stay here
> All squashed on the ground.

3. This passage is which genre, or type of literature?

Ⓕ nonfiction

Ⓖ poetry

Ⓗ biography

Ⓙ fable

4. What clues in the passage helped you decided what genre it is?

_____

_____

_____

_____

Sample Test 2: Reading Comprehension

Directions: Read the passage. Choose the best answer to the questions below.

> "Welcome to the first annual Neighborhood Guinea Pig Race!" Emily announced.
>
> Emily's guinea pig, Ruby, was entered in the first lane. Running in the second lane was Diego's guinea pig, Woody. Sofia entered her two guinea pigs. Otis was in lane three, and Macy was in lane four. While Sofia and Diego got their pets ready to race, Emily was having trouble with Ruby. Ruby was sound asleep and wouldn't budge from under her wood shavings. "Come out, little piggy," Emily encouraged, but Ruby wouldn't budge.
>
> "Why don't you try a carrot?" suggested Diego, holding out a small carrot. "That always works with Woody."
>
> Emily poked Ruby gently with the carrot and then stuck it under her nose. Sure enough, Ruby got up off her belly and followed the carrot.
>
> "It worked!" exclaimed Emily. "Thanks, Diego!"

1. What is the main problem in this story?

(A) Emily is impatient with Ruby.

(B) Ruby is lazy.

(C) Ruby won't come out of her cage for the race.

(D) Ruby likes carrots too much.

2. What are the names of Sofia's guinea pigs?

(F) Milo and Otis

(G) Ruby and Woody

(H) Woody and Otis

(J) Otis and Macy

3. Why does Ruby finally budge?

(A) Emily lures her out with a carrot.

(B) The race is about to start.

(C) She wakes up.

(D) Diego uses Woody to get her to come out.

Sample Test 2: Reading Comprehension

Directions: Read the passage. Choose the best answer to the questions below.

Earth and Venus are alike in many ways. Both planets have volcanoes. Venus has more volcanoes than any other planet. Scientists have mapped more than 1,600 volcanoes on Venus. Some scientists believe that there may be more than one million volcanoes on the planet.

Both planets look the same. They have clouds and a thick atmosphere. The two are almost the same size and have almost the same mass. Venus's orbit around the sun is much like Earth's.

Though Earth and Venus are alike, there are also some differences. Water does not exist on Venus. Also, the temperature on Venus is much hotter than on Earth.

On Earth, volcanoes erupt in a number of different ways. On Venus, however, almost all volcanoes erupt with flat lava flows. Scientists have not found information to show that any of Venus's volcanoes erupt and spew great amounts of ash into the sky.

4. What is the topic sentence of this passage?

(F) Both planets look the same.

(G) Though Earth and Venus are alike, there are also some differences.

(H) Earth and Venus are both planets that have volcanoes.

(J) Earth and Venus are alike in many ways.

5. How is Venus's climate different than Earth's?

(A) Venus gets more rain.

(B) Earth has more hot days during the year than Venus.

(C) The temperature on Venus is much hotter than on Earth.

(D) Venus has more cloudy days than Earth.

6. Which of the following states a fact about Earth and/or Venus?

(F) Water does not exist on Venus.

(G) It might be nice to visit Venus.

(H) Some people think Earth looks like Venus.

(J) It would be the same to live on Venus as it is here on Earth.

GO

Sample Test 2: Reading Comprehension 55

Directions: Read the passage. Choose the best answer to the questions that follow.

The Underground Railroad refers to a group of people who helped slaves escape to freedom. Those in charge of the escape effort were often called *conductors*, just like the conductors of a train. The people escaping were known as *passengers*, just like train passengers. And the places where the escaping slaves stopped for help were often called *stations*, just like the places trains stop.

Like a train ride, the Underground Railroad moved people along. However, the ways in which they moved was very different from a train ride. Those who escaped often followed routes that had been laid out by others before them. Unlike a train ride, some routes went underground through dirt tunnels without any sort of tracks.

Similar to a train ride, those traveling the Underground Railroad often traveled great distances. They had no train seats and no gentle rocking of the train car on the tracks, though. Instead, they had difficult trails to follow. They rarely traveled during the day, finding that it was safer to travel at night.

Escaping slaves had to be certain that they could find their way. They needed food and water to make the journey. Conductors often helped with this. One of the most famous Underground Railroad conductors was Harriet Tubman. She had escaped slavery herself and was dedicated to helping others escape.

Experts disagree about how well the Underground Railroad was organized. Still, it is believed that the system helped thousands of slaves reach freedom between 1830 and 1860.

Name _____ Date _____

Sample Test 2: Reading Comprehension

Directions: Use the passage on page 55 to help you answer the questions below.

7. What is the author's purpose in writing this article?

(A) to quiz the reader on train vocabulary

(B) to tell the reader about how the Underground Railroad worked

(C) to tell a story about Harriet Tubman

(D) to explain the meaning of the name *Underground Railroad*

8. What were people called who were in charge of groups of escaping slaves?

(F) conductors

(G) stations

(H) passengers

(J) masters

9. What two emotions below best describe how slaves traveling on the Underground Railroad might have felt?

(A) frightened and excited

(B) disappointed and mad

(C) carefree and happy

(D) silly and lighthearted

10. Because of the Underground Railroad

(F) other programs like it were set up.

(G) many people had jobs.

(H) conductors had to be found to run it.

(J) thousands of slaves escaped.

11. Which of the following is not a supporting detail for the passage?

(A) The Underground Railroad refers to a group of people who helped slaves escape to freedom.

(B) Still, it is believed that the system helped thousands of slaves reach freedom between 1830 and 1860.

(C) The people escaping were known as passengers, just like train passengers.

(D) The Underground Railroad offered free train rides to people.

12. Which of the following is not a way in which the Underground Railroad and trains are alike?

(F) They have passengers.

(G) They travel great distances.

(H) They stop at stations.

(J) They travel on tracks.

STOP

Practice Test 1: Reading
Part 1: Vocabulary

Directions: Choose the answer that means the same, or about the same, as the underlined word.

1. <u>grab</u> an apple

(A) reach for

(B) crunch

(C) eat

(D) break

2. give a <u>signal</u>

(F) radio

(G) poster

(H) gift

(J) sign

3. <u>thorough</u> cleaning

(A) quick

(B) necessary

(C) complete

(D) house

4. <u>explore</u> the island

(F) search

(G) find

(H) stalk

(J) look for

5. To <u>consult</u> someone is to _____.

(A) compliment

(B) get advice

(C) insult

(D) give advice

6. If someone is <u>generous</u>, he is _____.

(F) giving

(G) guilty

(H) selfish

(J) greedy

7. If something is <u>spoiled</u>, it is _____.

(A) crusty

(B) cooked

(C) sunburned

(D) ruined

8. She put on her <u>cloak</u>.

(F) hat

(G) cape

(H) sweater

(J) scarf

Name _____   Date _____

Practice Test 1: Reading
Part 1: Vocabulary

Directions: Choose the answer that means the same, or about the same, as the underlined word.

9. The girls <u>abandoned</u> their fort in the woods.

   (A) left alone on purpose

   (B) played with

   (C) amused

   (D) walked with

10. To demonstrate, Gina made a <u>circular</u> motion with her hand.

   (F) circus

   (G) in a circle

   (H) waving

   (J) slapping

11. Paulomi wants to <u>discontinue</u> her magazine subscription.

   (A) reorder

   (B) order

   (C) stop

   (D) pay for

12. My older brother went on an <u>expedition</u> to Central America to study pyramids.

   (F) journey with a purpose

   (G) vacation

   (H) trip

   (J) stroll

Directions: Choose the word that means the opposite of the underlined word.

13. a <u>weeping</u> child

   (A) young

   (B) laughing

   (C) skipping

   (D) sad

14. a <u>dangerous</u> snake

   (F) slimy

   (G) moist

   (H) harmless

   (J) long

15. friends and <u>foes</u>

   (A) friends

   (B) enemies

   (C) pets

   (D) parents

16. <u>quality</u> foods

   (F) salty

   (G) dessert

   (H) well-made

   (J) bad

17. <u>coarse</u> salt

   (A) natural

   (B) rough

   (C) tough

   (D) fine

GO

Practice Test 1: Reading
Part 1: Vocabulary

Directions: Read the two sentences. Choose the word that fits best in both sentences.

18. My _____ is in the closet.
Add a new _____ of paint.

- (F) hat
- (G) color
- (H) shirt
- (J) coat

19. The photography _____ meets today.
The cave man carried a _____.

- (A) group
- (B) club
- (C) spear
- (D) class

20. He will need new swimming _____.
Load those _____ in the van.

- (F) goggles
- (G) shoes
- (H) boxes
- (J) trunks

21. Our teacher tells us not to _____ anyone.
I had a cup of _____ at the party.

- (A) food
- (B) hit
- (C) punch
- (D) juice

Directions: Choose the answer in which the underlined word is used in the same way as in the box.

22. The sky was clear.

- (F) Clear away those dinner dishes.
- (G) The tower radioed that we were in the clear.
- (H) Clear skies and bright sun were forecast for today.
- (J) He said it would be clear sailing from here on in.

23. Watch out for that falling limb!

- (A) Andrew checked his watch for the time.
- (B) The captain asked him to take the first watch.
- (C) Watch your step.
- (D) We kept the watch fire burning all night.

Directions: Choose the answer that best defines the underlined part of the word.

24. disbelief   disorganized

- (F) absence of
- (G) more
- (H) less than
- (J) again

25. gentleness   kindness

- (A) quality of
- (B) less
- (C) more
- (D) opposite of

Name _____ Date _____

Practice Test 1: Reading
Part 1: Vocabulary

Directions: Choose the best answer to each question below.

26. Which of these words probably comes from the Latin word *crimen*, meaning *accusation*?

(F) cringe

(G) cry

(H) criminal

(J) crimp

27. Which of these words probably comes from the Greek word *mystikos*, meaning *seeing with the eyes closed*?

(A) musky

(B) mystic

(C) must

(D) muster

28. We hiked to a _____ campsite. Which word means the campsite was *far away*?

(F) remote

(G) pleasant

(H) crowded

(J) level

29. The girls were _____ to the show after they bought their tickets. Which word means that they were *allowed to enter*?

(A) going

(B) cast

(C) admitted

(D) shown

Directions: Read the paragraph. Choose the word that fits best in each numbered blank.

Mountain gorillas live in the _____ **(30)** in Rwanda, Uganda, and the Democratic Republic of the Congo. These _____, **(31)** beautiful animals are becoming very rare. They have lost much of their habitat as people move in and take over their land. Although there are _____ **(32)** laws protecting gorillas, poachers continue to hunt them. Scientists and park rangers are working hard to _____ **(33)** the mountain gorillas.

30. (F) deserts

(G) forests

(H) lakes

(J) valleys

31. (A) large

(B) small

(C) skinny

(D) violent

32. (F) loose

(G) easy

(H) strange

(J) strict

33. (A) chase away

(B) hunt

(C) protect

(D) kill

STOP

Practice Test 1: Reading
Part 2: Reading Comprehension

Directions: Read the passage. Choose the best answer to the questions that follow.

Ava's mom has errands to run, so Ava agrees to stay home to babysit for her little brother, who is asleep. Her mom also leaves Ava a list of chores to do while she is gone. Ava will be able to go swimming with her friends when her chores are finished and her mom gets back.

As soon as Ava's mom leaves, Ava starts calling her friends on the phone. She talks to Jade for 20 minutes and Amari for 15 minutes. She is supposed to call Tyler when she finishes talking to Isabel.

After talking on the phone, Ava watches some videos on the computer. Then, she listens to some music and writes a few e-mails.

Before Ava realizes it, two hours have passed and her mom is back home. Her mom walks in and finds the kitchen still a mess, crumbs all over the carpet, dusty furniture, and Ava's little brother coloring on the wall in his room.

1. Who was Ava going to call after Amari?

(A) Jade

(B) Tyler

(C) Isabel

(D) her mom

2. Which of the following is probably not a chore that Ava was supposed to do?

(F) dust

(G) listen for her brother

(H) clean her room

(J) clean the kitchen

3. What do you think the resolution to this problem will be?

(A) Ava's little brother will have to do all the chores.

(B) Ava will not get to go swimming with her friends.

(C) Ava's mom will drive her to the pool.

(D) Ava, her mom, and her brother will watch a movie.

GO

Name _____   Date _____

Practice Test 1: Reading
Part 2: Reading Comprehension

Directions: Read the passage. Choose the best answer to each question on the next page.

Quinn was running for class president. He and his friend Zack hung colored posters up in the hallways. The posters declared, "QUINN SHOULD WIN!"

A fifth grader walked by them as they hung one on the door to the library. He read the poster and asked, "Why? Why should you win?" and then walked away.

Quinn had never thought about why before. He knew that he was popular and that a lot of people would vote for him.

"I suppose you should have some issues," Zack commented. "More recess time? Hey, how about getting that gumball machine in the boys' bathroom you're always talking about?"

In the election meeting that afternoon, Mrs. Jacobs, the school principal, told them it was a great responsibility to be class president. All candidates running, she said, should be honest. "Let your platform speak for itself," she added.

At home, Quinn and Zack made up new campaign posters that said, "VOTE QUINN: New gumball machine in the boys' room. Everyone will play soccer at lunch. Taco day is abolished!"

The next day at school, some of Quinn's regular friends avoided him, especially the girls. When he asked J.D. if he wanted to play soccer at lunch, J.D. responded, "Of course, Your Majesty."

"What's the matter with everyone?" Quinn muttered while standing in the lunch line.

"I'll tell you what's wrong," said a small girl in line behind him. "Nobody likes your campaign promises. The girls couldn't care less if you're going to get a gumball machine in the boys' room. A lot of people like taco day. And, nobody wants to be told they have to play soccer at recess. Some people like to play other games. You only made promises about what you like."

Quinn thought about what he could do. He decided that if he wanted to know what his classmates wanted, he should take a poll. Later that day, he and Zack asked each fourth grader what they wanted most to change in their school. They made a bar graph so they could see what was important to fourth graders. Then, Quinn and Zack made up new campaign posters. Quinn's friends started talking to him again, and the next week he won the election. Quinn realized that listening to your classmates is the most important thing a class president can do.

GO

Practice Test 1: Reading
Part 2: Reading Comprehension

Directions: Use the passage on page 62 to help you answer the questions below.

4. What was Quinn's first campaign slogan?

(F) New gumball machine in the boys' room.

(G) Everyone will play soccer at lunch.

(H) Quinn should win!

(J) Taco day is abolished!

5. What is the main message of this story?

(A) Holding a public office is an important responsibility.

(B) School elections are very complicated.

(C) Popularity is more important than campaign promises.

(D) Girls and boys don't always like the same things.

6. What causes Quinn's friends to stop speaking to him?

(F) He puts up his campaign posters.

(G) He only makes promises for things he wants.

(H) He decides to run for class president.

(J) He changes his campaign promises.

7. Which of the following probably would have happened if Quinn hadn't changed his slogans?

(A) He would have won anyway.

(B) Mrs. Jacobs would have told him he couldn't run.

(C) Zack would have refused to speak to him.

(D) He would have lost the election.

8. Which genre is this story?

(F) western

(G) mystery

(H) drama

(J) nonfiction

9. What is the turning point in this story?

(A) The girl in line tells him what is wrong with his promises.

(B) Quinn decides to ask his classmates what they want.

(C) Quinn wins the election.

(D) Some of Quinn's friends refuse to talk to him.

GO

Name _____   Date _____

Practice Test 1: Reading
Part 2: Reading Comprehension

Directions: Read the passage. Choose the best answer to each question.

Perhaps you have heard that many types of bats have very small eyes and do not see well. Still, as they swoop through the night, they do not bump into objects and are able to find food, even though they can't see their prey. How is this possible? Echolocation!

You might recognize the beginning of the word *echolocation* as *echo*, and you might recognize the last part of the word as *location*. This gives you clues about how echolocation works. The bat sends out sounds. The sounds bounce off objects and return to the bat. Echolocation not only tells the bat that objects are nearby, it also tells the bat just how far away the objects are.

Bats are not the only creatures that use echolocation. Porpoises and some types of whales and birds use it as well. It is a very effective tool.

10. Which two words make up the word *echolocation*?

(F) *ech* and *olocation*

(G) *echolocate* and *tion*

(H) *echo* and *locate*

(J) *echo* and *location*

11. What is the main idea of this passage?

(A) Bats cannot see very well.

(B) Many animals use echolocation.

(C) Echolocation is an effective tool for bats and other animals.

(D) Bats are not the only creatures that use echolocation.

12. Bats have to use echolocation mainly because

(F) they have no eyes.

(G) they have poor eyesight.

(H) they have big ears.

(J) they fly past lots of obstacles.

Practice Test 1: Reading
Part 2: Reading Comprehension

Directions: Read the passage. Choose the best answer to each question that follows.

Earth revolves around the sun. It also spins on an invisible axis that runs through its center.

It takes $365\frac{1}{4}$ days, or one year, for Earth to revolve around the sun. Just as the moon moves in an orbit around Earth, Earth moves around the sun. Earth does not move in a perfect circle. Its orbit is an ellipse, which is a flattened circle, like an oval. As Earth revolves around the sun in an elliptical shape, it spins on its invisible axis.

Earth's axis of rotation is not straight up and down; it's tilted. This important feature produces the seasons on Earth. No matter where Earth is in its rotation around the sun, its axis is tilted in the same direction and at the same angle. So, as Earth moves, different parts of it are facing the sun and different parts are facing away. The North Pole is tilting toward the sun in June, so the northern half of Earth is enjoying summer. In December, the North Pole is tilted away from the sun, so the northern part of the world experiences winter.

This important relationship between Earth and the sun determines how hot and cold we are, when we plant our crops, and whether we have droughts or floods.

13. If it is summer in North America, what season would it be in Australia?

(A) spring

(B) summer

(C) winter

(D) fall

14. What would happen if Earth's axis were not tilted but straight up and down?

(F) Nothing would change.

(G) Earth wouldn't change seasons.

(H) It would always be summer on Earth.

(J) It would always be winter on Earth.

15. Based on the passage, which of the following statements is not true?

(A) Earth moves around the sun in an elliptical orbit.

(B) When the North Pole is tilting toward the sun, it is summer in the Northern Hemisphere.

(C) Earth revolves around the sun every six months.

(D) Earth is always tilted in the same direction and at the same angle.

GO

Practice Test 1: Reading
Part 2: Reading Comprehension

Directions: Read the passage. Choose the best answer to each question that follows.

Before Europeans arrived in the Northeast, thick forest covered the land. The Native Americans, including the Iroquois, the Wampanoag, and the Mohicans, made these forests their home.

During the winter, the Native Americans stayed close to home, telling stories, playing games, and living off the food they had collected earlier in the year. As the weather warmed, they fished in rivers and streams, gathered eggs, and hunted geese and other birds.

In the spring, the Native Americans also planted corn, beans, and pumpkins. They gathered wild fruits, herbs, and tree bark to use as medicines.

August was a time of harvest. The Native Americans would leave their villages and set out to hunt in the woods. The men hunted for bear, deer, and other game. The meat was dried and saved for the cold winter months.

The villagers returned home at the first sign of snow. The Native Americans relied on the forest to live and gave thanks for the food and shelter they received from it.

16. In the last sentence of the passage, what does the word *relied* mean?

- (F) expected
- (G) destroyed
- (H) counted on
- (J) remembered

17. The Native Americans prepared for winter by _____.

- (A) telling stories
- (B) gathering eggs
- (C) gathering tree bark
- (D) drying meat from the animals they hunted

18. How do you think the life of Europeans differed from that of the Native Americans at this time?

_____

_____

_____

_____

_____

_____

GO

Practice Test 1: Reading
Part 2: Reading Comprehension

Directions: Read the passage. Choose the best answer to each question on the next page.

Inventor Guglielmo Marconi came to the United States in 1899. Telegraph communication by wire was already in place, but Marconi wanted to show off his wireless communication—radio.

Marconi's invention could send Morse code without using any wires. He thought this would help with business communication. When introducing his work, he also planned to show how his invention could do things such as broadcasting a sporting event.

Other people had more and different ideas. These ideas led to programs that included spoken words and music being broadcast on the radio. Operas, comedy hours, and important speeches could be heard in many homes throughout the country. Two famous radio broadcasts were the "War of the Worlds" presentation on October 31, 1938, a fictional story that told about invading aliens; and President Roosevelt's radio announcement of the Japanese attack on Pearl Harbor on December 8, 1941.

In 1922, there were 30 radio stations that sent broadcasts. By 1923, the number had grown to an amazing 556! There was a problem with so many stations broadcasting, however. There was no regular way to do things. Radio station owners organized their stations any way they saw fit.

Even though stations organized into networks, broadcasting still was not organized. The United States government passed laws to regulate radio. This let station owners know which airwaves they could use. The laws also addressed what was okay to say on the radio and what was not appropriate.

Even though television and the Internet are widely used today, most homes and cars still have radios. It looks as though this kind of communication is here to stay, thanks to Mr. Marconi and his invention.

GO

Practice Test 1: Reading
Part 2: Reading Comprehension

Directions: Use the passage on page 67 to help you answer the questions below.

19. Which of the following came before there were 30 radio stations that sent broadcasts?

(F) There were an amazing 556 radio stations.

(G) The "War of the Worlds" program was broadcast.

(H) President Roosevelt announced the attack on Pearl Harbor.

(J) Guglielmo Marconi came to the United States.

20. Which of the following would be an appropriate title for this article?

(A) "Guglielmo Marconi"

(B) "Radio: How Did It Begin?"

(C) "Radio Is Here to Stay"

(D) "Wireless, Here We Go!"

21. Which of the following is a fact?

(F) Radio was the most helpful invention ever created.

(G) Mr. Marconi was a genius.

(H) Radios send signals without wires.

(J) Radio will never go away.

22. Which of the following is not a supporting detail found in this article?

(A) The United States government passed laws to regulate radio.

(B) Marconi won the Nobel Prize in 1909.

(C) Marconi wanted to introduce his wireless communication.

(D) Marconi came to the United States in 1899.

23. Why did the author most likely write this article?

(F) to inform the reader about the introduction of radio in the United States

(G) to prove how successful a life Marconi had

(H) to inspire us to invent more communication devices

(J) to inform us about all the possible radio shows there are to make

24. What can you infer about people's reactions to radio?

(A) They didn't like it and preferred to watch events.

(B) It took a long time for them to get used to the idea.

(C) They immediately liked it and were excited about it.

(D) They shunned Marconi and thought his invention was too modern.

STOP

Punctuation

Directions: Read each sentence. Choose the punctuation mark that is needed in the sentence. If no more punctuation is needed, choose "None."

Example

Do you think the film is scary

- (A) .
- (B) !
- (C) ?
- (D) None

Answer: C

---

1. The clouds were dark, and the wind was getting stronger.

- (A) !
- (B) .
- (C) ?
- (D) None

2. Jody please don't forget to feed the cat.

- (F) ?
- (G) !
- (H) ,
- (J) None

3. "Your brother just called," said Aziz.

- (A) .
- (B) ,
- (C) !
- (D) None

4. Alex Lucy, and Malia all went to the movies.

- (F) .
- (G) !
- (H) ,
- (J) None

5. "Please take out the trash" Mom said.

- (A) "
- (B) ,
- (C) .
- (D) None

6. How much money do we need

- (F) .
- (G) ?
- (H) ,
- (J) None

Look carefully at all the answer choices before you choose the one you think is correct. Make sure you completely fill in the circle for your answer choice.

Punctuation

Directions: Choose the line that has a punctuation error. If there is no error, choose "No mistakes."

1. Ⓐ Purple finches often build their nests
   Ⓑ in hanging baskets. like ferns.
   Ⓒ They lay four or five eggs.
   Ⓓ No mistakes

2. Ⓕ I found out how to plant a
   Ⓖ seed and make it grow. It
   Ⓗ grew into a beautiful plant.
   Ⓙ No mistakes

3. Ⓐ Shandra shook her head.
   Ⓑ She had missed the bus again,
   Ⓒ and she knew shed be late for school.
   Ⓓ No mistakes

4. Ⓕ 308 Market Street
   Ⓖ Farmland, MI 44567
   Ⓗ May 14, 2011
   Ⓙ No mistakes

5. Ⓐ Dear Sir,
   Ⓑ I am returning this watch. It has not worked since I got it in the mail.
   Ⓒ Please refund my money?
   Ⓓ No mistakes

6. Ⓕ I will expect a reply soon.
   Ⓖ Sincerely
   Ⓗ Albert Jones
   Ⓙ No mistakes

Directions: Choose the word or words that fit best in the blank and show correct punctuation.

7. **Please wash your _____ car today.**
   Ⓐ father's
   Ⓑ Father's
   Ⓒ fathers'
   Ⓓ fathers's

8. **_____ don't forget your backpack.**
   Ⓕ Rita
   Ⓖ Rita:
   Ⓗ Rita,
   Ⓙ Rita;

9. **We will be going to _____ this summer.**
   Ⓐ Washington: D.C.
   Ⓑ Washington, dc
   Ⓒ washington dc
   Ⓓ Washington, D.C.,

Capitalization and Punctuation

Directions: Choose the sentence that shows correct punctuation and capitalization.

1. (A) Lena whispered, "This is a great movie."

   (B) "Don't forget your money said Mother."

   (C) Are there seats up front?" asked Dylan?

   (D) "let's get popcorn" suggested Wanda.

2. (F) Mrs. Shields writes about sports for our local newspaper.

   (G) Did Dr. Robinson call yet.

   (H) Please give this to miss Jung.

   (J) This is Mr McCoy's bicycle.

Directions: Choose the best way to write the underlined part of each sentence. If the underlined part is correct, choose "Correct as it is."

3. **Somehow, the shoe landed on Felipe sanchez's lawn.**

   (A) felipe sanchez's lawn

   (B) Felipe Sanchez's lawn

   (C) Felipe sanchez's Lawn

   (D) Correct as it is

4. **Rachel bought a new necklace but she lost it.**

   (F) necklace but,

   (G) necklace, but

   (H) necklace. But

   (J) Correct as it is

5. **"Don't change the channel!" yelled Ben's little sister.**

   (A) channel" yelled

   (B) channel." yelled,

   (C) channel." yelled

   (D) Correct as it is

Remember to look for correct capitalization and punctuation!

Capitalization and Punctuation

Directions: Choose the best way to write the underlined part of each sentence. If the underlined part is correct, choose "Correct as it is."

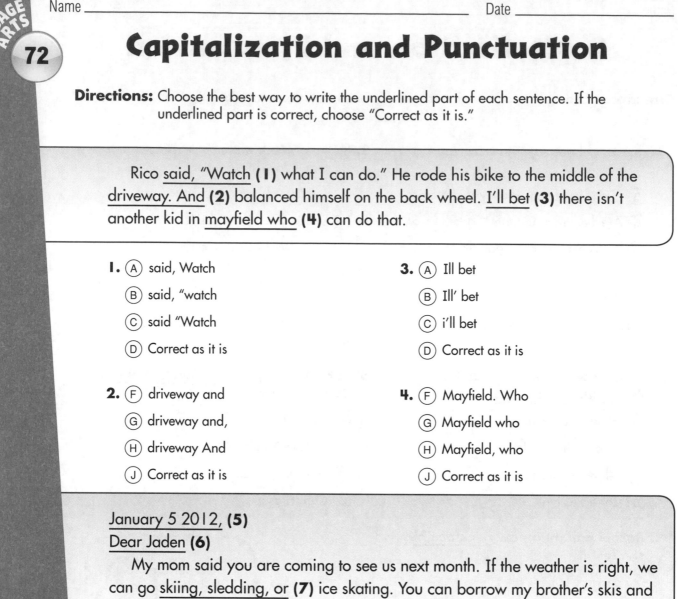

Rico <u>said, "Watch</u> **(1)** what I can do." He rode his bike to the middle of the <u>driveway. And</u> **(2)** balanced himself on the back wheel. <u>I'll bet</u> **(3)** there isn't another kid in <u>mayfield who</u> **(4)** can do that.

1. (A) said, Watch

   (B) said, "watch

   (C) said "Watch

   (D) Correct as it is

2. (F) driveway and

   (G) driveway and,

   (H) driveway And

   (J) Correct as it is

3. (A) Ill bet

   (B) Ill' bet

   (C) i'll bet

   (D) Correct as it is

4. (F) Mayfield. Who

   (G) Mayfield who

   (H) Mayfield, who

   (J) Correct as it is

<u>January 5 2012,</u> **(5)**
<u>Dear Jaden</u> **(6)**

   My mom said you are coming to see us next month. If the weather is right, we can go <u>skiing, sledding, or</u> **(7)** ice skating. You can borrow my brother's skis and skates.
See you soon.
<u>Your Cousin,</u> **(8)**
Sarah

5. (A) January 5, 2012

   (B) January 5 2012

   (C) January 5, 2012,

   (D) Correct as it is

6. (F) Dear Jaden

   (G) dear jaden

   (H) Dear Jaden,

   (J) Correct as it is

7. (A) skiing sledding or

   (B) skiing, sledding, or,

   (C) skiing sledding or,

   (D) Correct as it is

8. (F) Your Cousin

   (G) Your cousin,

   (H) your Cousin,

   (J) Correct as it is

Capitalization and Punctuation

Directions: Choose the answer that best fits in the blank and shows correct capitalization and punctuation.

1. Do you think we should go swimming, _____

- (A) Sam?
- (B) sam.
- (C) sam!
- (D) Sam.

2. The new mall will open on _____.

- (F) may 1 2012
- (G) May, 1 2012
- (H) may 1, 2012
- (J) May 1, 2012

Directions: Read the passage below. Choose the answer that shows the best way to write the underlined part.

(1) Can you imagine finding a bottle with a message inside—or perhaps one containing <u>money?</u> **(2)** <u>bottles</u> may travel thousands of miles in the ocean. **(3)** Not long ago, a child in <u>new york</u> found a bottle that had been washed up on the beach. **(4)** Inside was <u>1,700</u> **(5)** After waiting a year, the youngster was allowed to keep the money.

3. In sentence 1, <u>money?</u> is best written

- (A) money!
- (B) money.
- (C) Money?
- (D) Correct as it is

4. In sentence 2, <u>bottles</u> is best written

- (F) Bottles;
- (G) Bottles,
- (H) Bottles
- (J) Correct as it is

5. In sentence 3, <u>new york</u> is best written

- (A) New York
- (B) New York,
- (C) New york
- (D) Correct as it is

6. In sentence 4, <u>1,700</u> is best written

- (F) 1700.
- (G) $1,700!
- (H) $1,700?
- (J) Correct as it is

Capitalization and Punctuation

Directions: Rewrite the sentences below using the correct capitalization and punctuation.

1. tyson began singing the star-spangled banner

_____

_____

_____

2. vikram read an article about canadian geese in a magazine

_____

_____

_____

3. we sold school supplies to help raise money for the red cross

_____

_____

_____

4. i'm really glad you are here abby said

_____

_____

_____

5. will you tell dr singh i called

_____

_____

_____

6. riley will be the champion of west jefferson little league

_____

_____

_____

7. i suggest you go to the library to do research said mom

_____

_____

_____

8. has amina been reading james and the giant peach all afternoon

_____

_____

_____

Spelling

Directions: Choose the word that is spelled correctly and fits best in the blank.

Example

My teacher _____ that I practice my violin for one hour each day.

- (A) recommended
- (B) reccommended
- (C) reccomended
- (D) recomended

Answer: (A)

---

1. Tomorrow will be _____.

- (A) rainee
- (B) rainie
- (C) ranie
- (D) rainy

2. We went on a _____ walk.

- (F) nachur
- (G) nayture
- (H) nature
- (J) nachure

3. The garage needed a _____ cleaning.

- (A) thoroh
- (B) thurow
- (C) thourough
- (D) thorough

4. Jonas is going to a _____ movie.

- (F) horor
- (G) horror
- (H) horrorr
- (J) horrer

Read the directions carefully. Be sure you know whether you need to look for the correctly spelled word or the incorrectly spelled word.

Directions: Choose the phrase in which the underlined word is not spelled correctly.

5. (A) avoid <u>capture</u>

　　(B) hate to <u>complane</u>

　　(C) <u>empty</u> room

　　(D) <u>fourteen</u> points

6. (F) confusing <u>siginal</u>

　　(G) <u>sparkle</u> brightly

　　(H) <u>shallow</u> water

　　(J) find <u>something</u>

7. (A) <u>receeved</u> a call

　　(B) <u>furious</u> crowd

　　(C) cable <u>channel</u>

　　(D) white <u>chalk</u>

Spelling

Directions: Read each answer. Choose the answer that has a spelling error. If they are all correct, choose "No mistakes."

1. (A) conceited
   (B) invention
   (C) ceese
   (D) No mistakes

2. (F) carnevore
   (G) citrus
   (H) fascinate
   (J) No mistakes

3. (A) cricket
   (B) consider
   (C) asignment
   (D) No mistakes

Directions: Read each phrase. Choose the underlined word that is misspelled for how it is used in the phrase.

4. (F) bad <u>attitude</u>
   (G) high <u>sees</u>
   (H) <u>butter</u> and bread
   (J) <u>incorrect</u> answer

5. (A) <u>reed</u> a book
   (B) <u>grew</u> up
   (C) mountain <u>summit</u>
   (D) <u>tipped</u> over

6. (F) <u>active</u> puppy
   (G) <u>taking</u> notes
   (H) supporting <u>sentences</u>
   (J) buzzing <u>be</u>

Directions: Read each sentence. Choose the underlined part that is misspelled. If all words are spelled correctly, choose "No mistakes."

7. Some plants eat <u>meat</u> in <u>adition</u> to eating <u>their</u> own food. <u>No mistakes</u>
                (A)   (B)   (C)   (D)

8. <u>Usually,</u> the bones of birds' <u>wings</u> are <u>hollow.</u> <u>No mistakes</u>
     (F)   (G)   (H)   (J)

9. One <u>bauld</u> eagle nest can <u>weigh</u> as much as an <u>automobile.</u> <u>No mistakes</u>
       (A)   (B)   (C)   (D)

10. It is <u>said</u> that one <u>milyun</u> <u>matches</u> can be made from one tree. <u>No mistakes</u>
     (F)   (G)   (H)   (J)

Spelling

Directions: Read each answer. Choose the answer that has a spelling error. If none have an error, choose "No mistakes."

1. (A) reproduce
   (B) usualy
   (C) interest
   (D) No mistakes

3. (A) cautius
   (B) observe
   (C) information
   (D) No mistakes

2. (F) service
   (G) fountain
   (H) suceed
   (J) No mistakes

Directions: Read each phrase. Choose the underlined word that is misspelled for how it is used in the phrase.

4. (F) <u>groan</u> up
   (G) second <u>chance</u>
   (H) <u>spelling</u> bee
   (J) wrap <u>carefully</u>

5. (A) <u>terrible</u> food
   (B) famous <u>legend</u>
   (C) <u>dew</u> your homework
   (D) <u>amusing</u> play

Directions: Read each sentence. Choose the underlined part that is misspelled. If all words are spelled correctly, choose "No mistakes."

6. Alaskan huskies need five <u>thowsand</u> <u>calories</u> and up to four <u>quarts</u> of water

                                (F)   (G)   (H)

   a day. <u>No mistakes</u>
             (J)

7. <u>During</u> the winter in Japan, people make <u>elaborate</u> <u>stachues</u> out of ice and
   (A)   (B)   (C)

   snow. <u>No mistakes</u>
            (D)

8. The five-pound <u>kiwi</u> bird can lay an egg <u>weighing</u> more than a <u>pound</u>!
                 (F)   (G)   (H)

   <u>No mistakes</u>
     (J)

9. Harriet Tubman <u>asisted</u> slaves in <u>escaping</u> by using the <u>Underground</u>
                (A)   (B)   (C)

   <u>Railroad.</u> <u>No mistakes</u>
         (D)

Sample Test 3: Mechanics

Name _____ Date _____

Directions: Choose the punctuation mark that is needed in the sentence.

Example

Its more fun than scary.

- (A) ?
- (B) !
- (C) '
- (D) None

Answer: C

1. The puppy couldn't find the food dish.

- (A) ,
- (B) .
- (C) ?
- (D) None

2. Max said hed help me rake the leaves.

- (F) "
- (G) '
- (H) ?
- (J) None

3. Why isnt he here?

- (A) ?
- (B) .
- (C) '
- (D) None

Directions: Choose the line that has the punctuation error.

4. (F) Don't forget to feed the
(G) hamster before you leave,"
(H) Aunt Elaine said.
(J) No mistakes

5. (A) My violin competition was one of
(B) the best experiences Ive ever
(C) had. I felt very proud.
(D) No mistakes

Directions: Choose the answer that best completes the sentence.

6. Do you know what he made you for your _____

- (F) birthday?
- (G) birthday.
- (H) birthday!
- (J) birthday:

7. _____ take a walk this afternoon," Nora suggested.

- (A) Lets
- (B) Lets'
- (C) "Let's,
- (D) "Let's

GO

Sample Test 3: Mechanics

Directions: Choose the sentence that shows correct capitalization and punctuation.

8. (F) my sister takes good notes.

   (G) This is a great bird book

   (H) What kind of bird was that?

   (J) Did you put seed in the feeder.

9. (A) The tennis courts are full

   (B) Venus put our names on the list.

   (C) Did you remember your racket.

   (D) This can of tennis balls is new?

10. (F) Dad bought seeds plants, and fertilizer.

    (G) The shovel rake and hoe are in the garage.

    (H) We usually camp with Rashid, Ethan and, Annie.

    (J) The garden had corn, beans, and peas.

11. (A) I cant see the game from here.

    (B) Ellie wasn't able to play this week.

    (C) Don't' worry if you forgot.

    (D) The coach would'nt let us in.

Directions: Choose the answer that best fits in the blank and shows correct capitalization and punctuation.

12. Our neighbors got back from a long trip to _____

   (F) southern china.

   (G) southern China.

   (H) southern China?

   (J) southern China?

13. _____please take the trash out!" yelled Mom.

   (A) "Erik,

   (B) Erik,

   (C) "Erik

   (D) "erik,

14. Does that look like the _____

   (F) Grand Canyon.

   (G) Grand Canyon?

   (H) grand canyon?

   (J) grand canyon.

15. _____ he isn't going to join us.

   (A) No

   (B) No:

   (C) No;

   (D) No,

Sample Test 3: Mechanics

LANGUAGE ARTS 80

Directions: Choose the sentence that shows correct capitalization and punctuation. If the underlined part is correct, choose "Correct as it is."

16. The last thing I meant to do was <u>annoy the Andersons on arbor day.</u>

- (F) annoy the andersons on arbor day
- (G) Annoy the Andersons on arbor day
- (H) annoy the Andersons on Arbor Day
- (J) Correct as it is

17. <u>New zealand</u> is home to a playful bird called the *kea.*

- (A) New, Zealand
- (B) new zealand
- (C) New Zealand
- (D) Correct as it is

18. "Ouch! I've got a splinter in my <u>finger," cried Rosa.</u>

- (F) finger.," Cried Rosa
- (G) finger," cried rosa
- (H) finger, cried Rosa
- (J) Correct as it is

19. Potatoes are a healthful <u>food but potato</u> chips are not.

- (A) food. But potato
- (B) food, but potato
- (C) food; but potato
- (D) Correct as it is

Directions: Read the passage. Choose the answer that shows the best way to write the underlined section. If the underlined section is correct, choose "Correct as is."

People who live in <u>Nova Scotia Canada</u> **(20)** are called *Bluenoses.* This isnt **(21)** because of the color of their noses, however. This part of <u>Canada</u> **(22)** once sold large quantities of potatoes called *bluenose potatoes.* The potatoes got their name because each one had a blue end or <u>"nose. **(23)**</u>

20. (F) Nova Scotia, Canada
- (G) Nova Scotia, Canada,
- (H) Nova Scotia, canada
- (J) Correct as it is

21. (A) isnt'
- (B) is'nt
- (C) isn't
- (D) Correct as it is

22. (F) , Canada,
- (G) Canada,
- (H) , Canada
- (J) Correct as it is

23. (A) "nose.'
- (B) "nose".
- (C) "nose."
- (D) Correct as it is

GO

Name _____ Date _____

Sample Test 3: Mechanics

Directions: Choose the word that is spelled correctly and best fits in the blank.

24. This _____ leads to the gym.

- Ⓕ stareway
- Ⓖ stareweigh
- Ⓗ stairweigh
- Ⓙ stairway

25. Three _____ people live in the city.

- Ⓐ milion
- Ⓑ millun
- Ⓒ millione
- Ⓓ million

26. Did you finish the _____ yet?

- Ⓕ lesson
- Ⓖ leson
- Ⓗ lessin
- Ⓙ lessan

27. We planted _____ along the fence.

- Ⓐ daisyes
- Ⓑ daisies
- Ⓒ daisys
- Ⓓ daises

Directions: Read each phrase. Choose the phrase in which the underlined word is not spelled correctly.

28. Ⓕ traffic sounds
   Ⓖ five minutes
   Ⓗ amazing student
   Ⓙ loud grone

29. Ⓐ draw concloosions
   Ⓑ curious cat
   Ⓒ disappointing day
   Ⓓ make comparisons

30. Ⓕ excited kids
   Ⓖ venomous snakes
   Ⓗ dog hare
   Ⓙ detect sound

31. Ⓐ pioneer town
   Ⓑ save mony
   Ⓒ fine seafood
   Ⓓ rescue boat

32. Ⓕ mountain gorila
   Ⓖ crisp lettuce
   Ⓗ porcupine quills
   Ⓙ large building

Name _____ Date _____

Word Choice

Directions: Read each sentence. Choose the word or phrase that best fits in the sentence.

Example

Pablo was looking _____ to his family's camping trip.

- (A) foremost
- (B) forehead
- (C) former
- (D) forward

Answer: (D)

1. Carmen _____ left a chocolate bar on the camp table.

- (A) angry
- (B) carelessly
- (C) bravely
- (D) have

2 The water _____ in the fountain.

- (F) splash
- (G) having splashed
- (H) splashing
- (J) splashed

3. My mother _____ for three hours.

- (A) drive
- (B) driven
- (C) has drove
- (D) drove

Stay with your first answer choice.
You should change an answer only if you are sure the one you marked is incorrect.

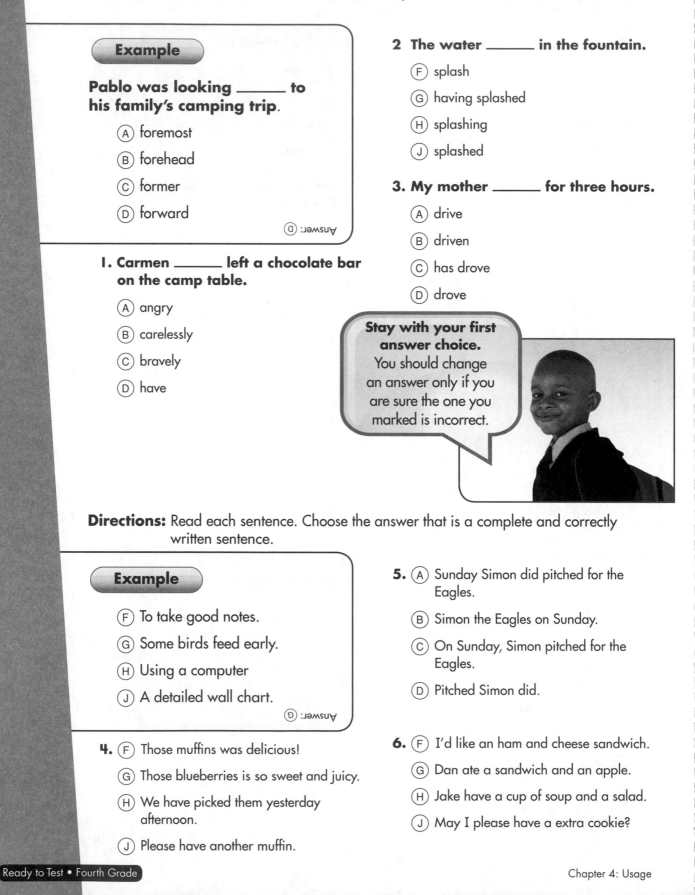

Directions: Read each sentence. Choose the answer that is a complete and correctly written sentence.

Example

- (F) To take good notes.
- (G) Some birds feed early.
- (H) Using a computer
- (J) A detailed wall chart.

Answer: (G)

4. (F) Those muffins was delicious!
   (G) Those blueberries is so sweet and juicy.
   (H) We have picked them yesterday afternoon.
   (J) Please have another muffin.

5. (A) Sunday Simon did pitched for the Eagles.
   (B) Simon the Eagles on Sunday.
   (C) On Sunday, Simon pitched for the Eagles.
   (D) Pitched Simon did.

6. (F) I'd like an ham and cheese sandwich.
   (G) Dan ate a sandwich and an apple.
   (H) Jake have a cup of soup and a salad.
   (J) May I please have a extra cookie?

Word Choice

Directions: Read each line. Choose the line that has a usage error. If there is no error, choose "No mistakes."

1. Ⓐ George Washington
   Ⓑ are called the father
   Ⓒ of our country.
   Ⓓ No mistakes

2. Ⓕ Binoculars are helpful
   Ⓖ because they let you
   Ⓗ observe things closely.
   Ⓙ No mistakes

3. Ⓐ We missed the
   Ⓑ baseball game I hope
   Ⓒ we make it to next week's game.
   Ⓓ No mistakes

4. Ⓕ The junior high
   Ⓖ play take place on
   Ⓗ Friday and Saturday night.
   Ⓙ No mistakes

5. Ⓐ He hasn't never made
   Ⓑ a mistake on any of
   Ⓒ his reading assignments.
   Ⓓ No mistakes

6. Ⓕ We haveta get more
   Ⓖ decorations for the hall
   Ⓗ in order to finish.
   Ⓙ No mistakes

Directions: Read each sentence. Choose the answer that shows the best way to write the underlined part. If the underlined part is correct, choose "No changes."

7. **Mr. Jacobs leading the school band.**
   Ⓐ leaded
   Ⓑ leads
   Ⓒ are leading
   Ⓓ No changes

8. **Antonio's family drove up the mountain on a long, whiny road.**
   Ⓕ wind
   Ⓖ windshield
   Ⓗ winding
   Ⓙ No changes

Directions: Read each sentence. Choose the answer that is a complete and correctly written sentence.

9. Ⓐ Ray and I raked the leaves into a huge pile.
   Ⓑ My friend Ann helped him and I.
   Ⓒ Her and I jumped onto the leaf pile.
   Ⓓ Ray's great picture of me and her.

10. Ⓕ Not all birds.
    Ⓖ Ostriches and penguins can't fly.
    Ⓗ Fly in a V-shaped group.
    Ⓙ Ducks and geese.

Sentences

Directions: Read the paragraph and answer the questions.

(1) "Boy, does this sound like a goofy assignment," I said to Kendra, <u>rolling</u> my eyes. **(2)** We were walking home after school talking about what Mr. Stewart had given us for homework.

(3) We were supposed to listen—just listen—for two hours this week. **(4)** We could do it any time we wanted, in short periods or long, and write down some of <u>the stuffs</u> we heard. **(5)** We also had to describe where we listened and the time of day.

(6) As we walked by a park, Kendra stopped for a moment and suggested, "Hey, I have an idea. <u>Let's us</u> start right now."

(7) For once she had something. **(8)** I told her it was a great idea, and then I spotted <u>an bench</u> beside the fountain. **(9)** "Let's get started," I said.

---

1. In sentence 1, <u>rolling</u> is best written

- (A) rollering.
- (B) rolleded.
- (C) rolled.
- (D) Correct as it is

2. In sentence 4, <u>the stuffs</u> is best written

- (F) the stuff.
- (G) a stuffs.
- (H) an stuff.
- (J) Correct as it is

3. In sentence 6, <u>Let's us</u> is best written

- (A) Lets.
- (B) Lets us.
- (C) Let's.
- (D) Correct as it is

4. In sentence 8, <u>an bench</u> is best written

- (F) an benches.
- (G) a bench.
- (H) a benches.
- (J) Correct as it is

Sentences

Directions: Read each sentence. Choose the answer that names the simple subject.

Example

It was mostly <u>black</u> with red <u>marks</u> on its <u>wings</u>.
Ⓐ   Ⓑ   Ⓒ   Ⓓ

Answer: Ⓐ

1. <u>Everyone</u> <u>drinks</u> orange <u>juice</u> <u>for</u> breakfast.
   Ⓐ   Ⓑ   Ⓒ Ⓓ

2. <u>Most</u> <u>students</u> <u>enjoy</u> <u>camping</u>.
   Ⓕ   Ⓖ   Ⓗ   Ⓙ

3. <u>Charlotte</u> <u>lost</u> <u>her</u> job because <u>she</u> showed up late.
   Ⓐ   Ⓑ Ⓒ   Ⓓ

4. <u>My</u> <u>dad</u> <u>cooked</u> <u>spaghetti and meatballs</u> for dinner.
   Ⓕ   Ⓖ   Ⓗ   Ⓙ

Directions: Reach each sentence. Choose the answer that names the simple predicate.

5. A <u>good</u> <u>breakfast</u> <u>is</u> <u>important</u>.
   Ⓐ   Ⓑ   Ⓒ   Ⓓ

6. I <u>took</u> Jake's <u>dog</u> Ben <u>for</u> a <u>walk</u>.
   Ⓕ   Ⓖ   Ⓗ   Ⓙ

7. <u>Studying</u> <u>helps</u> <u>you</u> <u>get</u> good grades.
   Ⓐ   Ⓑ   Ⓒ Ⓓ

8. <u>Ramona</u> <u>performed</u> a <u>dance</u> routine for the <u>talent</u> show.
   Ⓕ   Ⓖ   Ⓗ   Ⓙ

Sentences

Directions: Read the underlined sentences. Choose the answer that best combines them.

1. The traffic was loud.
The neighbors were loud.
I couldn't sleep.

(A) The traffic was loud and the neighbors were loud. I couldn't sleep.

(B) The traffic was loud. The neighbors were loud, but I couldn't sleep.

(C) The traffic and neighbors were loud, so I couldn't sleep.

(D) The traffic was loud and so were the neighbors; but I couldn't sleep.

2. Our town's name is Lost City.
It has an unusual history.

(F) Lost City has an unusual history, and it is our town.

(G) An unusual history, our town is Lost City.

(H) Our town, Lost City, has an unusual history.

(J) With an unusual history, our town is Lost City.

Directions: Read each sentence. Choose the best way of expressing the idea.

3. (A) The founders of Lost City from Baltimore came.

(B) The founders of Lost City came from Baltimore.

(C) Coming from Baltimore were the founders of Lost City.

(D) From Baltimore the founders of Lost City came.

4. (F) Mary she rode the bus all the way into the city.

(G) Rode the bus all the way into the city Mary did.

(H) All the way into the city, Mary rode the bus.

(J) Mary rode the bus all the way into the city.

5. (A) Though once calm in the morning, the seas were choppy by afternoon.

(B) The seas became choppy in the afternoon, and it was calm in the morning.

(C) The seas were calm in the morning, but by the afternoon they had become choppy.

(D) The seas were calm in the morning, because they were choppy in the afternoon.

If you are not sure which answer is correct, say each one to yourself. The correct answer usually sounds best.

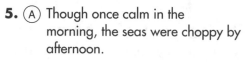

Sentences

Directions: Read the passage, and answer the questions that follow.

> **(1)** Serious storms are hurricanes that occur over the ocean. **(2)** The warm tropical ocean water is warm. **(3)** During the summer and early fall, a low-pressure area can form above the waves. **(4)** The warm air zips up above the waves. **(5)** The moist air zips above the waves. **(6)** Cooler air in. **(7)** This causes the air to spin. **(8)** Air pressure in the center drops. **(9)** More warm, moist air is sucked up into the system. **(10)** It creates wind, rain, and clouds. **(11)** Inside the wall, the system's eye is calm. **(12)** But around the eye, the rain, wind, and clouds swirl in the fierce hurricane

1. Sentence 1 is best written

(A) Serious storms that occur over the ocean are hurricanes.

(B) Serious storms, hurricanes, occur over the ocean.

(C) Hurricanes are serious storms that occur over the ocean.

(D) Correct as it is

2. Which sentence incorrectly repeats a word or group of words?

(F) sentence 1

(G) sentence 2

(H) sentence 3

(J) sentence 4

3. Which of these is not a sentence?

(A) sentence 2

(B) sentence 6

(C) sentence 9

(D) sentence 11

4. How can sentences 4 and 5 best be joined without changing their meanings?

(F) Zipping up above the waves, the water is warm and moist.

(G) The warm and moist air zips up above the waves.

(H) The warm air and the moist air zips up above the waves.

(J) The warm, moist air zips up above the waves.

Sentences

Directions: Write **S** before each line that is a simple sentence or complete thought. Write **F** before each line that is a sentence fragment or incomplete thought.

1. _____ You should know better.

2. _____ Walking faster all the time.

3. _____ Wait outside.

4. _____ Caught the ball and threw it to second base.

5. _____ Every house in town.

6. _____ The dog jumped over the fence.

7. _____ They will arrive soon.

8. _____ Can you close the window?

9. _____ A few people in this club.

10. _____ He can read well.

A **compound** sentence is made up of two complete thoughts, or simple sentences, that are joined by a conjunction.

Directions: Use the conjunctions *and, or,* or *but* after the comma to complete each sentence.

11. Sasha flew to Chicago, _____ she took a train to Milwaukee.

12. I can go to the game, _____ I have to be home by 10.

13. Finish your homework, _____ you won't be allowed to play outside.

14. Some athletes are paid well, _____ others do not make much money.

15. His favorite food is pizza, _____ his favorite drink is lemonade.

Sentences

Directions: Choose the best answer to identify what type of sentence it is. Choose **DE** for declarative, **IN** for interrogative, **IM** for imperative, and **EX** for exclamatory.

1. He quickly looked around to see if anyone was watching him.

- (A) DE
- (B) IN
- (C) IM
- (D) EX

2. He fled toward the barn.

- (F) DE
- (G) IN
- (H) IM
- (J) EX

3. Can you keep a secret?

- (A) DE
- (B) IN
- (C) IM
- (D) EX

4. Not a chance!

- (F) DE
- (G) IN
- (H) IM
- (J) EX

5. Do not stop reading until you reach the end of this story.

- (A) DE
- (B) IN
- (C) IM
- (D) EX

6. Jack stood on the deck of the ship.

- (F) DE
- (G) IN
- (H) IM
- (J) EX

7. Get back in your room.

- (A) DE
- (B) IN
- (C) IM
- (D) EX

Do you need some help telling the different kinds of sentences apart?

- A **declarative** sentence makes a statement and ends with a period.
- An **interrogative** sentence asks a question and ends with a question mark.
- An **imperative** sentence expresses a command or request and ends with a period.
- An **exclamatory** sentence shows excitement or emotion and ends with an exclamation mark.

Name _____ Date _____

Paragraphs

Directions: Read the paragraph. Choose the best topic sentence for the paragraph.

Example

_____ Most are in the highlands of the Southwest. The horses have great difficulty finding food during the winter months. Snow covers the grass and small bushes that they feed on. Their numbers grow smaller each year.

Ⓐ Horses have soft fur.

Ⓑ Horses are interesting animals.

Ⓒ There are about 20,000 wild horses living in our country.

Ⓓ Horses can be ridden for work or for recreation.

Answer: Ⓒ

1. _____ Some said that if people dreamed of the same thing three nights in a row the dream was bound to come true. Others believed that if a person told about the dream before breakfast it would bring bad luck.

Ⓐ People dream for lots of reasons.

Ⓑ Long ago, people had many superstitions about dreams.

Ⓒ Dreams can be about many different things.

Ⓓ People used to be very superstitious.

Directions: Choose the answer that best develops the topic sentence below.

2. Birds eat many different things.

Ⓕ Their colors vary from drab to colorful. Some drab birds have small patches of color.

Ⓖ Small birds generally eat seeds and insects. Larger birds eat small animals and even fish.

Ⓗ They also fly in different ways. Gulls soar, but hummingbirds flap their wings often.

Ⓙ Even in cities, birds can survive. Some hawks now make their homes in skyscrapers.

Remember, a paragraph should focus on one idea. The correct answer is the one that best fits with the rest of the paragraph.

Paragraphs

Directions: Read each paragraph. Choose the sentence that does not belong.

(1) The sleepy little fishing town doubled in size almost overnight. (2) Harriet Johnson decided to build a resort on the cliffs near the beach. (3) With her fortune, she hired hundreds of workers to complete the job. (4) Many of them decided to stay when the job was finished. (5) Mrs. Johnson lived to be 97 years old. (6) These workers helped build the logging industry that exists even today.

1. (A) sentence 2

   (B) sentence 3

   (C) sentence 4

   (D) sentence 5

(1) Loch Ness is a long and very deep lake in Scotland. (2) Since the year 565, many people there have told of seeing a strange animal with a long, snakelike neck and a small head. (3) Most of those who have seen it say the Loch Ness Monster is dark, has a hump like a camel, and is about 50 feet long. (4) Camels live in desert regions and can go long periods of time without drinking water.

2. (F) sentence 1

   (G) sentence 2

   (H) sentence 3

   (J) sentence 4

Directions: Read each paragraph. Choose the sentence that best fits in the blank.

3. In Tennessee, there is a large, beautiful lake inside a giant cave. _____ Years ago, people named it the "Lost Sea." In the 1800s, Native Americans and Southern soldiers would hide in the cave by the lake. This cave was once even used as a dance hall.

   (A) Tennessee also has beautiful mountains.

   (B) Lakes are usually filled with fresh water.

   (C) Caves can contain stalactites or stalagmites.

   (D) It is the world's largest underground lake.

4. You've heard of "raining cats and dogs," but how about fish? In an English town called *Appin*, thousands of herring fish fell from the sky one day in 1817. _____ Today, scientists think a storm sucked the fish up from the ocean and dumped them inland.

   (F) No one then could explain how this happened.

   (G) Fish are usually found in water.

   (H) Herring are a type of fish that people eat.

   (J) There weren't many modern conveniences in 1817.

Name _____ Date _____

Paragraphs

Directions: Read the paragraph and answer the questions.

(1) One important reformer of the mid-1800s was Margaret Fuller. **(2)** As a young woman, Margaret Fuller taught school and wrote articles for magazines and newspapers. **(3)** She would hold public meetings with women to talk about issues that were important to them. **(4)** Women enjoyed talking together about what interests them. **(5)** In 1845, Margaret Fuller also wrote a book on her ideas about women's rights. **(6)** Many people were excited about her ideas. **(7)** Sadly, Margaret Fuller died in 1850 onboard a boat sailing for America.

1. Choose the best first sentence for this paragraph.

(A) During the 1800s, many people introduced new inventions.

(B) A reformer is someone who works to make conditions better than they have been.

(C) Many important people lived during the 1800s.

(D) Margaret is kind of an old-fashioned name.

2. Which sentence should be left out of this paragraph?

(F) sentence 3

(G) sentence 4

(H) sentence 1

(J) sentence 7

3. Which of the following would be most appropriate in a letter asking for information about sports programs available through a local community education program?

(A) I have heard that you have a lot of neat programs for people in the community. I think this is a wonderful service you are providing that is much needed by those who can't afford to get such education anywhere else.

(B) I am a very athletic person and am interested in what sports programs you will be offering during the summer. Please send me a schedule of programs that includes costs and times of meetings.

(C) My family just moved here from Nebraska, and I am excited about meeting new people. I love to do active things.

(D) I have volunteered in many places in the past and am wondering if you take volunteer instructors. Please send me a volunteer form.

Paragraphs

Directions: Read the paragraph, and answer the questions.

(1) Thomas Jefferson accomplished many great things. (2) He is probably best known as the main author of the Declaration of Independence. (3) Jefferson was a person of integrity, and many people trusted him. (4) He was a member of the Continental Congress and a minister to France. (5) He became secretary of state in 1790 and vice president in 1797. (6) Jefferson served as president of the United States from 1801 until 1809. (7) His wife was not alive to be his first lady. (8) This great man continued to work for his principles until he passed away in 1826.

1. What is the topic sentence of the paragraph?

(A) sentence 1

(B) sentence 2

(C) sentence 3

(D) sentence 4

2. Which of these could not be added after sentence 2?

(F) Jefferson was tall, with reddish hair.

(G) He was only 33 years old when he helped write the Declaration of Independence.

(H) The Declaration of Independence was the first step in a war against Britain.

(J) Benjamin Franklin helped Jefferson with some of the ideas in the document.

3. Which sentence does not belong in the paragraph?

(A) sentence 5

(B) sentence 6

(C) sentence 7

(D) sentence 8

4. Which of these could be added after sentence 6?

(F) He was president for seven years.

(G) During his presidency, he helped the United States purchase the Louisiana Territories.

(H) Some people liked him and some didn't.

(J) He was only the eighth president of the United States.

Cover the answer choices, and read the question. Think about your answer before you look at the choices. Then, choose the option that is closest to your answer.

Name _____   Date _____

Study Skills

Directions: Use the dictionary entries to answer the questions below.

save [sāv] *v.* 1. to rescue from harm or danger 2. to keep in a safe condition 3. to set aside for future use; store 4. to avoid
saving [sā´vĭng] *n.* 1. rescuing from harm or danger 2. avoiding excess spending; economy 3. something saved
savory [sā´və-rē] *adj.* 1. appealing to the taste or smell 2. salty to the taste

Dictionaries have guide words that appear at the top corners of each page. Guide words tell you the first and last word on each page.

1. The *a* in *saving* sounds most like the a in _____.

(A) pat

(B) ape

(C) heated

(D) naughty

2. Which sentence uses *save* in the same way as definition number 3?

(F) Firefighters save lives.

(G) She saves half of all she earns.

(H) Going by jet saves eight hours of driving.

(J) The life jacket saved the boy from drowning.

3. Which sentence uses *savory* in the same way as definition number 2?

(A) The savory stew made me thirsty.

(B) The savory bank opened an account.

(C) This flower has a savory scent.

(D) The savory dog rescued me.

4. Look at these guide words from a dictionary page.

| pace | packing |

Which of the following could be found on this page?

(F) package

(G) pac

(H) pact

(J) pad

5. Look at these guide words from a dictionary page.

| fourth | fragile |

Which of the following could be found on this page?

(A) frail

(B) fourteenth

(C) fracture

(D) fountain

Study Skills

Directions: Choose the best answer to each question below.

1. **If a book's call number is 683.2, on which shelf in the library would you find it?**

   (A) 220–285

   (B) 540–599

   (C) 600–685

   (D) 686–734

2. **If a book's call number is 234.48, on which shelf in the library would you find it?**

   (F) 800–890

   (G) 540–599

   (H) 220–285

   (J) 200–232

3. **The following call numbers appear on different books. Which of these books would you find on shelf 540–599?**

   (A) 589.88

   (B) 539.1

   (C) 501.35

   (D) 600.5

If you can't find your answer among the choices, reread the question. It is possible you misread it the first time.

Directions: Study this entry from an electronic card catalog. Use it to answer the questions below.

Author: Lyons, Nick
Title: Confessions of a fly-fishing addict/Nick Lyons.
Publisher: New York: Simon & Schuster, c1989
Descript: 200 p. :22cm
Subjects: Fly fishing
Add Title: Confessions of a fly-fishing addict
ISBN: 0671683792289
Call Number: 799.12 Lyo: 9/89

4. **Choose the label for the shelf on which you would look for this book.**

   (F) 500–600

   (G) 600–700

   (H) 700–800

   (J) 800–900

5. **What is the call number for this book?**

   (A) 799.12

   (B) 1989

   (C) 200

   (D) 0671683792289

6. **In what year was this book published?**

   (F) 2000

   (G) 1989

   (H) 1799

   (J) 2005

Study Skills

Directions: Use the picture of the encyclopedias to answer the questions.

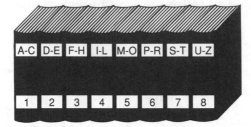

A-C D-E F-H I-L M-O P-R S-T U-Z
1 2 3 4 5 6 7 8

1. In which volume would you find information about different types of flags?

(A) Volume 2

(B) Volume 3

(C) Volume 5

(D) Volume 7

2. Which of the following topics would be found in Volume 5?

(F) information about the moon

(G) how to knit

(H) world climate regions

(J) the life of Marian Anderson

3. Where would you find an article about Thomas Jefferson?

(A) Volume 7

(B) Volume 4

(C) Volume 1

(D) Volume 3

4. Which of the following topics would be found in Volume 1?

(F) bears

(G) democracy

(H) North America

(J) Underground Railroad

Directions: Choose the answer you think is correct.

Table of Contents

Chapter	Page
1 Kinds of Bugs......................	1
2 Bug Bodies	15
3 Bug Senses	29
4 What Bugs Eat.................	37

5. Which chapter probably tells about how bugs find food?

(A) Chapter 1

(B) Chapter 2

(C) Chapter 3

(D) Chapter 4

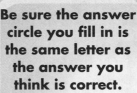

Be sure the answer circle you fill in is the same letter as the answer you think is correct.

Name _____   Date _____

Study Skills

Directions: Based on the graph below, choose the best answer.

REGULAR ICE CREAM   6 Years of Production
United States

Millions of gallons

920
900
880
860
840
820

Year 1   Year 2   Year 3   Year 4   Year 5   Year 6

USDA-NASS

1. Which year showed the highest ice cream production?

  (A) Year 3

  (B) Year 4

  (C) Year 5

  (D) Year 6

2. Approximately how many millions of gallons of ice cream were produced in Year 3?

  (F) 897 million gallons

  (G) 900 million gallons

  (H) 880 million gallons

  (J) 890 million gallons

3. Which year deviates from a pattern of increasing production?

  (A) Year 1

  (B) Year 2

  (C) Year 3

  (D) Year 4

4. Based on the graph, which of the following statements is true?

  (F) Ice cream production decreased overall from Year 1 to Year 6.

  (G) Ice cream production increased at a steady rate.

  (H) Ice cream production increased overall from Year 1 to Year 6.

  (J) One hundred million more gallons of ice cream were produced in Year 6 than Year 1.

Every part of a true sentence must be true.

Name _____ Date _____

Sample Test 4: Usage

Directions: Choose the word or phrase that best fits in the sentence.

1. The horn players _____ in the city finals.

- (A) competes
- (B) is competing
- (C) compete
- (D) competing

2. Which of the following is a complete and correctly written sentence?

- (F) I was late because the bus broke down.
- (G) I was late even though the bus broked down.
- (H) I was late the bus broke down.
- (J) I was late because the bus is broke.

Directions: Read each line. Choose the line that has a usage error. If there is no error, choose "No mistakes."

3. (A) When I went to college,

   (B) everyone was surprised when

   (C) I choosed art as my major.

   (D) No mistakes

4. (F) Although all snakes

   (G) have teeths, very few

   (H) of them have fangs.

   (J) No mistakes

5. (A) Her cousin, Alyson,

   (B) is the most politest person

   (C) I have ever met.

   (D) No mistakes

Directions: Choose the answer that names the simple subject.

6. Some children like fruit better than vegetables.

   (F)   (G)   (H)   (J)

Directions: Choose the answer that names the simple predicate.

7. Kenzo said his homework assignment would be a breeze.

   (A)   (B)   (C)   (D)

GO

Sample Test 4: Usage

Directions: Choose the answer that best combines the underlined sentences.

8. Cole walked three miles today.
Sierra walked three miles today.

(F) Cole walked three miles today, and so did Sierra.

(G) Three miles were walked today by both Cole and Sierra.

(H) Cole and Sierra walked three miles today.

(J) Cole walked three miles today; Sierra did, too.

9. Audrey painted the fence.
Audrey cleaned the yard.

(A) Audrey painted the fence; she cleaned the yard.

(B) Audrey painted the fence; then, she cleaned the yard.

(C) Audrey painted the fence, and Audrey cleaned the yard.

(D) Audrey painted the fence and cleaned the yard.

10. Sasha prepared lunch.
The lunch was hot.
The lunch was delicious.

(F) Sasha prepared lunch. The lunch was hot and delicious.

(G) Sasha prepared a hot and delicious lunch.

(H) Sasha prepared a lunch, which was hot and delicious.

(J) Sasha prepared a lunch that was hot and also delicious.

Directions: Choose the best way of expressing the idea in each item below.

11. (A) Toward San Francisco a group of pioneers thought they were headed.

(B) San Francisco, they thought the pioneers were headed.

(C) A group of pioneers thought they were headed toward San Francisco.

(D) A group of pioneers toward San Francisco were headed.

12. (F) Baltimore was soon known for its fine seafood.

(G) Soon, Baltimore was known for its fine seafood.

(H) For its fine seafood Baltimore was known soon.

(J) Baltimore, for its fine seafood, was soon known.

GO

Name _____ Date _____

Sample Test 4: Usage

Directions: Choose the best topic sentence for the paragraph below.

13. _____ **Soap was once money to the people of Mexico. Lumps of coal were used as coins by the people of England. Stone money was used on the Pacific Ocean island of Yep. Even food has been used as money. In Russia, "coins" of cheese could be used to buy things.**

   (A) Soap can be made from animal fat.

   (B) For some people today, making soap is a fun and interesting hobby.

   (C) Money was not always made of metals or paper, as it is today.

   (D) Money has been around for a long time.

Directions: Choose the answer that best develops the topic sentence below.

14. **During colonial days, there were no bathtubs or showers in houses.**

   (F) Colonial days were during the time that European people first settled in America.

   (G) There weren't any cars, either. People had to travel by horse.

   (H) People today take lots of baths. In fact, some people even have swimming pools and hot tubs in their houses.

   (J) They were not missed, however. People of that time thought that baths were unhealthy.

Directions: Choose the sentence that does not belong in the paragraph.

(1) Rain is the biggest danger to baby birds. **(2)** During rainy weather, the parents have to leave the nest in search of food. **(3)** Baby birds usually eat chewed-up worms and bugs. **(4)** The baby birds are left uncovered. **(5)** The babies get chilled. **(6)** Thousands have been known to die during long rainstorms.

15. (A) sentence 1

   (B) sentence 3

   (C) sentence 4

   (D) sentence 6

GO

Sample Test 4: Usage

Directions: Read the passage, and answer the questions.

---

(1) People in the city of Rabaul, Papua New Guinea, live in a huge volcanic crater. (2) Because of this, they know they need an escape plan in case of an eruption.

(3) In the fall of 1994, people began to notice signs of an eruption. (4) Recognized the signs. (5) Birds flew away from their nests, the ground shook in an up-and-down motion rather than side-to-side, and sea snakes slithered out of the ocean.

(6) On the day of the eruption, earthquakes shook Rabaul. (7) More than 50,000 people left the area. (8) Volcanic ash filled the sky. (9) When the smoke cleared, about three-fourths of the houses on the island <u>been</u> flattened. (10) The island suffered greatly, but because of good planning, only a few people lost their lives.

---

16. How is sentence 2 best written?

- (F) They know they need an escape plan, because of this, in case of an eruption.
- (G) They know, because of this, that they need an escape plan in case of an eruption.
- (H) An escape plan in case of eruption because of this they need.
- (J) Correct as it is

17. Which sentence could be added after sentence 5?

- (A) Animals can sense an earthquake long before people can feel the tremors.
- (B) Sea snakes are snakes that live in water.
- (C) The snakes slithered in a side-to-side motion.
- (D) The ocean nearby is filled with many creatures.

18. Which of the following is not a complete sentence?

- (F) sentence 1
- (G) sentence 2
- (H) sentence 3
- (J) sentence 4

19. In sentence 9, <u>been</u> is best written _____.

- (A) have been
- (B) beened
- (C) had been
- (D) Correct as it is

Name _____ Date _____

Sample Test 4: Usage

Directions: Use the dictionary definition to answer the questions that follow.

crutch [kruch] *n.* A support made to help with walking usu. held under the arm and sometimes used in pairs 2. The leg rest on a sidesaddle 3. A device used as a support or prop *v.* 1. To support or prop up

20. The *u* in crutch sounds most like the vowel sound in _____.

(F) urge

(G) us

(H) took

(J) horrid

21. In which of these sentences is *crutch* used as a verb?

(A) David had to use a crutch after he sprained his foot.

(B) He crutched the table with a tall stick.

(C) Lee used his blanket as a crutch to make him braver.

(D) Ravi threw her leg around the crutch as she sat in the saddle.

Directions: Study the table of contents from the book *Sunken Treasures*. Choose the best answer to the questions that follow.

Chapter	Pages
1: Types of Treasures	1
2: Places Treasure Are Found....................	14
3: Treasure Hunters and Experts..................	28
4: How Treasure Ship Sank......................	46
5: Missing Sunken Treasures...	62
6: Sunken Treasure Web Site References......	75
7: Sunken Treasure Book References..........	83
8: Sunken Treasure Periodical References.....	92

22. Which of the following sentences might be found in Chapter 1?

(F) Treasure ranges from ancient oil lamps to gold and jewels.

(G) One valuable site is www.yo-ho-matey.com.

(H) The Caribbean is a place many people think of when they hear the words sunken treasure.

(J) Many treasure ships sank during fierce battles.

23. Yoshi wants to do more investigating about sunken treasures. In which chapters should she look?

(A) Chapters 1, 2, and 3

(B) Chapters 3, 4, and 5

(C) Chapters 4, 5, and 6

(D) Chapters 6, 7, and 8

STOP

Making an Outline

Directions: The outline below is for a report about owls. Study the outline, and answer the questions that follow.

Owls

I. _____

    A. Great Horned Owl

    B. Snowy Owl

    C. Barn Owl

II. Body Characteristics

    A. Size

    B. Body Covering

    C. _____

    D. Eyes, Talons, and Beaks

III. Eating Habits

    A. Mice

    B. Other Small Rodents

1. Which of the following best fits in the blank in part I?

Ⓐ Owl Migration

Ⓑ Owl Habitats

Ⓒ Types of Owls

Ⓓ Owl Eating Habits

2. Which of the following best fits in the blank next to section II C?

Ⓕ Feather Variations

Ⓖ Grasses and Leaves

Ⓗ Trees

Ⓙ Nocturnal

3. Explain how the organization of the outline would help you write a report about owls.

_____

_____

_____

_____

_____

_____

_____

_____

_____

_____

_____

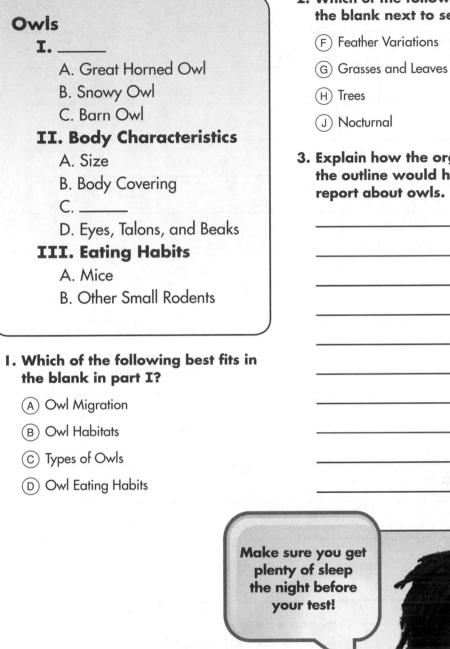

Make sure you get plenty of sleep the night before your test!

Name _____   Date _____

Writing a Personal Narrative

Directions: Describe what it was like when you did something for the first time. Some ideas include playing a new sport, learning how to play an instrument, acting in a play, or starting a new hobby. Include details or feelings you had during the experience.

_____

_____

_____

_____

_____

_____

_____

_____

_____

_____

_____

_____

_____

_____

_____

A **personal narrative** is a true story that is based on a person's experiences. It should have a clear beginning, middle, and end.

Writing Using Figurative Language

Directions: Read the poem. Then, fill in the blanks to complete the similes from the poem.

With fur like a snowstorm
And eyes like the night,
Two giant old bears
Sure gave me a fright.

They came up behind me
As quiet as mice,
And tapped on my shoulder.
Their paws were like ice.

As high as a kite,
I jumped in the air,
And turned round to see
Those bears standing there.

"We're sorry we scared you,"
The bears said so cool.
"We just came to ask you
To fill up our pool!"

1. fur like _____

2. eyes like _____

3. as quiet as _____

4. paws like _____

5. as high as a _____

Directions: Write your own similes using these words as a guide.

6. a lunch as _____ **as** _____

7. a friend like a _____

8. a coat as _____ **as** _____

9. a winter day like a _____

10. with _____ **like sunshine**

Figurative language is language used for descriptive effect. This poem uses similes.
Similes use the words *like* or *as* to compare things that may seem unlike each other.

For example, *Her lips were as red as cherries.*

Writing with Details

Directions: This is the beginning of a story. Read it and use your own ideas to help you finish the story.

It was finally getting cooler. After a blazing hot day, the sun had gone down. Hannah still couldn't believe their car had broken down. She also couldn't believe her father had decided to walk three miles through the desert for help. The map showed a town up ahead, but they hadn't seen any cars go by for more than an hour. Hannah was alone with her mother and her sister, Abigail.

1. What problem does Hannah's family have?

_____
_____
_____
_____
_____

2. Describe two ways that this story might turn out.

_____
_____
_____
_____
_____
_____
_____
_____

3. What are some of the sounds, sights, and feelings that Hannah's family might have experienced?

_____
_____
_____
_____
_____
_____
_____
_____
_____
_____
_____
_____

4. Use the details from your answer to questions 1–3 to write the ending to the story on a separate piece of paper.

Writing a Persuasive Essay

Directions: Read the paragraph about a book one student really liked. Then, answer each question below.

> I really liked the book *The Wizard of Oz* and think others will like it, too. It was very exciting, especially the part where Dorothy went to the Wicked Witch's castle and made the witch melt. I also liked the way the characters worked together to solve their problems. Finally, when Dorothy says, "There's no place like home," I thought about my home and family and the many wonderful things I have.

1. What is the title of a book or movie you really liked?

_____

_____

2. Why do you think that others should read or watch it?

_____

_____

_____

_____

_____

_____

3. What are some specific parts of the book or movie that you think others would enjoy?

_____

_____

_____

_____

_____

_____

4. Now, write a few paragraphs using the information from questions 2 and 3 to convince others to read this book or watch the movie. Explain why you liked it, and include examples to support your reasons. Be sure to use as many details as possible to persuade readers.

_____

_____

_____

_____

_____

_____

_____

_____

_____

_____

_____

_____

_____

Writing a Narrative Procedure

Directions: Read the paragraph below about how to plant a seed. Then, think of something you know how to do well. Write a narrative procedure that explains how to do it. Use paragraphs and words such as *first, next, then, finally,* and *last.*

I found out how to plant a seed and make it grow. First, I found a spot where the plant would get the right amount of sunshine. Next, I dug a hole and put the seed into the soil. I covered the seed with soil, and then I watered it. After a couple of weeks, it began to grow into a beautiful plant.

_____

_____

_____

_____

_____

_____

_____

_____

_____

_____

_____

_____

A **narrative procedure** explains how to do something. It uses clear steps that are easy to follow.

Sample Test 5: Writing

Directions: Follow the instructions for each item below.

1. Describe something in nature. For example, you could describe a sunset, a tree in the fall, or a stormy sky. Use at least two similes in your description.

_____

_____

_____

_____

_____

_____

2. Write a paragraph that explains how to do something. Be sure to include words such as *first, next,* and *last.*

_____

_____

_____

_____

_____

_____

_____

_____

_____

_____

GO

Sample Test 5: Writing

Directions: Write about a time when you had to make a difficult decision. Include descriptions of places and people, interesting details, and feelings you had during your experience.

_____

_____

_____

_____

_____

_____

_____

_____

_____

_____

_____

_____

_____

_____

_____

_____

_____

_____

_____

_____

_____

STOP

Name _____ Date _____

Practice Test 2: Language
Part 1: Mechanics

Directions: Read each sentence. Choose the punctuation mark that is needed in the sentence. If no more punctuation is needed, choose "None."

1. I ate the whole box I had such a stomachache.

- Ⓐ ,
- Ⓑ !
- Ⓒ ;
- Ⓓ None

2. Oranges lemons, and grapefruits are citrus fruits.

- Ⓕ ?
- Ⓖ ,
- Ⓗ ;
- Ⓙ None

3. "That closet needs a thorough cleaning! my mom said.

- Ⓐ "
- Ⓑ .
- Ⓒ '
- Ⓓ None

4. We've been waiting anxiously.

- Ⓕ .
- Ⓖ '
- Ⓗ ?
- Ⓙ None

Directions: Choose the line that has a punctuation error. If there is no error, choose "No mistakes."

5. Ⓐ The bus will pick us up
   Ⓑ at 830 A.M. sharp for
   Ⓒ the field trip to the zoo.
   Ⓓ No mistakes

6. Ⓕ Sara wanted to adopt
   Ⓖ another greyhound but
   Ⓗ she simply didn't have room.
   Ⓙ No mistakes

Directions: Choose the word or words that fit best in the blank and show correct punctuation.

7. _____ we won't be seeing that film.

- Ⓐ No,
- Ⓑ No
- Ⓒ No;
- Ⓓ No:

8. _____ and Rodrigo all went to get their hair cut.

- Ⓕ Max Henry
- Ⓖ Max Henry,
- Ⓗ Max, Henry,
- Ⓙ Max Henry;

Practice Test 2: Language
Part 1: Mechanics

Directions: Read each sentence. Choose the sentence that shows correct punctuation and capitalization.

9. (A) Tell Mrs Jensen I called

   (B) Miss. Richards will be late.

   (C) Our coach is Mr. Wannamaker

   (D) Dr. Pearl was here earlier.

10. (F) Will you please take the garbage out.

   (G) Dont let Destiny forget her chores.

   (H) She borrowed *The Cricket in Times Square* from the library.

   (J) This house looks like a pigsty

11. (A) "I think you did a wonderful job," Dad said.

   (B) "The *world book* encyclopedia is a good place to look."

   (C) "I will help you look in *National Geographic* when you get home.

   (D) Your report will be perfect when your done," Dad insisted.

12. (F) Jin hurt his thumb, yesterday, while playing soccer.

   (G) However, he still scored two goals.

   (H) He is one of the best players in clear lake, Michigan.

   (J) Jin wants to play soccer in College someday.

Directions: Read each sentence. Choose the answer that fits best in the blank and shows correct capitalization and punctuation.

13. **The play will be held on Wednesday, _____ nights.**

   (A) Thursday, and Friday,

   (B) Thursday, and, Friday

   (C) Thursday, and Friday

   (D) Thursday and Friday,

14. **_____ for the cool camera.**

   (F) Thank you,

   (G) thank you

   (H) Thank, you

   (J) Thank you

15. **Our project is due on _____.**

   (A) october 28 2012

   (B) October 28, 2012

   (C) October 28 2012

   (D) October, 28, 2012

16. **Please send that to _____.**

   (F) Mankato, Minnesota

   (G) mankato Minnesota

   (H) mankato minnesota

   (J) mankato, Minnesota,

GO

Practice Test 2: Language
Part 1: Mechanics

Directions: Read each passage. Choose the correct answer for each question.

Dear grandma

(1) Guess where we went today? (2) We went to see the Statue of Liberty. (3) I couldn't believe how big it is. (4) Theres a huge torch in the statue's hand. (5) I could see the statue as we sailed across to it. (6) It looked big from the boat, but it was gigantic when I stood in front of it.

(7) Yesterday, we took the elevator up to the top of the Empire State Building. (8) We used telescopes to look out across the city. (9) We were up so high!

(10) Dad says it's time to go. (11) We're going to Central Park today to skate row on the lake, and feed ducks. (12) I'm going to mail your letter in the hotel lobby. (13) See you soon?

Love,
Delia

---

17. At the beginning of Delia's letter, Dear grandma is best written _____.

(A) Dear Grandma

(B) Dear Grandma,

(C) Dear Grandma.

(D) Correct as it is

18. In sentence 4, Theres is best written _____.

(F) There's

(G) Theres'

(H) Theres's

(J) Correct as it is

19. In sentence 11, skate row on the lake, and feed ducks. is best written

(A) skate row on the lake and feed ducks,

(B) skate row on the lake and feed ducks.

(C) skate, row on the lake, and feed ducks.

(D) Correct as it is

20. In sentence 13, See you soon? is best written

(F) See you Soon.

(G) See you soon

(H) See you soon.

(J) Correct as it is

Name _____ Date _____

Practice Test 2: Language
Part 1: Mechanics

Directions: Choose the word that is spelled correctly and fits best in the blank.

21. The train _____ arrived.

Ⓐ finaly

Ⓑ finnaly

Ⓒ finely

Ⓓ finally

22. Please _____ your work.

Ⓕ revew

Ⓖ reeview

Ⓗ review

Ⓙ revyoo

23. He is my best _____.

Ⓐ frind

Ⓑ frend

Ⓒ friend

Ⓓ freind

24. Please _____ your papers in number order.

Ⓕ arange

Ⓖ arainge

Ⓗ arrainge

Ⓙ arrange

Directions: Read each phrase. Choose the phrase in which the underlined word is not spelled correctly for how it is used.

25. Ⓐ the hardest job

Ⓑ blond hare

Ⓒ a good citizen

Ⓓ invite them

26. Ⓕ no trouble

Ⓖ an unusual bird

Ⓗ the local seen

Ⓙ a lively conversation

27. Ⓐ a stormy knight

Ⓑ ordered food

Ⓒ a funny story

Ⓓ a pineapple cake

28. Ⓕ a train passenger

Ⓖ the threatened species

Ⓗ numerous ants

Ⓙ time two go

29. Ⓐ a spring day

Ⓑ a ruff road

Ⓒ Tuesday morning

Ⓓ bird migration

GO ▶

Practice Test 2: Language
Part 1: Mechanics

Directions: Read each choice. Choose the answer that has a spelling error. If they are all correct, choose "No mistakes."

30. (F) broil

(G) acident

(H) dwarf

(J) No mistakes

31. (A) jury

(B) knuckle

(C) pollite

(D) No mistakes

32. (F) wildernes

(G) structure

(H) republic

(J) No mistakes

Directions: Read each phrase. Choose the underlined word that is misspelled for how it is used in the phrase.

33. (A) <u>ad</u> numbers

(B) <u>brilliant</u> diamond

(C) <u>distant</u> planet

(D) <u>nibble</u> cheese

34. (F) <u>compound</u> word

(G) <u>baron</u> wasteland

(H) science <u>laboratory</u>

(J) <u>publish</u> a book

35. (A) blood <u>vessel</u>

(B) olive <u>oil</u>

(C) length of <u>chord</u>

(D) <u>mosquito</u> net

Directions: Read each sentence. Choose the underlined part that is misspelled. If all words are spelled correctly, choose "No mistakes."

36. We <u>should</u> <u>probly</u> go inside before the <u>thunderstorm</u> starts. <u>No mistakes</u>
    (F)   (G)   (H)   (J)

37. Our dog <u>always</u> <u>houls</u> at the moon on <u>Thursday</u> nights. <u>No mistakes</u>
    (A)   (B)   (C)   (D)

38. The <u>weather</u> <u>forecast</u> for this weekend looks <u>postitive</u>. <u>No mistakes</u>
    (F)   (G)   (H)   (J)

39. Jazmin was <u>completing</u> a <u>puzzle</u> with her <u>classmate</u> Myles. <u>No mistakes</u>
    (A)   (B)   (C)   (D)

STOP

Practice Test 2: Language
Part 2: Usage

Directions: Choose the word or phrase that fits best in the sentence.

1. The ball _____ down the steps.

Ⓐ rolled

Ⓑ roll

Ⓒ rolling

Ⓓ having rolled

Directions: Choose the answer that is a complete and correctly written sentence.

2. Ⓕ Last night at 7 o'clock in the school auditorium.

Ⓖ The third annual school talent show.

Ⓗ Our class put on the funniest skit of the show.

Ⓙ Heard my parents laughing and applauding.

Directions: Read each line. Choose the line that has a usage error. If there is no error, choose "No mistakes."

3. Ⓐ Me and Paige want to

Ⓑ go horseback riding this

Ⓒ Saturday if the weather is good.

Ⓓ No mistakes

4. Ⓕ It wasn't no bother to

Ⓖ retype that paper since

Ⓗ I had to do mine, too.

Ⓙ No mistakes

5. Ⓐ Please clean up the dinner

Ⓑ dishes before you start

Ⓒ watching television.

Ⓓ No mistakes

Directions: Read the sentence. Choose the answer that names the simple subject.

6. The show must go on if we want to win the state theater competition.
　Ⓕ　Ⓖ　　　　　　Ⓗ　　　　　　　　　　　　　Ⓙ

Directions: Read the sentence. Choose the answer that names the simple predicate.

7. Please turn in papers that include your name and the date.
　Ⓐ　Ⓑ　　Ⓒ　　　　Ⓓ

GO ▶

Practice Test 2: Language
Part 2: Usage

Directions: Read the underlined sentences. Choose the answer that best combines them.

8. The tiny squirrel peeked from behind the tree.
The tiny squirrel scurried away.

  (F) The tiny squirrel peeked and scurried away from behind the tree.

  (G) The tiny squirrel peeked from behind the tree; it scurried away.

  (H) The tiny squirrel peeked from behind the tree and scurried away.

  (J) The tiny squirrel peeked from behind the tree and the tiny squirrel scurried away.

9. Mariah arrived at 6 o'clock.
Sylvia arrived at 6 o'clock.

  (A) Mariah arrived at 6 o'clock; so did Sylvia.

  (B) Mariah arrived at 6 o'clock, and Sylvia arrived at 6 o'clock.

  (C) Mariah arrived at 6 o'clock, as did Sylvia.

  (D) Mariah and Sylvia arrived at 6 o'clock.

10. Addy has a bicycle.
Her bike is shiny.
Her bike is green.

  (F) Addy has a bicycle. It is shiny and green.

  (G) Addy has a shiny, green bicycle.

  (H) Addy has a shiny bicycle. Addy has a green bicycle.

  (J) Addy has a bicycle, which is shiny and green.

Directions: Read each sentence. Choose the best way of expressing the idea.

11. (A) Having burned dead wood and heavy brush.

  (B) They burn dead wood and heavy brush.

  (C) Dead wood and heavy brush they burn.

  (D) Dead wood will burn heavy brush.

12. (F) The large truck, which brought the furniture to our house.

  (G) The truck was large that brought the furniture to our house.

  (H) The truck brought the furniture to our house, and was large.

  (J) The large truck brought the furniture to our house.

GO

Practice Test 2: Language
Part 2: Usage

Directions: Read the paragraph, and choose the best topic sentence for it.

_____ One scientist found out that cars painted pink or any light shade seem to be safer. The light colors are more easily seen. Cars of two or three different colors may be even safer.

13. (A) Cars can come in many colors.

(B) I prefer my cars to be red.

(C) Scientists counted car accidents to look for ways to prevent them.

(D) Scientists study natural phenomenon.

Directions: Choose the answer that best develops the topic sentence below.

The Gulf Stream is made up of a flow of warm ocean water a thousand times as great as the flow of the Amazon River.

14. (F) Scientists have mapped the Gulf Stream's course up the Atlantic Coast.

(G) Hot springs also have warm water.

(H) The Amazon River is in South America.

(J) Water also flows down rivers and streams toward the oceans.

Directions: Read the paragraph. Choose the sentence that fits best in the blank.

One of the nicest things about summer evenings is being able to watch fireflies or try to catch them. _____ Some scientists think the lights are used to scare away birds that might eat the fireflies. Others think the fireflies use their lights to say "hello" to their future mates.

15. (A) My grandma likes to sit on the porch in the evening.

(B) I usually catch fireflies in a big jam jar.

(C) Fireflies need to have lots of air if you catch them and put them in a jar.

(D) Did you ever wonder why fireflies light up?

GO

Practice Test 2: Language
Part 2: Usage

Directions: Read the passage. Choose the best answer for each question.

(1) There are more than 15,000 active volcanoes in the world. (2) Still, know everything there is to know about volcanoes scientists do not. (3) The study of volcanoes is called *volcanology*, and people who study volcanoes are called *volcanologists*.

(4) How does a volcano form? (5) Hot liquid rock, called *magma*, bubbles toward the surface through rock. (6) Once magma has arrived at Earth's surface, it is called *lava*. (7) Lava builds up until it forms a mountain in the shape of a cone. (8) The spot where lava comes up to Earth's surface through the cone is called a *volcano*.

(9) Some volcanic eruptions calm, but other destructive. (10) Large pieces of rock can be thrown out of the volcano. (11) People near an erupting volcano can be in great danger from <u>flowing</u> lava and volcanic bombs.

16. Sentence 2 is best written

F Scientists still don't know everything there is to know about volcanoes.

G Scientists don't know everything there is to know about volcanoes still.

H Scientists don't still know everything there is to know about volcanoes.

J Correct as it is

17. Which of these is not a sentence?

A sentence 8

B sentence 9

C sentence 10

D sentence 11

18. Which sentence could be added after sentence 10?

F Some people collect these rocks after the eruption.

G Dust is also thrown out and can cloud the air.

H Rocks are also formed from flowing lava.

J Many people like to bring back rock souvenirs when they visit a volcano.

19. In sentence 11, <u>flowing</u> is best written

A flowdering

B flowering

C flowed

D Correct as it is

GO

Name _____   Date _____

Practice Test 2: Language
Part 2: Usage

Directions: Use the map to answer the questions below.

	1	2	3	4
A	Wood Lane 🌲🌲🌲		library	house
B	🌲🌲🌲 Apple Street	house May Street	house Yellow Lane	🌲🌲🌲 March Lane
C	house	pool	house	
D	pool		factory	factory

Maple Street
Pine Street
Acorn Street
Jones Street
Bell Street

Legend

library	🏛	swimming pool	≈
woods	🌲🌲🌲	house	🏠
		factory	🏭

N
W ——— E
S

20. Near which coordinate is the library located?

- (F) B-2
- (G) A-3
- (H) D-3
- (J) C-1

21. Where are the factories located?

- (A) west of Apple Street
- (B) on the north side of the city
- (C) on the south side of the city
- (D) south of Bell Street

22. How many wooded areas does this town have?

- (F) 1
- (G) 2
- (H) 3
- (J) 4

23. If you walked from the library toward one of the swimming pools, you would be going

- (A) southeast.
- (B) northwest.
- (C) northeast.
- (D) southwest.

24. If you walked from the factories toward Maple Street, you would be going

- (F) north
- (G) south
- (H) west
- (J) east

GO ▶

Practice Test 2: Language
Part 2: Usage

Directions: Choose the best answer for each question.

25. Where would you look to find the phone number for a plumber?

(A) encyclopedia

(B) newspaper

(C) telephone book

(D) atlas

26. Which resource would you use to find out when Hanukkah occurs this year?

(F) encyclopedia

(G) calendar

(H) dictionary

(J) atlas

27. Where would you look to find a word that means the same as another word?

(A) dictionary

(B) crossword puzzle

(C) encyclopedia

(D) thesaurus

28. Which would you find in the glossary of a book?

(F) the year the book was published

(G) the meanings of words from the book

(H) the titles of the book chapters

(J) the topics found in the book and where to find them

Directions: Choose the word or name that would come first if the list were arranged in alphabetical order.

29. (A) annoy

(B) hoot

(C) horn

(D) ancient

30. (F) Joling, Beth

(G) Omar, Elijah

(H) Appleton, John

(J) Harkness, Dan

Directions: Read the sentences. Choose the answer that shows key words that should be included in notes on Frederick Douglass.

31. Frederick Douglass was probably born in 1818. He became a well-known author, speaker, and reformer on the subject of the abolition of slavery.

(A) Frederick Douglass; well-known speaker; slavery

(B) Frederick Douglass; born 1818; reformer; abolition of slavery

(C) 1818; author; speaker; abolition

(D) probably; 1818; author; abolition

STOP

Practice Test 2: Language
Part 3: Writing

Directions: Follow the instructions for each item below.

1. On the lines below, write a persuasive paragraph. You could try to persuade your parents of something, or pretend you are writing a letter to the school paper. Be sure to state your position clearly. Use examples and reasons to support your argument.

_____

_____

_____

_____

_____

_____

_____

_____

2. Imagine what it would be like to fly. Write a paragraph that describes your experience.

_____

_____

_____

_____

_____

_____

_____

_____

STOP

Number Sense

Directions: Read and work each problem. Find the correct answer. Fill in the circle.

Example

What is the next number in this sequence?
2 4 6 8 10 12 . . .

- (A) 16
- (B) 14
- (C) 20
- (D) 13

Answer: (B)

---

1. Yusef is in line to take his turn at the long jump. There are 13 people in line, and he is in the middle. What is his place in line?

- (A) fifth
- (B) tenth
- (C) seventh
- (D) sixth

2. There are an even number of events in which students can participate at the May Day fair. Which of the following could be the number of events?

- (F) 11
- (G) 15
- (H) 21
- (J) 22

3. What is 547 rounded to the nearest hundred?

- (A) 550
- (B) 560
- (C) 500
- (D) 600

4. Colleen found 16 shells on Saturday and 17 shells on Sunday. Al found 12 shells on Saturday and 22 shells on Sunday. Who found the greater number of shells altogether?

- (F) Al
- (G) Colleen
- (H) They found the same number of shells.
- (J) Not enough information

5. Which group of numbers is in order from least to greatest?

- (A) 4, 34, 16, 66, 79
- (B) 13, 24, 35, 44, 65
- (C) 76, 89, 45, 13, 12
- (D) 3, 56, 12, 98, 10

Look at all the answers before you mark one. You need to know what your choices are!

Number Sense

Directions: Read and work each problem. Find the correct answer. Fill in the circle.

1. What number goes in the box on the number line shown?

215   218   220   □

- Ⓐ 230
- Ⓑ 224
- Ⓒ 222
- Ⓓ 228

2. Which number is between 456,789 and 562,325?

- Ⓕ 572,325
- Ⓖ 564,331
- Ⓗ 455,644
- Ⓙ 458,319

3. If these numbers are put in order from greatest to least, what is the number exactly in the middle?

45   55   50   65   30   35   75

- Ⓐ 45
- Ⓑ 50
- Ⓒ 35
- Ⓓ 30

4. Look at the numbers below. If these numbers are ordered from least to greatest, which answer choice would correctly fit?

33,616   255,500
4,580,000   _____

- Ⓕ 887,140,000
- Ⓖ 88,846
- Ⓗ 3,540,939
- Ⓙ 2,193

5. What is $15.67 rounded to the nearest dollar?

- Ⓐ $15.00
- Ⓑ $15.50
- Ⓒ $16.00
- Ⓓ $15.60

6. Choose the most reasonable answer. What is the average number of books in a bookstore?

- Ⓕ 100
- Ⓖ 1,000,000
- Ⓗ 10,000
- Ⓙ 600

7. Which of the following will have a remainder when divided by 6?

- Ⓐ 12
- Ⓑ 42
- Ⓒ 36
- Ⓓ 46

8. Which point on this number line shows 654?

A   B   C   D

645   650

- Ⓕ A
- Ⓖ B
- Ⓗ C
- Ⓙ D

Number Sense

25 40 45 65 70 95 110

Directions: Read and work each problem. Find the correct answer. Fill in the circle.

1. Which number is between 211,356 and 320,198?

- (A) 301,495
- (B) 355,121
- (C) 210,387
- (D) 202,457

2. If these numbers are put in order from greatest to least, what number is exactly in the middle?
70 95 40 25 45 110 65

- (F) 45
- (G) 70
- (H) 65
- (J) 40

3. Which of the following is an odd number and a multiple of 3?

- (A) 6
- (B) 9
- (C) 24
- (D) 11

4. 768 =

- (F) seven sixty-eight
- (G) seventeen hundred sixty-eight
- (H) seven hundred sixty-eight
- (J) seven thousand sixty-eight

5. What is the numeral for one million, three hundred fifty-two thousand, twenty-one?

- (A) 1,535,221
- (B) 15,352,210
- (C) 150,352,021
- (D) 1,352,021

6. What is the word name for 1,382,004?

- (F) one million, three hundred eighty-two thousand, four
- (G) one million, three hundred eighty-two thousand, four hundred
- (H) one hundred thousand, three hundred eighty-two, four
- (J) one hundred million, three hundred eighty-two thousand, four hundred

7. Which of these will have a remainder when it is divided by 8?

- (A) 40
- (B) 45
- (C) 24
- (D) 56

8. Maria is fourteenth in line to buy a movie ticket. Exactly how many people are in front of her in line?

- (F) 13
- (G) 15
- (H) 14
- (J) 12

Name _____   Date _____

Number Sense

Directions: Read and work each problem. Find the correct answer. Fill in the circle.

1. If you arranged these numbers from least to greatest, which number would be last?

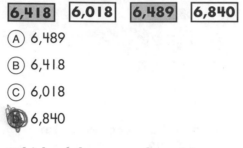

- (A) 6,489
- (B) 6,418
- (C) 6,018
- (D) 6,840

2. Which of these numbers is even and a multiple of 12?

- (F) 35
- (G) 145
- (H) 144
- (J) 148

3. Which number is missing from the sequence below?
36, 45, 54, _____, 72, 81

- (A) 60
- (B) 63
- (C) 59
- (D) 64

4. What is 42 in written form?

- (F) fourteen two
- (G) four two
- (H) forty-two
- (I) fourty-two

5. Which of the following number sentences is not true?

- (A) 5,428 > 5,482
- (B) $\frac{1}{4} = \frac{3}{12}$
- (C) 1.2 < 2.6
- (D) 8,222,504 > 8,201,756

6. If you are counting by fives, what number comes after 695?

- (F) 690
- (G) 700
- (H) 705
- (J) 675

7. 795,643 =

- (A) seven hundred million, ninety-five thousand, six hundred forty-three
- (B) seven hundred ninety-five thousand, six hundred forty-three
- (C) seven hundred ninety-five million, six thousand forty-three
- (D) seven hundred ninety-five, six hundred forty-three

8. Extend the number pattern.
2.5, 2.8, 3.1, 3.4, _____

- (A) 3.2
- (B) 3.9
- (C) 3.5
- (D) 3.7

Name _____ Date _____

Number Sense

Directions: Read and work each problem. Find the correct answer. Fill in the circle.

1. **Which number is between 3,489 and 4,662?**
   - (A) 4,668
   - (B) 3,482
   - (C) 3,625
   - (D) 3,261

2. **Which of these numbers would come after 4.8 on a number line?**
   - (F) 4.7
   - (G) 5.1
   - (H) 4.6
   - (J) 3.9

3. **Takeo is planning to meet his brothers at the baseball field between 2:10 and 2:35. At which of the following times might his brothers arrive?**
   - (A) 3:20
   - (B) 2:45
   - (C) 2:05
   - (D) 2:30

4. **Which number is missing from the sequence below?**
   6, 12, 18, 24, 30, _____, 42
   - (F) 32
   - (G) 40
   - (H) 36
   - (J) 39

5. **What is the numeral for three million, one hundred thirty-six thousand, fifteen?**
   - (A) 3,136,015
   - (B) 3,136,150
   - (C) 3,036,015
   - (D) 336,015

6. **If these numbers are put in order from least to greatest, what is the number exactly in the middle?**
   92 77 18 67 36 25 104
   - (F) 67
   - (G) 77
   - (H) 92
   - (J) 36

18,25,3,6,6

Here's a tip to narrow down your choices: Think about tossing out the high and low numbers, and consider the ones in the middle.

Name _____   Date _____

Number Sense

Directions: Read and work each problem. Find the correct answer. Fill in the circle.

1. What is the word name for 6,703,405?

(A) six million, seven zero three thousand, four hundred five

(B) six million, seven hundred three thousand, four hundred fifty

(C) six million, seven hundred three thousand, four hundred five

(D) six million, seven hundred three, four hundred five

2. Extend the number pattern. 56, 53, 50, 47, 44, _____

(F) 40

(G) 41

(H) 43

(J) 45

3. Find the missing number. 18, 26, 34, _____, 50, 58

(A) 38

(B) 40

(C) 42

(D) 44

4. What is the numeral for four million, eight hundred two thousand, sixteen?

(F) 4,802,160

(G) 4,082,016

(H) 4,802,016

(J) 4,802,160

5. Which of the following will have a remainder when divided by 8?

(A) 54

(B) 32

(C) 88

(D) 64

6. Which number sentence is not true?

(F) $\frac{1}{3} = \frac{5}{15}$

(G) $6.25 = 6\frac{3}{4}$

(H) $\frac{2}{3} = \frac{4}{6}$

(J) $\frac{3}{4} > \frac{1}{4}$

7. How many of these numbers are greater than 218?

| 222 | 245 | 212 | 245 |

(A) 1

(B) 2

(C) 3

(D) 4

8. Which number sentence is not true?

(F) $\frac{3}{12} = \frac{1}{4}$

(G) $5.26 < 5.1$

(H) $12.75 = 12\frac{3}{4}$

(J) $25\% > 18\%$

Number Sense

Directions: Read and work each problem. Find the correct answer. Fill in the circle.

1. **Which number is between 3,000,000 and 3,500,000?**

   Ⓐ 3,548,000
   Ⓑ 3,259,336
   Ⓒ 3,620,469
   Ⓓ 2,986,999

2. **Which number is less than 52,000 and has a 7 in the ones place?**

   Ⓕ 51,070
   Ⓖ 48,687
   Ⓗ 52,317
   Ⓙ 38,763

3. **Which number is greater than 750 and has a 1 in the tens place?**

   Ⓐ 816
   Ⓑ 751
   Ⓒ 419
   Ⓓ 781

4. **Which number is less than 6?**

   Ⓕ 6.7
   Ⓖ 5.83
   Ⓗ 6.0009
   Ⓙ 7.1

5. **Which number is even and has a 0 in the thousands place?**

   Ⓐ 36,089
   Ⓑ 509,663
   Ⓒ 364,081
   Ⓓ 20,428

6. **Which number is between 580 and 680 and is made of all even numbers?**

   Ⓕ 626
   Ⓖ 582
   Ⓗ 647
   Ⓙ 544

7. **Which number is odd and has a 2 in the ten thousands place?**

   Ⓐ 26,058
   Ⓑ 32,555
   Ⓒ 25,451
   Ⓓ 289,463

8. **Which number is less than 3?**

   Ⓕ 3.8
   Ⓖ $2\frac{7}{8}$
   Ⓗ $4\frac{1}{3}$
   Ⓙ 3.01

Number Concepts

Directions: Read and work each problem. Find the correct answer. Fill in the circle.

1. Which image shows 8 × 3?

Ⓐ [image of stars with some crossed out]

Ⓑ [image of stars, circled]

Ⓒ [image of stars]

Ⓓ None of these

2. Which number can be expressed as (14 + 5) + (9 × 3) − 1?

Ⓕ 30

Ⓖ 31

Ⓗ 46

Ⓙ 45 [circled]

3. Which of the following expressions does not equal 24?

Ⓐ 8 × 3

Ⓑ 4 × 6

Ⓒ 2 × 12

Ⓓ 2 × 2 × 3 [circled]

4. Shawn is collecting stones for a project. On the first day, he collects 100. On the second day, he collects 20. On the third day, he finds 3 stones. Which number shows how many stones he collected in all?

Ⓕ 23

Ⓖ 123 [circled]

Ⓗ 1,023

Ⓙ 24

5. Which number can be expressed as the following?
(8 × 2) + 4

Ⓐ 10

Ⓑ 14

Ⓒ 20 [circled]

Ⓓ 23

If you are stuck, skip the problem and come back to it at the end of the lesson.

Number Concepts

Directions: Read and work each problem. Fill in the circle.

1. **Which number makes this number sentence true?**
   □ × 8 = 72

   (A) 11

   (B) 8

   (C) 9

   (D) 7

2. **Which number makes this number sentence true?**
   □ + 79 = 129

   (F) 50

   (G) 60

   (H) 51

   (J) 49

3. **Which number makes this number sentence true?**
   685 − □ = 660

   (A) 30

   (B) 25

   (C) 20

   (D) 35

4. **Which number makes this number sentence true?**
   □ ÷ 11 = 11

   (F) 2

   (G) 22

   (H) 112

   (J) 121

5. **Which number makes this number sentence true?**
   6 × □ = 72

   (A) 8

   (B) 12

   (C) 9

   (D) 14

6. **Which number makes this number sentence true?**
   □ + 390 = 426

   (F) 36

   (G) 46

   (H) 34

   (J) 26

7. **Which number makes this number sentence true?**
   2,455 − □ = 2,097

   (A) 348

   (B) 358

   (C) 318

   (D) 352

8. **Which number makes this number sentence true?**
   □ ÷ 20 = 30

   (F) 1,600

   (G) 550

   (H) 800

   (J) 600

Number Concepts

Directions: Read and work each problem. Find the correct answer. Fill in the circle.

Example

18 □ 9 = 9
Which operation sign belongs in the box?

(A) +

(B) −

(C) ×

(D) ÷

Answer: (B)

1. 120 □ 10 = 12
Which operation sign belongs in the box?

(A) +

(B) −

(C) ×

(D) ÷

2. 17 + □ = 67
120 − □ = 70
Which number completes both number sentences?

(F) 50

(G) 40

(H) 60

(J) 70

3. $\frac{2}{20} = \frac{3}{□}$
What does the □ equal?

(A) 10

(B) 20

(C) 30

(D) 40

4. 69 □ 24 = 45
20 □ 12 = 8
Which operation sign belongs in both boxes?

(F) +

(G) −

(H) ×

(J) ÷

5. 5,000 □ 7,000 = 12,000
350,000 □ 36,000 = 386,000
Which operation sign belongs in both boxes?

(A) +

(B) −

(C) ×

(D) ÷

6. $\frac{1}{4} = \frac{□}{8}$
What does the □ equal?

(F) 36

(G) 24

(H) 12

(J) 32

7. 324 □ 4 = 81
Which operation sign belongs in the box?

(A) +

(B) −

(C) ×

(D) ÷

Number Concepts

Directions: Look for a pattern in the IN and OUT numbers in each table. Decide which function you need to use to get from each IN number to the OUT number below it. Fill in the table. Then, write the rule for getting from the IN number to the OUT number.

1.

IN	30	18	72	46	_____	16	100
OUT	15	9	36	_____	44	8	_____

Rule: _____

2.

IN	28	57	108	_____	52	39	66
OUT	34	_____	114	9	58	_____	72

Rule: _____

3.

IN	80	250	66	130	_____	600	11
OUT	75	245	_____	_____	93	595	6

Rule: _____

4.

IN	3	11	50	9	22	12	_____
OUT	12	_____	200	36	_____	48	32

Rule: _____

Number Concepts

MATH
134

Directions: Choose the equation that best describes the text. Mark the space for your choice.

Example

Annalise's class is studying 12 types of rocks. The class has 5 rocks left to study. How many rocks have they studied already?

Ⓐ □ + 12 = 5

Ⓑ 12 − 5 = □

Ⓒ 12 + 5 = □

Ⓓ □ − 5 = 12

Answer: B

1. Mr. Yakov ordered some books from an online bookstore. Each of the four books he ordered was $13.95. What was his total?

Ⓐ $13.95 × 4 = □

Ⓑ $13.95 ÷ 4 = □

Ⓒ $13.95 + 4 = □

Ⓓ $13.95 − □ = 4

2. Each of Joey's three cousins received a piggybank. He is giving them all his pennies for their banks. Joey has 285 pennies. How many will each cousin get?

Ⓕ 3 ÷ □ = 285

Ⓖ 285 × 3 = □

Ⓗ 285 + 285 + 285 = □

Ⓙ 285 ÷ 3 = □

3. Evan collects stamps. His dad gave him his grandpa's stamp book, which contained 1,872 stamps. In 2009, Evan collected 136 stamps. In 2010, he collected 255 stamps. In 2011, he collected 119 stamps. How many stamps does he now have altogether?

Ⓐ 136 + 255 + 119 = □

Ⓑ □ + 136 + 255 + 119 = 1,872

Ⓒ 1,872 + 136 + 255 + 119 = □

Ⓓ 1,872 − 136 − 255 − 119 = □

4. The Toodles Toy Company received a shipment of 41,100 action figures. They plan to ship the figures out to all 60 of their stores. How many action figures will each store receive?

Ⓕ 41,100 × 60 = □

Ⓖ 41,100 ÷ 60 = □

Ⓗ 41,000 − 60 = □

Ⓙ □ ÷ 41,000 = 60

5. Abe's Art Supply had a paint sale. Before the sale, they had 132 tubes of Peacock Blue paint. On Friday, they sold 44 tubes. On Saturday, they sold 30 tubes, and on Sunday, they sold 16 tubes. How many tubes of Peacock Blue were left after the sale?

Ⓐ 132 − 44 − 30 − 16 = □

Ⓑ 132 + 44 + 30 + 16 = □

Ⓒ 132 ÷ □ = 44 + 30 + 16

Ⓓ 132 − 44 + 30 + 16 = □

Number Concepts

Directions: Choose the equation that best describes the text. Mark the space for your choice.

1. **Asher bought 3 puzzles that cost $2.50 and 2 that cost $4.00. How much did he spend on puzzles altogether?**

   Ⓐ ($2.50 + 3) + ($4.00 + 2) = ☐

   Ⓑ ($2.50 × 3) + ($4.00 × 2) = ☐

   Ⓒ ($2.50 × 3) × ($4.00 × 2) = ☐

   Ⓓ ($2.50 × 3) ÷ ($4.00 × 2) = ☐

2. **Olivia's soccer team raised $278 last summer and $301 this summer. How much more money do they need to reach their goal of $750?**

   Ⓕ $750 + ($278 − $301) = ☐

   Ⓖ $750 − ☐ = $278 + $301

   Ⓗ $750 + $278 + $301 = ☐

   Ⓙ $750 − $278 − $301 = ☐

3. **Lima wants to plant a garden that will be 8 feet by 11 feet. What will the perimeter of her garden be?**

   Ⓐ 8 + 8 + 11 + 11 = ☐

   Ⓑ 8 × 8 × 11 × 11 = ☐

   Ⓒ 8 + 11 = ☐

   Ⓓ 11 ÷ ☐ = 8

4. **What will the area of Lima's garden be? (Use the information in question 3.)**

   Ⓕ (8 × 11) = (8 × 11) = ☐

   Ⓖ 11 − 8 = ☐

   Ⓗ 8 × 11 = ☐

   Ⓙ 8 + 8 + 11 + 11 = ☐

5. **In his orchard, Mr. Waxhaw plans to plant 12 rows with 16 apple trees in each. How many apple trees will he need?**

   Ⓐ 12 + 12 + 16 + 16 = ☐

   Ⓑ 12 + 16 = ☐

   Ⓒ 12 ÷ ☐ = 16

   Ⓓ 12 × 16 = ☐

6. **Mrs. Howard has 144 colored pencils. There are 20 students in her class, but 2 are absent. How many colored pencils will each student get?**

   Ⓕ 144 × (20 − 2) = ☐

   Ⓖ 144 ÷ (20 − 2) = ☐

   Ⓗ 144 ÷ 20 = ☐

   Ⓙ 144 − 20 − 2 = ☐

Fractions and Decimals

Directions: Read and work each problem. Show each fraction in simplest form. Find the correct answer. Fill in the circle.

Example

$\frac{1}{4}$ is equal to which of the following?

(A) 0.04

(B) 0.40

(C) 0.25

(D) 0.50

Answer: Ⓒ

---

1. Which of these figures is $\frac{4}{7}$ shaded?

(A)

(B)

(C)

(D)

2. Which point represents $\frac{3}{4}$?

A B   C   D
1   2   3   4

(F) A

(G) B

(H) C

(J) D

3. Bea traveled 99.5 miles in one weekend. If she traveled 46.9 miles on Saturday, how far did she travel on Sunday?

(A) 52.6 miles

(B) 146.4 miles

(C) 34 miles

(D) Not enough information

4. Which mixed number below is the same as $\frac{82}{9}$?

(F) $1\frac{9}{9}$

(G) $1\frac{1}{9}$

(H) $9\frac{1}{9}$

(J) 9

Pay close attention to the numbers in the denominator.
Also, look closely at the placement of the decimal points. If you misread, you may choose the wrong answer.

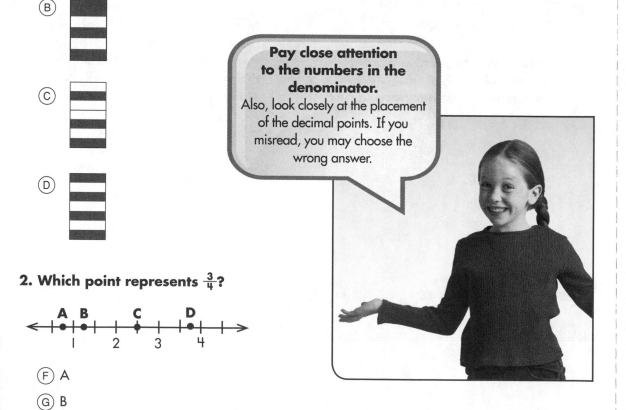

Fractions and Decimals

Directions: Read each problem. Find the correct answer. Fill in the circle.

1. Which of the following numbers has a 5 in the hundredths place?

- (A) 505.21
- (B) 251.32
- (C) 31.335
- (D) 63.251

2. Which picture shows a fraction equivalent to $\frac{3}{10}$?

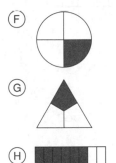

- (F)
- (G)
- (H)
- (J)

3. Which of these has a value greater than $\frac{1}{8}$?

- (A) $\frac{1}{16}$
- (B) $\frac{9}{4}$
- (C) $\frac{1}{32}$
- (D) $\frac{1}{64}$

4. Which number shows how much of the figure below is shaded?

- (F) $\frac{1}{2}$
- (G) $\frac{2}{10}$
- (H) $\frac{5}{1}$
- (J) $\frac{5}{100}$

5. Which fraction shows how many of the shapes are shaded?

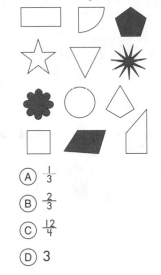

- (A) $\frac{1}{3}$
- (B) $\frac{2}{3}$
- (C) $\frac{12}{4}$
- (D) 3

6. Which of the decimals below names the smallest number?

- (F) 2.15
- (G) 2.05
- (H) 2.50
- (J) 2.21

7. Which fraction and decimal set below shows equal amounts?

- (A) $\frac{1}{8}$ and 0.125
- (B) $\frac{3}{4}$ and 0.34
- (C) $\frac{1}{2}$ and 0.25
- (D) $\frac{2}{10}$ and 0.02

8. How would 4.75 be represented as a fraction in simplest terms?

- (F) $4\frac{3}{4}$
- (G) $4\frac{7}{5}$
- (H) $4\frac{3}{5}$
- (J) $4\frac{75}{100}$

Name _____   Date _____

Fractions and Decimals

Directions: Read and work each problem. Show each fraction in simplest form. Find the correct answer. Fill in the circle.

1. Which fraction represents 4 divided by 5?

Ⓐ $\frac{5}{4}$

Ⓑ $\frac{3}{5}$

Ⓒ $\frac{4}{5}$

Ⓓ $\frac{5}{5}$

2. Which fraction shows how much of this figure is shaded?

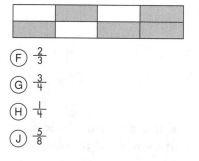

Ⓕ $\frac{2}{3}$

Ⓖ $\frac{3}{4}$

Ⓗ $\frac{1}{4}$

Ⓙ $\frac{5}{8}$

3. Which fraction shows how many of the shapes are shaded?

□ ■ ○ □ ● ○ ■ ● ■ ●

Ⓐ $\frac{2}{5}$

Ⓑ $\frac{3}{5}$

Ⓒ $\frac{7}{10}$

Ⓓ $\frac{1}{2}$

4. Joaquim is eating a pizza. The pizza has eight slices, and Joaquim eats two. What fraction of the pizza did he eat?

Ⓕ $\frac{1}{4}$

Ⓖ $\frac{3}{8}$

Ⓗ $\frac{8}{2}$

Ⓙ $\frac{1}{8}$

5. Which picture shows a fraction equivalent to $\frac{4}{5}$?

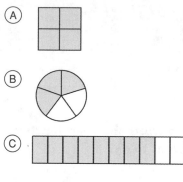

Ⓐ

Ⓑ

Ⓒ

Ⓓ

6. Which statement is true?

Ⓕ $\frac{1}{2} < \frac{1}{4}$

Ⓖ $\frac{3}{4} = 0.75$

Ⓗ $1 > \frac{5}{4}$

Ⓙ $0.25 = \frac{1}{2}$

7. Which fraction is shown by the X on this number line?

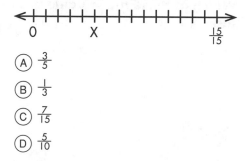

0   X $\frac{15}{15}$

Ⓐ $\frac{3}{5}$

Ⓑ $\frac{1}{3}$

Ⓒ $\frac{7}{15}$

Ⓓ $\frac{5}{10}$

Properties

Directions: Read each problem. Find the correct answer. Fill in the circle.

Example

Which number has an 8 in the thousands place?

(A) 81,428

(B) 78,643

(C) 42,638

(D) 29,821

Answer: (B)

---

1. Two thousand fifty-six can be shown as _____.

(A) 20,056

(B) 256

(C) 2.56

(D) 2,056

2. What is 365 rounded to the nearest ten?

(F) 400

(G) 360

(H) 370

(J) 300

Do two answer choices look a lot alike? One of them is probably correct!

3. What does the 4 in 42,678 mean?

(A) 4,000

(B) 400

(C) 40,000

(D) 4

4. What is the standard form of forty-two thousand, nine hundred one?

(F) 42,910

(G) 42,901

(H) 4,291

(J) 429,100

5. What is the standard form of 5,000 + 70 + 9?

(A) 579,000

(B) 5,790

(C) 5,079

(D) 579

6. What is another name for 651?

(F) 6 thousands, 5 tens, and 1 one

(G) 6 hundreds, 1 ten, and 5 ones

(H) 6 tens and 5 ones

(J) 6 hundreds, 5 tens, and 1 one

Properties

MATH
140

Directions: Read ands work each problem. Find the correct answer. Fill in the circle.

1. What is the meaning of 690?

(A) 69 hundreds

(B) 6 hundreds and 9 ones

(C) 69 tens

(D) 6 hundreds and 9 tens

2. What is another name for 8 hundreds, 4 tens, and 3 ones?

(F) 8,430

(G) 843

(H) 834

(J) 8,043

3. What is the expanded numeral for 265?

(A) 200 + 60 + 5

(B) 260 + 5

(C) 2 + 6 + 5

(D) 200 + 65

4. What is another way to write ten thousands?

(F) 10 + 1,000

(G) 1,000

(H) ten 1,000

(J) 10,000

5. How can you write 56,890 in expanded notation?

(A) 5 + 6 + 8 + 9 + 0

(B) 50,000 + 6,000 + 800 + 90

(C) 56,000 + 8,900

(D) 0.5 + 0.06 + 0.0008 + 0.0009

6. What is another name for 7 thousands and 5 hundreds?

(F) 5,700

(G) 7,050

(H) 570

(J) 7,500

7. How can you write 9,876 in expanded notation?

(A) 9,800 + 76 + 0

(B) 9,800 + 70 + 60

(C) 9,000 + 870 + 60

(D) 9,000 + 800 + 70 + 6

8. How many hundreds are in 9,451?

(F) 9

(G) 4

(H) 5

(J) 1

Properties

Directions: Read and work each problem. Find the correct answer. Fill in the circle.

1. **Which number comes next in this pattern?**
   5, 15, 45, _____

   (A) 50

   (B) 60

   (C) 135

   (D) None of these

2. **The only charge to use the pool is the $3.00 parking fee. Which of these number sentences should be used to find how much money the parking lot made on a day when 82 cars were parked there?**

   (F) 82 + $3.00 =

   (G) 82 − $3.00 =

   (H) 82 × $3.00 =

   (J) 82 ÷ $3.00 =

3. **What is 788 rounded to the nearest hundred?**

   (A) 700

   (B) 780

   (C) 790

   (D) 800

4. **Which equation would you use to find out the number of minutes in one week?**

   (F) 24 × 60

   (G) (7 × 24) × 60

   (H) (7 × 24) × 365

   (J) 365 ÷ 60

5. **How many thousands are in 5,708?**

   (A) 8

   (B) 0

   (C) 7

   (D) 5

> Read each problem carefully, and be sure you understand what it is asking.

Properties

Directions: Read and work each problem. Find the correct answer. Fill in the circle.

1. There are two numbers whose product is 98 and quotient is 2. What are the two numbers?

   (A) 49 and 8

   (B) 14 and 2

   (C) 14 and 7

   (D) 96 and 2

2. Look at the problem below. Which of these symbols goes in the box to get the smallest answer?
   150 ☐ 6 =

   (F) +

   (G) −

   (H) ×

   (J) ÷

3. Which letter is missing from this pattern?
   C D E __ G C D E F G

   (A) C

   (B) A

   (C) G

   (D) F

4. Which number sentence goes with 5 + 32 = 37?

   (F) 37 − 32 = 5

   (G) 37 + 5 = 42

   (H) 32 × 5 = 160

   (J) 32 ÷ 8 = 4

5. The ☐ stands for what number?
   5 × ☐ = 200

   (A) 100

   (B) 40

   (C) 4

   (D) 25

6. Which equation will have the greatest answer?

   (F) 357 − 6 =

   (G) 615 − 485 =

   (H) 888 − 777 =

   (J) 915 − 769 =

7. Each column in the number pattern below equals 21. Which numbers are missing?
   ```
   3  5  2  1  6
   2  7  8  9  1
   9  7  4  6  7
   _  1  7  _  7
   ```

   (A) 6 and 8

   (B) 7 and 5

   (C) 1 and 7

   (D) 4 and 3

8. Suppose you are estimating by rounding to the nearest ten. Which numbers should you use to estimate if you are rounding numbers between 23 and 46?

   (F) 30 and 50

   (G) 30 and 40

   (H) 20 and 50

   (J) 20 and 40

Properties

Directions: Find the pattern in each row of numbers. Continue the pattern to fill in the blanks. Then, draw a line to match the pattern to the correct rule.

Pattern	Rule
1. 1, 3, 5, ___, ___, 11, 13	−11
2. 70, ___, 50, ___, ___, 20, 10	+12
3. 1, 8, 15, 22, ___, ___, ___	+8
4. 36, 33, 30, ___, ___, ___, ___	−9
5. 115, 100, 85, ___, ___, ___, ___	+2
6. 64, 55, 46, ___, ___, ___, ___	−10
7. 17, 25, 33, ___, ___, ___, ___	−3
8. 96, ___, 84, 78, ___, ___, ___	−15
9. 88, ___, 66, ___, 44, ___, ___	−6
10. 12, 24, 36, ___, ___, ___, ___	+7

Properties

Directions: Choose a variable for the unknown amount. Then, write a number sentence to represent the problem. Finally, find the solution.

Example

Kyle made a dozen muffins. His little sisters ate 5 of them. How many muffins are left?

Variable: Let c = number of muffins left

Number sentence: $c + 5 = 12$

Solution: $c = 7$

A **variable** is an amount that is not known. It is often represented by a letter. Variables are used in number sentences to represent a situation.

1. **Julie is playing a board game. She rolls a 3 on the first die. What must she roll on the second die to move 9 spaces?**

   Variable: _____

   Number sentence: _____

   Solution: _____

2. **Rashad has a bag with 4 grapes. His father puts another handful into the bag. Rashad now has 13 grapes. How many grapes did his father give him?**

   Variable: _____

   Number sentence: _____

   Solution: _____

3. **A factory has 314 workers. The owner gave each worker a bonus of $500. What was the total amount of bonuses that the owner gave his workers?**

   Variable: _____

   Number sentence: _____

   Solution: _____

4. **Kayla's cat had 7 kittens. So far, she has given away 5 of them. How many kittens are left?**

   Variable: _____

   Number sentence: _____

   Solution: _____

Properties

Directions: Identify the property that makes each of these number sentences true. Write *A* for the associative property and *C* for the commutative property.

The **commutative property** says you can switch the order of the numbers and still get the same answer.	The **associative property** says you can change the grouping of the numbers and still get the same answer.
$5 + 10 = 10 + 5$ $15 = 15$ $5 \times 2 = 2 \times 5$ $10 = 10$	$(3 + 5) + 6 = 3 + (5 + 6)$ $8 + 6 = 3 + 11$ $14 = 14$ $(3 \times 5) \times 6 = 3 \times (5 \times 6)$ $15 \times 6 = 3 \times 30$ $90 = 90$

_____ 1. $59 + 43 = 43 + 59$

_____ 2. $(7 + 8) + 6 = 7 + (8 + 6)$

_____ 3. $(5 + 2) + 3 = 3 + (5 + 2)$

_____ 4. $5 \times (8 \times 6) = (5 \times 8) \times 6$

_____ 5. $3 \times 2 \times 9 = 9 \times 2 \times 3$

_____ 6. $412 \times (13 \times 15) = 412 \times (15 \times 13)$

_____ 7. $421 + 13 = 13 + 421$

_____ 8. $(3 + 8) + 14 = 3 + (8 + 14)$

_____ 9. $12 \times (3 \times 4) = (12 \times 3) \times 4$

_____ 10. $62 \times 18 = 18 \times 62$

Properties

Directions: Rewrite each of the expressions in an equivalent form using the property indicated.

1. 15 + 225 = _____ commutative

2. (6 + 8) + 20 = _____ associative

3. 3 + 9 = _____ commutative

4. 37 × (59 × 3) = _____ associative

5. (1 × 2) × 18 = _____ associative

6. 17 × 56 = _____ commutative

7. 4 × 3 = _____ commutative

8. 5 + 8 + 6 = _____ commutative

9. 7 × (4 × 3) = _____ associative

10. 7 × (4 × 3) = _____ commutative

11. 26 + 13 = _____ commutative

12. 11 × (4 × 2) = _____ associative

Sample Test 6: Concepts

Directions: Read and work each problem. Show each fraction in simplest form. Find the correct answer. Fill in the circle.

Example

Which of these is the best estimate of 767 ÷ 7 = □?

Ⓐ 10

Ⓑ 11

Ⓒ 100

Ⓓ 110

Answer: Ⓓ

---

1. In this pyramid, each number is the product of the two numbers directly below it. Which number is missing from the pyramid?

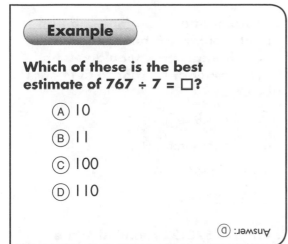

Ⓐ 6

Ⓑ 4

Ⓒ 8

Ⓓ None of these

2. How many hundreds are in 100,000?

Ⓕ 10

Ⓖ 100,000

Ⓗ 100

Ⓙ 1,000

3. Which of the following fraction groups are ordered correctly from least to greatest?

Ⓐ $1\frac{1}{8}, \frac{7}{8}, \frac{5}{8}, \frac{8}{8}$

Ⓑ $\frac{2}{3}, \frac{2}{5}, \frac{2}{4}, \frac{5}{6}$

Ⓒ $\frac{1}{2}, \frac{1}{3}, \frac{1}{4}, \frac{1}{6}$

Ⓓ $\frac{2}{10}, \frac{2}{8}, \frac{2}{5}, \frac{2}{3}$

4. What is 10,962 in written form?

Ⓕ nineteen thousand, sixty-two

Ⓖ ten thousand, nine hundred sixty-two

Ⓗ one thousand, nine hundred sixty-two

Ⓙ ten thousand, nine six two

5. Which of the following is not a multiple of 3 that is less than 30?

Ⓐ 15

Ⓑ 6

Ⓒ 18

Ⓓ 19

6. Which number correctly completes the following related number sentences?

6 – 2 = □

2 + □ = 6

6 – □ = 2

□ + 2 = 6

Ⓕ 4

Ⓖ 2

Ⓗ 3

Ⓙ 6

GO

Sample Test 6: Concepts

Directions: Read and work each problem. Find the correct answer. Fill in the circle.

7. Which fraction names the greatest number?

(A) $\frac{3}{4}$

(B) $\frac{2}{3}$

(C) $\frac{7}{8}$

(D) $\frac{1}{2}$

8. What is 500,003,300 in expanded form?

(F) 500,000,000 + 3,000 + 3

(G) 500,000,000 + 30,000 + 30

(H) 500,000 + 3,300

(J) 500,000,000 + 3,000 + 300

9. Which equation would you use to solve the following problem? Tyrone and Lawrence have a total of 26 CDs. They each have the same number of CDs. How many CDs does Tyrone have?

(A) $26 \times 2 = \square$

(B) $26 + 2 = \square$

(C) $26 - 2 = \square$

(D) $26 \div 2 = \square$

10. What fraction goes in the box on the number line below?

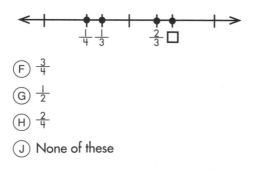

(F) $\frac{3}{4}$

(G) $\frac{1}{2}$

(H) $\frac{2}{4}$

(J) None of these

11. If you made 20 muffins and had to fit them into 4 boxes to give to your friends, how would you find the number of muffins to fit in each box?

(A) divide 20 by 4

(B) subtract 4 from 20

(C) multiply 20 by 4

(D) add 20 and 4

12. What is $73.52 rounded to the nearest dollar?

(F) $73.50

(G) $74.00

(H) $73.00

(J) $75.00

13. Which number makes these number sentences true?
9 + $\square$ = 15
42 ÷ 7 = $\square$

(A) 6

(B) 4

(C) 12

(D) 9

14. Which of these is between 673,904 and 678,042?

(F) 675,864

(G) 673,901

(H) 672,075

(J) 678,069

STOP

Addition

Directions: Choose the correct answer to each equation. Choose "None of these" if the correct answer is not given.

Example

$$\begin{array}{r} 31 \\ +25 \\ \hline \end{array}$$

(A) 6

(B) 56

(C) 54

(D) None of these

Answer: (B)

1.
$$\begin{array}{r} 282 \\ 422 \\ +116 \\ \hline \end{array}$$

(A) 810

(B) 830

(C) 710

(D) None of these

2.
$$\begin{array}{r} 995 \\ +226 \\ \hline \end{array}$$

(F) 967

(G) 1,221

(H) 769

(J) None of these

3. 281 + 93 =

(A) 212

(B) 374

(C) 188

(D) None of these

4.
$$\begin{array}{r} 5,989 \\ +2,697 \\ \hline \end{array}$$

(F) 8,686

(G) 8,668

(H) 3,292

(J) None of these

5.
$$\begin{array}{r} 45 \\ +22 \\ \hline \end{array}$$

(A) 23

(B) 67

(C) 990

(D) None of these

6.
$$\begin{array}{r} 76 \\ +23 \\ \hline \end{array}$$

(F) 99

(G) 53

(H) 3

(J) None of these

7. 96 + 52 + 48 =

(A) 196

(B) 4

(C) 148

(D) None of these

8. 7 + □ = 71

(F) 10

(G) 78

(H) 64

(J) None of these

Name _____ Date _____

Addition

Directions: Add the numbers.

1. 362
    +119

2. 428
    +358

3. 524
    +167

4. 665
    +219

5. 92
    29
    +64

6. 85
    27
    +78

7. 38
    25
    +63

8. 51
    49
    +73

The answer in an addition problem is always larger than the numbers being added.

Addition

Directions: Mark the space for the correct answer to each addition problem. Choose "None of these" if the answer is not given.

1. 1,524 + 2,341 =

   (A) 4,865

   (B) 3,865

   (C) 2,865

   (D) None of these

2. 66 + 77 + 88 =

   (F) 99

   (G) 211

   (H) 231

   (J) None of these

3. 14,588
    + 5,405

   (A) 19,993

   (B) 19,985

   (C) 19,983

   (D) None of these

4. 999
    +222

   (F) 1,111

   (G) 1,121

   (H) 1,021

   (J) None of these

5. 2,007 + 1,542 =

   (A) 3,549

   (B) 3,565

   (C) 3,445

   (D) None of these

6. 101 + 202 + 303 =

   (F) 404

   (G) 505

   (H) 606

   (J) None of these

7. 11,205 + 99 =

   (A) 11,303

   (B) 11,304

   (C) 11,305

   (D) None of these

8. 12 + 542 + 98 =

   (F) 552

   (G) 640

   (H) 652

   (J) None of these

Subtraction

Directions: Subtract the numbers.

1. 96
  −27

6. 422
  −158

2. 35
  −19

7. 535
  −348

3. 87
  −68

8. 723
  −158

4. 45
  −18

9. 427
  −114

5. 311
  −127

10. 989
  −819

Subtraction

Directions: Mark the space for the correct answer to each subtraction problem. Choose "None of these" if the correct answer is not given.

1. 422
   −104
   - (A) 218
   - (B) 312
   - (C) 318
   - (D) None of these

2. 6,000 − 250 =
   - (F) 5,000
   - (G) 5,750
   - (H) 5,650
   - (J) None of these

3. 309 − 45 =
   - (A) 246
   - (B) 266
   - (C) 364
   - (D) None of these

4. 1,589
   − 678
   - (F) 911
   - (G) 901
   - (H) 921
   - (J) None of these

5. 88 − 46 =
   - (A) 24
   - (B) 42
   - (C) 36
   - (D) None of these

6. 4,532
   −2,698
   - (F) 1,844
   - (G) 1,804
   - (H) 1,834
   - (J) None of these

7. 511
   − 12
   - (A) 498
   - (B) 501
   - (C) 502
   - (D) None of these

8. 96 − 68 =
   - (F) 28
   - (G) 38
   - (H) 22
   - (J) None of these

Subtraction

Directions: Mark the space for the correct answer to each subtraction problem. Choose "None of these" if the correct answer is not given.

1. 693
   − 95
   - (A) 788
   - (B) 598
   - (C) 608
   - (D) None of these

2. 1,360 − 952 =
   - (F) 408
   - (G) 435
   - (H) 480
   - (J) None of these

3. 654 − 33 − 8 =
   - (A) 631
   - (B) 615
   - (C) 621
   - (D) None of these

4. 191
   − 61
   - (F) 30
   - (G) 131
   - (H) 130
   - (J) None of these

5. 3,006 − 1,981 =
   - (A) 1,115
   - (B) 1,079
   - (C) 1,025
   - (D) None of these

6. 1,429
   − 335
   - (F) 1,094
   - (G) 1,940
   - (H) 1,904
   - (J) None of these

7. 982 − 529 =
   - (A) 463
   - (B) 453
   - (C) 467
   - (D) None of these

8. 8,633 − 6,003 =
   - (F) 2,600
   - (G) 2,630
   - (H) 2,000
   - (J) None of these

Adding and Subtracting Fractions

Directions: Choose the correct answer to each equation in simplest form. Choose "None of these" if the correct answer is not given.

Example

$\frac{4}{5} + \frac{4}{5} =$

(A) $\frac{5}{8}$

(B) $1\frac{3}{5}$

(C) 1

(D) None of these

Answer: (B)

1. $2\frac{1}{5}$
$+1\frac{3}{5}$

(A) 4

(B) $3\frac{4}{5}$

(C) $3\frac{2}{5}$

(D) None of these

2. $\frac{3}{4} - \frac{1}{4} = \square$

(F) $\frac{4}{4}$

(G) 1

(H) $\frac{1}{2}$

(J) None of these

3. $\frac{1}{10} + \frac{5}{10} = \square$

(A) $\frac{10}{6}$

(B) $\frac{3}{5}$

(C) $\frac{6}{10}$

(D) None of these

4. $\frac{5}{8} + \frac{7}{8} + \frac{1}{8} = \square$

(F) $\frac{13}{8}$

(G) $\frac{13}{24}$

(H) $1\frac{5}{8}$

(J) None of these

5. $\frac{6}{6} - \frac{6}{6} = \square$

(A) 0

(B) $\frac{12}{6}$

(C) 6

(D) None of these

6. $\square - \frac{2}{9} = \frac{5}{9}$

(F) $1\frac{1}{9}$

(G) $\frac{3}{9}$

(H) $\frac{7}{9}$

(J) None of these

7. $\frac{7}{9}$
$-\frac{6}{9}$

(A) $1\frac{4}{9}$

(B) $\frac{13}{9}$

(C) $\frac{1}{9}$

(D) None of these

> Look closely at the operation sign. Add whole numbers together first, then fractions. Remember to reduce to simplest form.

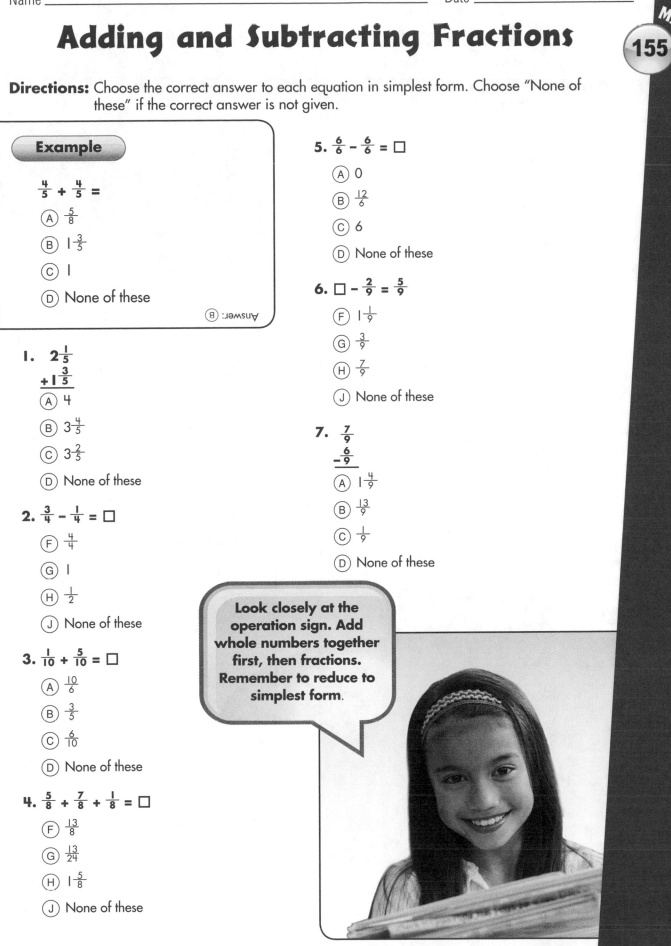

MATH
156

Adding and Subtracting Fractions

Directions: Choose the correct answer to each equation in simplest form. Choose "None of these" if the correct answer is not given.

1. $\frac{5}{6}$
    $+\square$
    $1\frac{2}{3}$

    (A) $\frac{5}{6}$

    (B) 1

    (C) $\frac{7}{6}$

    (D) None of these

2. $\square - \frac{2}{3} = 0$

    (F) $\frac{2}{3}$

    (G) $1\frac{2}{3}$

    (H) 0

    (J) None of these

3. $1\frac{3}{14}$
    $-\frac{1}{14}$

    (A) $1\frac{2}{7}$

    (B) $1\frac{1}{7}$

    (C) $\frac{1}{7}$

    (D) None of these

4. $1\frac{1}{12} - \frac{9}{12} =$

    (F) $\frac{1}{6}$

    (G) $\frac{2}{12}$

    (H) $1\frac{1}{2}$

    (J) None of these

5. $1\frac{7}{9}$
    $+\frac{5}{9}$

    (A) $2\frac{3}{9}$

    (B) $1\frac{12}{9}$

    (C) $2\frac{1}{3}$

    (D) None of these

6. $\frac{2}{3} - \square = \frac{1}{3}$

    (F) $\frac{3}{3}$

    (G) $\frac{1}{3}$

    (H) 1

    (J) None of these

7. $\frac{1}{24} + \frac{5}{24} =$

    (A) $\frac{1}{4}$

    (B) $\frac{4}{24}$

    (C) $\frac{6}{24}$

    (D) None of these

8. $\frac{3}{11} + \frac{9}{11} + \frac{1}{11} =$

    (F) $\frac{12}{11}$

    (G) $1\frac{2}{11}$

    (H) $\frac{5}{11}$

    (J) None of these

9. $\frac{2}{4} + \square = 1$

    (A) $\frac{1}{4}$

    (B) $\frac{2}{4}$

    (C) $1\frac{1}{2}$

    (D) None of these

10. $\frac{2}{7} + \frac{5}{7} =$

    (F) $\frac{7}{7}$

    (G) 0

    (H) 1

    (J) None of these

Adding and Subtracting Decimals

Directions: Choose the correct answer to each equation. Choose "None of these" if the correct answer is not given.

Example

$$6.211$$
$$+9.938$$

(A) 16.149

(B) 161.49

(C) 160.149

(D) None of these

Answer: (A)

---

1. 0.6 – 0.6 =

(A) 0

(B) 0.12

(C) 1

(D) None of these

2. $\$0.57$
$+\$0.68$

(F) 1.25

(G) $1.25

(H) 125

(J) None of these

3. 0.6537
–0.4325

(A) 1.0862

(B) 0.2212

(C) 0.22

(D) None of these

4. □ – 5.07 = 10.01

(F) 15.08

(G) 5.07

(H) 4.94

(J) None of these

5. 1.5 + 2.9 =

(A) 1.4

(B) 4.4

(C) 1.109

(D) None of these

6. $3.07 – $1.85 =

(F) 122

(G) $4.92

(H) $1.22

(J) None of these

7. $24.59
$19.57
+$28.36

(A) $72.32

(B) 72.52

(C) $72.52

(D) None of these

8. 12.053 + □ = 17.002

(F) 15.059

(G) 29.055

(H) 4.949

(J) None of these

Double-check the letter of your answer choice before filling in the circle.

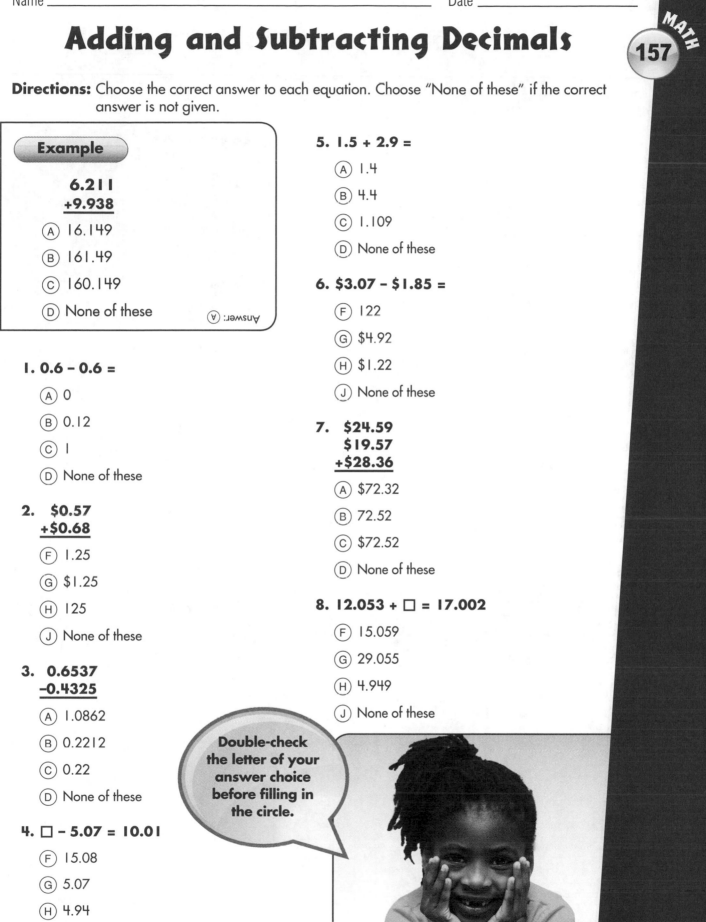

Adding and Subtracting Decimals

Directions: Choose the correct answer to each equation. Choose "None of these" if the correct answer is not given.

1. 12.682
   – 4.295
   - (A) 8.837
   - (B) 8.413
   - (C) 8.383
   - (D) None of these

2. 0.5487 – □ = 0.2408
   - (F) 0.3087
   - (G) 3.079
   - (H) 0.3079
   - (J) None of these

3. 1 + 0.1 =
   - (A) 0.11
   - (B) 1.1
   - (C) 1.01
   - (D) None of these

4. $15.79
   +$14.03
   - (F) $29.82
   - (G) $29.72
   - (H) $1.76
   - (J) None of these

5. $2.25
   $8.75
   +$5.13
   - (A) $15.13
   - (B) $16.13
   - (C) $15.88
   - (D) None of these

6. 5.0014 + □ = 13.5532
   - (F) 8.5518
   - (G) 7.5522
   - (H) 7.4678
   - (J) None of these

7. 1.6 + 4.09 =
   - (A) 6.5
   - (B) 5.69
   - (C) 5.015
   - (D) None of these

8. $22.19 – $18.34 =
   - (F) $3.25
   - (G) $4.25
   - (H) $3.85
   - (J) None of these

Multiplication and Division

Directions: Read and work each problem. Find the correct answer. Fill in the circle.

Example

Find 45 × 32.

- (A) 1,440
- (B) 1,120
- (C) 77
- (D) 1,395

Answer: (A)

---

1. Find 67 × 7.

- (A) 469
- (B) 479
- (C) 509
- (D) 74

2. Find 185 ÷ 5.

- (F) 37
- (G) 36
- (H) 180
- (J) 190

3. Find 88 ÷ 8.

- (A) 8
- (B) 0
- (C) 1
- (D) 11

4. Find 46 × 82.

- (F) 3,772
- (G) 3,672
- (H) 3,662
- (J) 128

5. Find 444 ÷ 6.

- (A) 78
- (B) 63
- (C) 74
- (D) 64

6. Find 22 × 12.

- (F) 240
- (G) 264
- (H) 242
- (J) 44

7. Find 34 × 57.

- (A) 91
- (B) 1,918
- (C) 1,938
- (D) 2,451

8. Find 42 ÷ 7.

- (F) 49
- (G) 294
- (H) 35
- (J) 6

Do you want to check your answers in a division problem? Just multiply your answer by the divisor.

Multiplication and Division

Directions: Work each problem, and choose the best answer.

1. 559
   × 4

(A) 2,236

(B) 2,206

(C) 2,336

(D) 2,263

2. 46
   ×21

(F) 926

(G) 699

(H) 968

(J) 966

3. 144 ÷ 8 =

(A) 16

(B) 18

(C) 14

(D) 22

4. 16)192

(F) 122

(G) 16

(H) 10

(J) 12

5. 58 ÷ 4 =

(A) 14

(B) 18

(C) 14 R2

(D) 14 R4

6. 612
   × 25

(F) 15,000

(G) 15,300

(H) 13,500

(J) 15,030

7. 6)360

(A) 10

(B) 36

(C) 600

(D) 60

8. 80 × 62 =

(F) 4,960

(G) 4,962

(H) 9,460

(J) 4,902

Multiplication and Division

Directions: Mark the space for the correct answer to each problem. Choose "None of these" if the correct answer is not given.

1. 54 ÷ 18 =
- Ⓐ 72
- Ⓑ 36
- Ⓒ 3
- Ⓓ None of these

2. 99 ÷ 3 =
- Ⓕ 66
- Ⓖ 33
- Ⓗ 11
- Ⓙ None of these

3. 659
  × 13
- Ⓐ 8,657
- Ⓑ 8,765
- Ⓒ 8,675
- Ⓓ None of these

4. 23⟌138
- Ⓕ 6 R1
- Ⓖ 6 R2
- Ⓗ 6
- Ⓙ None of these

5. 1,212
  ×   17
- Ⓐ 20,604
- Ⓑ 20,640
- Ⓒ 20,064
- Ⓓ None of these

6. 12⟌158
- Ⓕ 13
- Ⓖ 13 R1
- Ⓗ 13 R2
- Ⓙ None of these

7. 352
  ×   0
- Ⓐ 0
- Ⓑ 1
- Ⓒ 352
- Ⓓ None of these

8. 6 × ☐ = 114
- Ⓕ 108
- Ⓖ 19
- Ⓗ 684
- Ⓙ None of these

Multiplication and Division

Directions: Mark the space for the correct answer to each problem. Choose "None of these" if the correct answer is not given.

1. $16 \times \square = 144$

   (A) 8

   (B) 9

   (C) 9 R2

   (D) None of these

2. 4,803
   $\times$ 14

   (F) 67,242

   (G) 67,247

   (H) 57,242

   (J) None of these

3. $25\overline{)525}$

   (A) 11

   (B) 19

   (C) 20

   (D) None of these

4. $154 \div 11 =$

   (F) 14

   (G) 143

   (H) 165

   (J) None of these

5. 3,999
   $\times$ 10

   (A) 39,909

   (B) 39,990

   (C) 39,099

   (D) None of these

6. 251
   $\times$ 91

   (F) 21,841

   (G) 22,840

   (H) 22,841

   (J) None of these

7. $20\overline{)1,040}$

   (A) 51

   (B) 51 R6

   (C) 51 R8

   (D) None of these

8. $\square \div 18 = 8$

   (F) 144

   (G) 26

   (H) 2 R2

   (J) None of these

Factors and Multiples

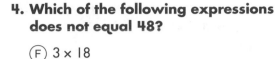

Directions: Read each problem. Choose and mark the best answer.

1. Which of the following expressions does not equal 12?

- (A) 4 × 3
- (B) 6 × 6
- (C) 2 × 6
- (D) 2 × 2 × 3

2. Which of the following expressions does not equal 54?

- (F) 9 × 6
- (G) 5 × 4
- (H) 3 × 18
- (J) 2 × 27

3. Which of the following expressions does not equal 20?

- (A) 20 × 1
- (B) 4 × 5
- (C) 2 × 10
- (D) 2 × 2 × 4

4. Which of the following expressions does not equal 48?

- (F) 3 × 18
- (G) 6 × 8
- (H) 2 × 24
- (J) 4 × 12

5. List all the factors of 15.

- (A) 1, 15
- (B) 1, 3, 15
- (C) 1, 3, 5, 15
- (D) 5, 10, 15, 20

6. Complete the table of multiples. What common multiple of 3 and 4 is in the table?

Multiples of 3	15	18		24			33
Multiples of 4	12	16			28	32	

- (F) 21
- (G) 24
- (H) 30
- (J) 33

A **factor** is a number that divides evenly into another number.
A **multiple** is the result of a number multiplied by any whole number.

Name _____ Date _____

Factors and Multiples

Directions: Read each problem. Choose and mark the best answer.

1. Which of the following expressions does not equal 36?

(A) 3×11

(B) 2×18

(C) 6×6

(D) $2 \times 2 \times 3 \times 3$

2. List all the factors of 24.

(F) 1, 2, 6

(G) 1, 2, 3, 4, 6, 12

(H) 1, 2, 3, 4, 6, 8, 12, 24

(J) 0, 1, 2, 3, 4, 5, 6, 12, 14, 24

3. Complete the table of multiples. What common multiples of 6 and 9 are in the table?

Multiples of 6	30	36			54	60	
Multiples of 9		27	36			63	

(A) 36 and 54

(B) 36 and 63

(C) 27 and 54

(D) 42 and 54

4. Which of the following numbers is not a multiple of 9?

(F) 99

(G) 64

(H) 72

(J) 45

5. Which of the following expressions does not equal 48?

(A) 6×8

(B) 3×24

(C) $2 \times 2 \times 2 \times 2 \times 3$

(D) 4×12

6. List all the factors of 10.

(F) 1, 10

(G) 1, 2, 10

(H) 1, 2, 5, 10

(J) 0, 1, 2, 5, 10

7. Which of the following numbers is not a multiple of 12?

(A) 36

(B) 144

(C) 84

(D) 62

8. List all the factors of 36.

(F) 6, 36

(G) 1, 3, 6, 36

(H) 1, 2, 3, 4, 6, 9, 12, 18, 36

(J) 0, 18, 36

Factors and Multiples

Directions: Read each problem. Choose and mark the best answer.

> **Example**
>
> Complete the factor tree for 25.
>
>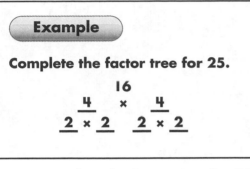
>
> 16
> 4 × 4
> 2 × 2   2 × 2

1. Complete the factor tree for 28.

28
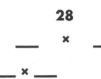
__ × __
__ × __

2. Complete the factor tree for 18.

18
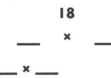
__ × __
__ × __

3. Complete the factor tree for 54.

54
__ × __
__ × __   __ × __

4. Complete the factor tree for 36.

36
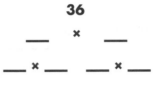
__ × __
__ × __   __ × __

5. A number with no factors but 1 and itself is called a *prime number*. For example, 3 is a prime number because its only factors are 1 and 3. Another prime number is 5. Circle each prime number you find below.

1	2	3	4	5	6	7	8	9	10
11	12	13	14	15	16	17	18	19	20
21	22	23	24	25	26	27	28	29	30

Sample Test 7: Computation

Directions: Choose the correct answer to each equation. Remember to reduce fraction answers to simplest form. Choose "None of these" if the correct answer is not given.

Example

145
× 32

(A) 4,640

(B) 725

(C) 177

(D) None of these

Answer: A

1. 0.4
−0.4

(A) 0

(B) 1.8

(C) 1

(D) None of these

2. 5 × 40 =

(F) 240

(G) 45

(H) 200

(J) None of these

3. 5,951 + 3,291 =

(A) 2,660

(B) 9,242

(C) 924.4

(D) None of these

4. 97)488

(F) 5.3

(G) 47,336

(H) 5 R3

(J) None of these

5. $4\frac{6}{11}$
$+3\frac{2}{11}$

(A) 8

(B) $1\frac{4}{11}$

(C) $7\frac{8}{11}$

(D) None of these

6. 48 ÷ 4 =

(F) 42

(G) 192

(H) 12

(J) None of these

7. $6.27
−$2.89

(A) $9.16

(B) $3.38

(C) $18.12

(D) None of these

8. 879 + □ = 922

(F) 43

(G) 1,801

(H) 1.04

(J) None of these

9. 463 − 72 =

(A) 391

(B) 33,336

(C) 535

(D) None of these

GO

Sample Test 7: Computation

Directions: Read and work each problem. Find the correct answer. Fill in the circle.

10. 45 + 62 + 71 =

   Ⓕ 178

   Ⓖ 2,790

   Ⓗ 168

   Ⓙ None of these

11. 12 × 8 =

   Ⓐ 4

   Ⓑ 96

   Ⓒ 20

   Ⓓ None of these

12. 78
    +46

   Ⓕ 32

   Ⓖ 114

   Ⓗ 122

   Ⓙ None of these

13. 18.2 – 9.53 =

   Ⓐ 8.67

   Ⓑ 867

   Ⓒ 86.7

   Ⓓ None of these

14. 5)‾82‾

   Ⓕ 30 R2

   Ⓖ 36

   Ⓗ 36 R2

   Ⓙ None of these

15. 124
    × 53

   Ⓐ 71

   Ⓑ 177

   Ⓒ 6,572

   Ⓓ None of these

16. $\frac{18}{15} - \frac{9}{15} =$

   Ⓕ $\frac{28}{15}$

   Ⓖ $\frac{13}{15}$

   Ⓗ $\frac{3}{5}$

   Ⓙ None of these

17. 794
    × 18

   Ⓐ 476

   Ⓑ 384

   Ⓒ 1,292

   Ⓓ None of these

18. 125 – □ = 106

   Ⓕ 231

   Ⓖ 19

   Ⓗ 13,250

   Ⓙ None of these

19. $\frac{7}{10} - \frac{2}{10} =$

   Ⓐ $\frac{9}{10}$

   Ⓑ $\frac{1}{2}$

   Ⓒ $\frac{14}{10}$

   Ⓓ None of these

STOP

Symmetry

Directions: Choose the best answer to each question below.

An object or shape has a **line of symmetry** when the two sides can be folded along a line and match up perfectly. Each side is a mirror image of the other. For example:

This rhombus has two lines of symmetry.

This arrow has one line of symmetry.

1. Which of the figures below does not show a line of symmetry?

Ⓐ
Ⓑ
Ⓒ
Ⓓ

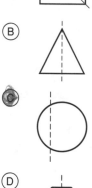

2. Which of these letters has a line of symmetry?

Ⓕ **Q**
Ⓖ **P**
Ⓗ **F**
Ⓙ **M**

3. Look at the letters below. Which one does not have a line of symmetry?

Ⓐ **O**
Ⓑ **T**
Ⓒ **G**
Ⓓ **X**

4. Which of the figures below does not have a line of symmetry?

Ⓕ
Ⓖ
Ⓗ
Ⓙ

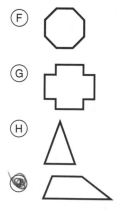

Symmetry

Directions: Read each problem. Find the correct answer. Fill in the circle.

1. Which of the following figures below does not show a line of symmetry?

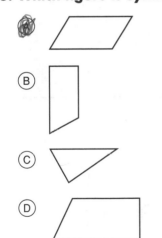

Ⓐ
Ⓑ
Ⓒ
Ⓓ

2. Which of the following letters has a line of symmetry?

Ⓕ **R**
Ⓖ **W**
Ⓗ **J**
Ⓙ **S**

3. Which figure is symmetrical?

Ⓐ
Ⓑ
Ⓒ
Ⓓ

4. Which letter has a line of symmetry?

Ⓕ **J**
Ⓖ **L**
Ⓗ **U**
Ⓙ **Q**

5. Which of these words contains a letter that does not have a line of symmetry?

Ⓐ **DRIVE**
Ⓑ **MIME**
Ⓒ **WATCH**
Ⓓ **COVE**

6. Which of the following figures below has more than one line of symmetry?

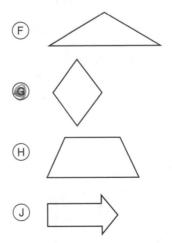

Ⓕ
Ⓖ
Ⓗ
Ⓙ

Reflection and Rotation

Directions: For the drawings below, write *reflection* or *rotation* to describe how the figure was moved.

Reflection is one kind of symmetry. In reflection, a figure is flipped, creating a mirror image.

E Ǝ

Rotation is another kind of symmetry. In rotation, a figure is rotated around a fixed point.

5 ꞁ

1. reflection

_____

4. rotation

_____

2. reflection

_____

5. reflection

_____

3. rotation

_____

6. reflection

_____

Name _____ Date _____

Shapes and Figures

Directions: Classify the shapes below as **quadrilateral, trapezoid, parallelogram, rectangle, square,** or **rhombus**.

A **quadrilateral** is any figure with 4 sides and 4 angles. Some quadrilaterals have special names.

trapezoid—a quadrilateral with 1 set of parallel sides

parallelogram—a quadrilateral with 2 sets of parallel sides and opposite sides of equal length

rectangle—a quadrilateral with 4 right angles and opposite sides of equal length

square—a quadrilateral with 4 right angles and 4 equal sides

rhombus—a quadrilateral with 4 equal sides and 2 pairs of parallel sides

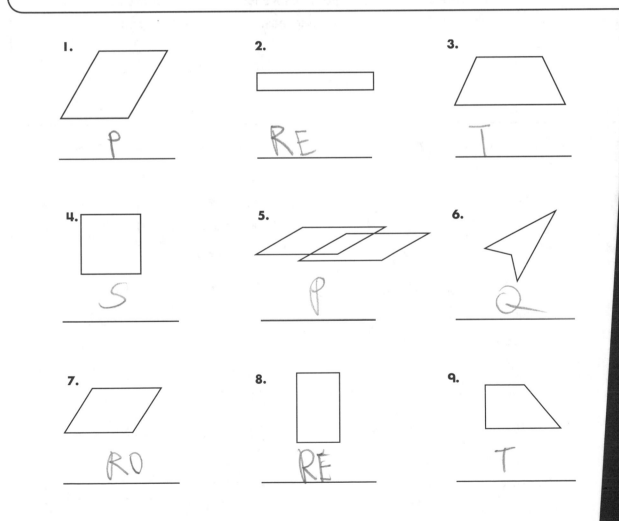

1. _P_

2. _RE_

3. _T_

4. _S_

5. _P_

6. _Q_

7. _RO_

8. _RE_

9. _T_

Shapes and Figures

Directions: Choose the best answer to each question below.

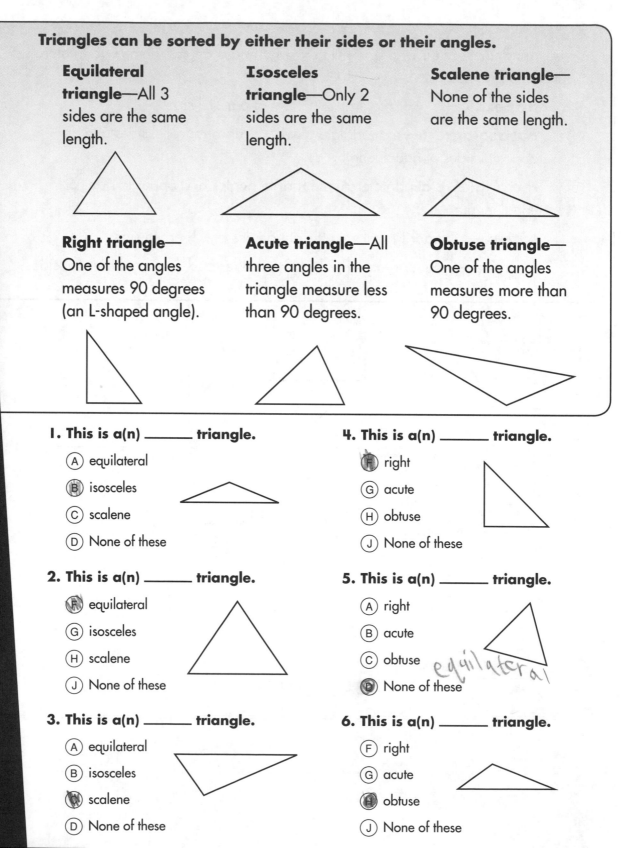

Triangles can be sorted by either their sides or their angles.

Equilateral triangle—All 3 sides are the same length.

Isosceles triangle—Only 2 sides are the same length.

Scalene triangle—None of the sides are the same length.

Right triangle—One of the angles measures 90 degrees (an L-shaped angle).

Acute triangle—All three angles in the triangle measure less than 90 degrees.

Obtuse triangle—One of the angles measures more than 90 degrees.

1. This is a(n) _____ triangle.
- (A) equilateral
- (B) isosceles
- (C) scalene
- (D) None of these

2. This is a(n) _____ triangle.
- (F) equilateral
- (G) isosceles
- (H) scalene
- (J) None of these

3. This is a(n) _____ triangle.
- (A) equilateral
- (B) isosceles
- (C) scalene
- (D) None of these

4. This is a(n) _____ triangle.
- (F) right
- (G) acute
- (H) obtuse
- (J) None of these

5. This is a(n) _____ triangle.
- (A) right
- (B) acute
- (C) obtuse
- (D) None of these

equilateral

6. This is a(n) _____ triangle.
- (F) right
- (G) acute
- (H) obtuse
- (J) None of these

Shapes and Figures

Directions: Read each problem. Find the correct answer. Fill in the circle.

1. Dylan drew a shape with 4 sides. Two sides were the same length, and one corner was 90 degrees. What shape did Dylan draw?

   Ⓐ parallelogram
   Ⓑ rectangle
   Ⓒ triangle
   Ⓓ hexagon

2. Which pair of shapes are similar?

   Ⓕ
   Ⓖ
   Ⓗ
   Ⓙ

3. How many sides does a rectangle have?

   Ⓐ 0
   Ⓑ 2
   Ⓒ 3
   Ⓓ 4

4. The steering wheel on a car is most shaped like a

   Ⓕ cube.
   Ⓖ sphere.
   Ⓗ square.
   Ⓘ circle.

5. How many sides does a circle have?

   Ⓐ 12
   Ⓑ 2
   Ⓒ 1
   Ⓓ 0

6. Kim made one straight cut across the trapezoid. Which pair of figures could be the two cut pieces of the trapezoid?

   Ⓕ
   Ⓖ
   Ⓗ
   Ⓙ

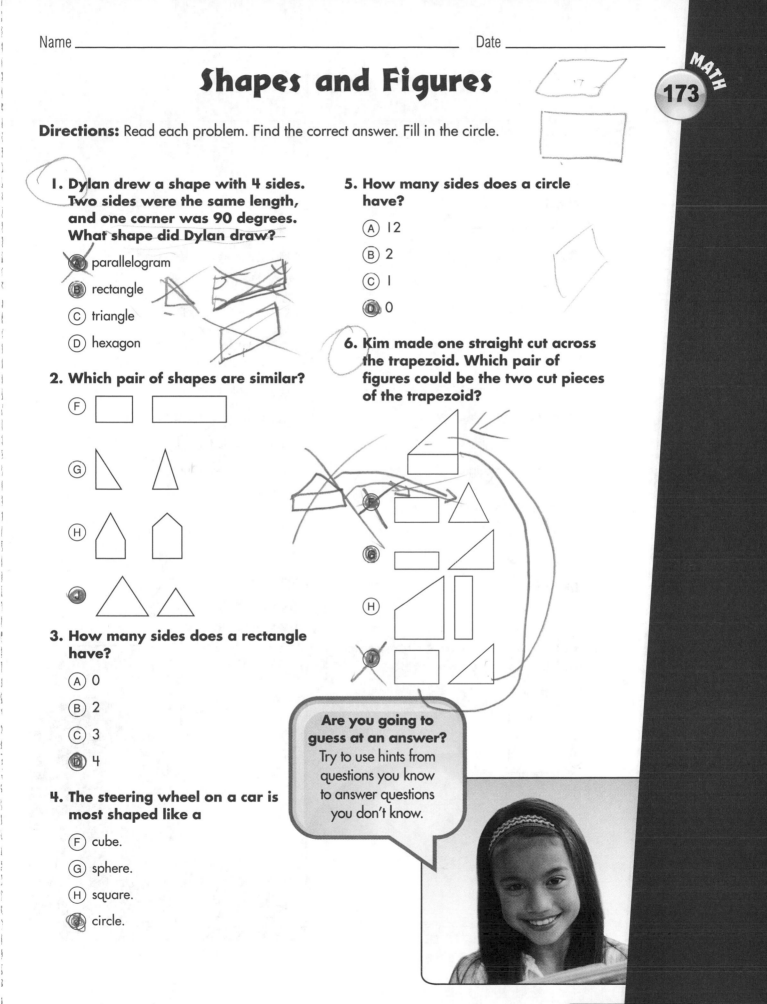

Are you going to guess at an answer? Try to use hints from questions you know to answer questions you don't know.

Name _____   Date _____

Shapes and Figures

Directions: Read each description below. Choose the answer that best fits the description.

1. a quadrilateral with 1 set of parallel sides

(A) a parallelogram

(B) a trapezoid

(C) a cube

(D) a square

2. a triangle with no sides of equal length

(F) an isosceles triangle

(G) an equilateral triangle

(H) a right triangle

(J) a scalene triangle

3. a polygon with six sides

(A) a pentagon

(B) an octagon

(C) a hexagon

(D) a quadrilateral

4. a quadrilateral with 4 right angles and 4 sides of equal length

(F) a rhombus

(G) a right triangle

(H) a rectangle

(J) a square

5. a quadrilateral with 4 equal sides and 2 pairs of parallel sides

(A) a rhombus

(B) a trapezoid

(C) a hexagon

(D) a rectangular prism

6. a triangle with one angle measuring more than 90°

(F) a scalene triangle

(G) an obtuse triangle

(H) an acute triangle

(J) an isosceles triangle

Should you change your answer? Only if you are sure of the correction!

Shapes and Figures

Directions: In the space below, use any combination of these basic geometric shapes to create a drawing of a real-life person, place, or thing.

3-D Shapes

Directions: Read each problem. Find the correct answer. Fill in the circle.

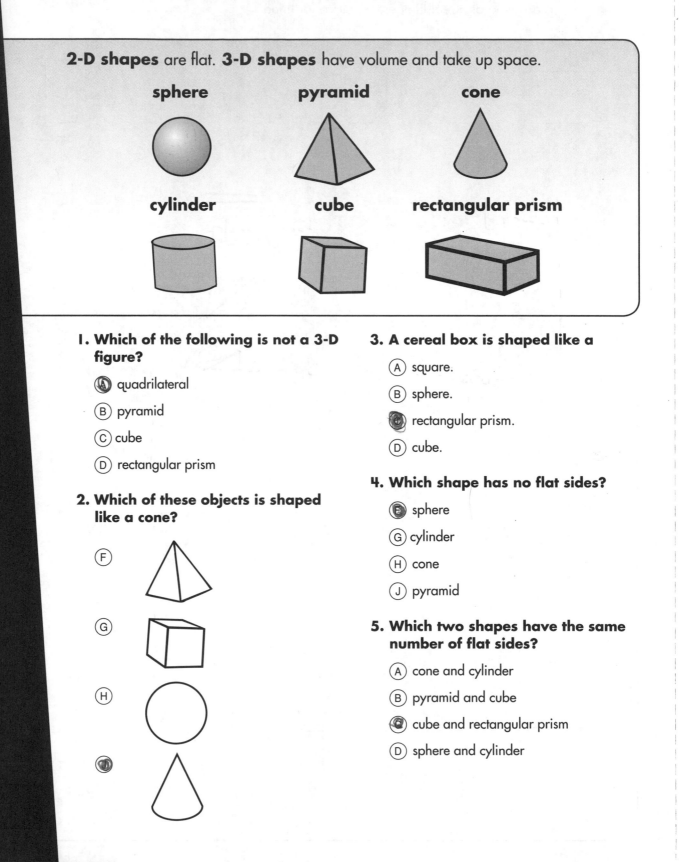

2-D shapes are flat. 3-D shapes have volume and take up space.

sphere   pyramid   cone

cylinder   cube   rectangular prism

1. Which of the following is not a 3-D figure?

(A) quadrilateral

(B) pyramid

(C) cube

(D) rectangular prism

2. Which of these objects is shaped like a cone?

(F)

(G)

(H)

(J)

3. A cereal box is shaped like a

(A) square.

(B) sphere.

(C) rectangular prism.

(D) cube.

4. Which shape has no flat sides?

(F) sphere

(G) cylinder

(H) cone

(J) pyramid

5. Which two shapes have the same number of flat sides?

(A) cone and cylinder

(B) pyramid and cube

(C) cube and rectangular prism

(D) sphere and cylinder

3-D Shapes

Directions: Read each problem. Find the correct answer. Fill in the circle.

1. A roll of paper towels is shaped like a

Ⓐ sphere.

Ⓑ pyramid.

Ⓒ cone.

● cylinder.

2. Four faces of a pyramid are triangles. What shape is the fifth face?

Ⓕ a triangle

● a square

Ⓗ a rectangle

Ⓙ a circle

3. Which of the following is shaped like a rectangular prism?

Ⓐ a sheet of paper

● a dictionary

Ⓒ a cup

Ⓓ a cube of sugar

4. Which 2-D shape matches the 3-D shape below?

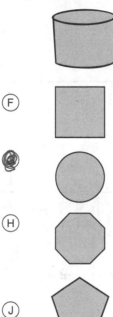

Ⓕ

●

Ⓗ

Ⓙ

5. Imagine that you were creating an ice-cream cone out of clay. What two 3-D figures would you use?

Ⓐ a cone and a cube

Ⓑ a pyramid and a sphere

Ⓒ a sphere and a cylinder

● a cone and a sphere

6. What two shapes make up the faces of a rectangular prism?

Ⓕ squares and rectangles

Ⓖ rectangles and triangles

Ⓗ parallelograms and squares

Ⓙ cubes and rectangles

Name _____   Date _____

3-D Shapes

A **face** is a flat surface. An **edge** is where two flat faces meet. A **vertex** is where three or more edges meet. Different 3-D shapes have different numbers of faces, edges, and vertices.

Edge

face

vertex

Directions: This chart lists the number of faces, edges, and vertices each shape has. Fill in the missing information.

Faces	1	6	6	5		2
Edges	0	12	12	8	0	0
Vertices	0	8	8	5		0

Directions: For each 2-D shape listed below, write the 3-D shape(s) that has at least one face with that shape.

1. square _____

2. rectangle _____

3. triangle _____

4. circle _____

3-D Shapes

Directions: For each shape listed below, find an object in the room with the shape. If you cannot find the shape in the room, think of a real-life object with the shape. Write what the object is, and then draw the shape.

1. cylinder _____

bottle

4. cone _____

funnel

2. sphere _____

ball

5. pyramid _____

arrow top

3. rectangular prism _____

pillow

6. cube _____

box

Perimeter, Area, and Volume

Directions: Work each problem, and choose the best answer.

Perimeter is the distance around the edge of a shape. You can find the perimeter of a rectangle by using this formula: (2 × length) + (2 × width). For example, this rectangle has a length of 18 and a width of 5. To find the perimeter:

$2 \times 18 = 36$
$2 \times 5 = 10$
$36 + 10 = 46$

5 ⎢⎯⎯⎯⎯⎯⎯⎯⎯⎯⎯⎢
     18

1. A rectangle has a length of 2 and width of 27. What is the perimeter?

- (A) 29
- (B) 58
- (C) 25
- (D) 54

2. A rectangle has a length of 3 and width of 18. What is the perimeter?

- (F) 21
- (G) 54
- (H) 42
- (J) 15

3. A rectangle has a length of 12 and width of 36. What is the perimeter?

- (A) 48
- (B) 96
- (C) 74
- (D) 76

4. A rectangle has a length of 15 and width of 24. What is the perimeter?

- (F) 54
- (G) 39
- (H) 62
- (J) 78

5. A rectangle has a length of 4 and width of 18. What is the perimeter?

- (A) 22
- (B) 14
- (C) 44
- (D) 36

6. A rectangle has a length of 20 and width of 30. What is the perimeter?

- (F) 50
- (G) 100
- (H) 80
- (J) 70

7. A rectangle has a length of 6 and width of 12. What is the perimeter?

- (A) 36
- (B) 18
- (C) 6
- (D) 78

8. A rectangle has a length of 8 and width of 9. What is the perimeter?

- (F) 17
- (G) 34
- (H) 80
- (J) 36

Perimeter, Area, and Volume

Directions: Read and work each problem. Find the correct answer. Fill in the circle.

> **Area** is the amount of space inside a flat shape. It is measured in square units. You can find the area of a rectangle by using this formula: length × width. For example, this rectangle has a length of 20 units and a width of 12 units. To find the area:
>
> 20 units × 12 units = 240 square units
>
> The rectangle has an area of 240 square units.
>
> 20
> 12

1. A rectangle has a length of 12 and width of 13. What is the area?

- (A) 624
- (B) 156
- (C) 50
- (D) 25

2. A rectangle has a length of 52 and width of 33. What is the area?

- (F) 1,716
- (G) 170
- (H) 85
- (J) 3,432

3. A rectangle has a length of 19 and width of 5. What is the area?

- (A) 386
- (B) 576
- (C) 380
- (D) 95

4. A rectangle has a length of 27 and width of 63. What is the area?

- (F) 90
- (G) 180
- (H) 1,701
- (J) 6,804

5. A rectangle has a length of 81 and width of 13. What is the area?

- (A) 1,053
- (B) 8,836
- (C) 188
- (D) 6,730

6. A rectangle has a length of 26 and width of 25. What is the area?

- (F) 625
- (G) 650
- (H) 676
- (J) 2,601

7. A square has one side with a length of 62. What is the area?

- (A) 248
- (B) 3,844
- (C) 15,376
- (D) Not enough information

8. A square has a perimeter of 16. What is the area?

- (F) 256
- (G) 64
- (H) 16
- (J) Not enough information

MATH
182

Perimeter, Area, and Volume

Directions: Read and work each problem. Find the correct answer. Fill in the circle.

I. The area of the rectangle is 216 square inches. What is the length of *b*?

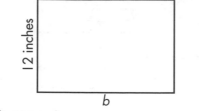

- Ⓐ 102 inches
- Ⓑ 96 inches
- Ⓒ 18 inches
- Ⓓ 9 inches

2. The perimeter of the rectangle is 150 feet. What is the area?

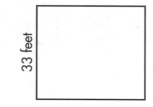

- Ⓕ 1,386 square feet
- Ⓖ 2,772 square feet
- Ⓗ 3,861 square feet
- Ⓙ 4,950 square feet

3. What is the perimeter of the figure below?

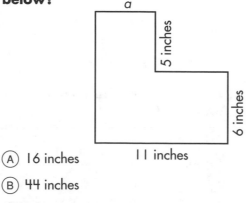

- Ⓐ 16 inches
- Ⓑ 44 inches
- Ⓒ 21 inches
- Ⓓ Not enough information

4. If you know that side *a* of the figure in question 3 is 5 inches, what is the area of the entire figure?

- Ⓕ 91 square inches
- Ⓖ 55 square inches
- Ⓗ 330 square inches
- Ⓙ Not enough information

5. The area of the figure below is 28 square inches, and *x* = *y*. What is the length of *x*?

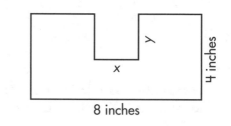

- Ⓐ 1 inch
- Ⓑ 2 inches
- Ⓒ 4 inches
- Ⓓ Not enough information

Perimeter, Area, and Volume

Directions: Determine the volume of the figures below.

1.

height = _____   width = _____

length = _____

Volume = _____

2.

width = _____

height = _____

length = _____

Volume = _____

3.

height = _____   width = _____

length = _____

Volume = _____

4.

height = _____   width = _____

length = _____

Volume = _____

5.

height = _____   width = _____

length = _____

Volume = _____

> One way to find volume is to use the following rule:
>
> volume = length × width × height

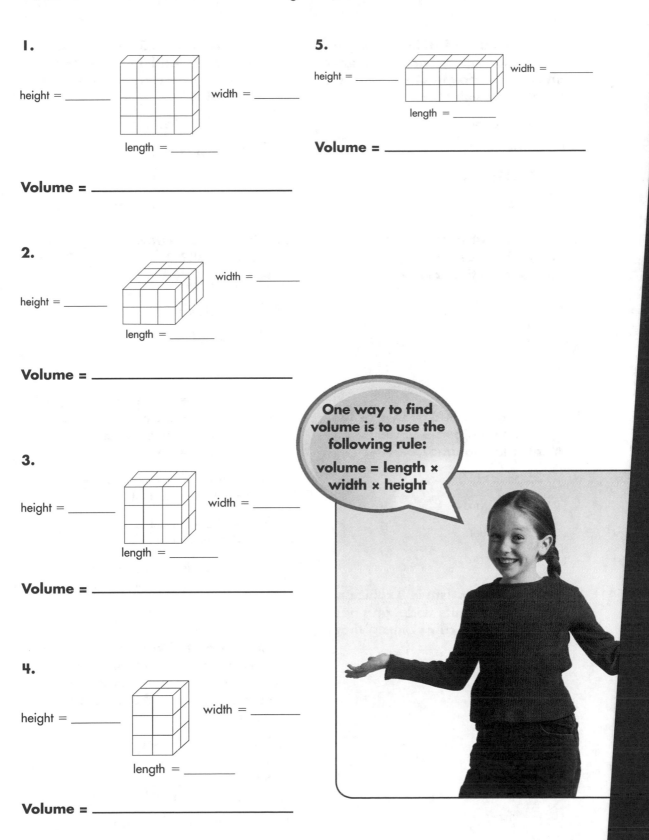

Perimeter, Area, and Volume

Directions: Read the description of each shape, and determine its volume.

1. **A rectangular prism has a length of 4 cubic units, a width of 3 cubic units, and a height of 4 cubic units. What is the volume?**

    Ⓐ 11 cubic units

    Ⓑ 28 cubic units

    Ⓒ 48 cubic units

    Ⓓ 121 cubic units

2. **A rectangular box is 12 inches long, 12 inches wide, and 6 inches tall. What is the volume?**

    Ⓕ 864 cubic inches

    Ⓖ 246 cubic inches

    Ⓗ 144 cubic inches

    Ⓙ 30 cubic inches

3. **A rectangular shed is 3 yards tall, 4 yards wide, and 5 yards long. What is the volume?**

    Ⓐ 35 cubic feet

    Ⓑ 12 cubic yards

    Ⓒ 32 cubic feet

    Ⓓ 60 cubic yards

4. **A rectangular prism is 8 cubic units long, 4 cubic units wide, and has a volume of 96 cubic units. What is the height?**

    Ⓕ 2 cubic units

    Ⓖ 3 cubic units

    Ⓗ 4 cubic units

    Ⓙ 5 cubic units

5. **An aquarium is 28 inches long, 12 inches wide, and 14 inches tall. How many cubic inches of water can it hold?**

    Ⓐ 54 cubic inches

    Ⓑ 560 cubic inches

    Ⓒ 728 cubic inches

    Ⓓ 4,704 cubic inches

6. **What is the volume of a cube that is 3 feet tall?**

    Ⓕ 9 cubic feet

    Ⓖ 27 cubic feet

    Ⓗ 81 cubic feet

    Ⓙ Not enough information

7. **A cube has a volume of 64 cubic units. If you know the cube is 4 cubic units long, what are the width and height?**

    Ⓐ The width is 4 cubic units, and the height is 4 cubic units.

    Ⓑ The width is 2 cubic units, and the height is 8 cubic units.

    Ⓒ The width is 8 cubic units, and the height is 2 cubic units.

    Ⓓ Not enough information

8. **The flat roof of a rectangular building has an area of 1,500 square feet. If the building is 20 feet tall, what is the building's volume?**

    Ⓕ 30,000 cubic feet

    Ⓖ 3,000 cubic feet

    Ⓗ 1,520 cubic feet

    Ⓙ Not enough information

Name _____ Date _____

Using Coordinates

Directions: The students in Room 14 are going on a scavenger hunt at Willow Lake. Each team needs to find the objects below. Write the item from the word list that is found at each coordinate.

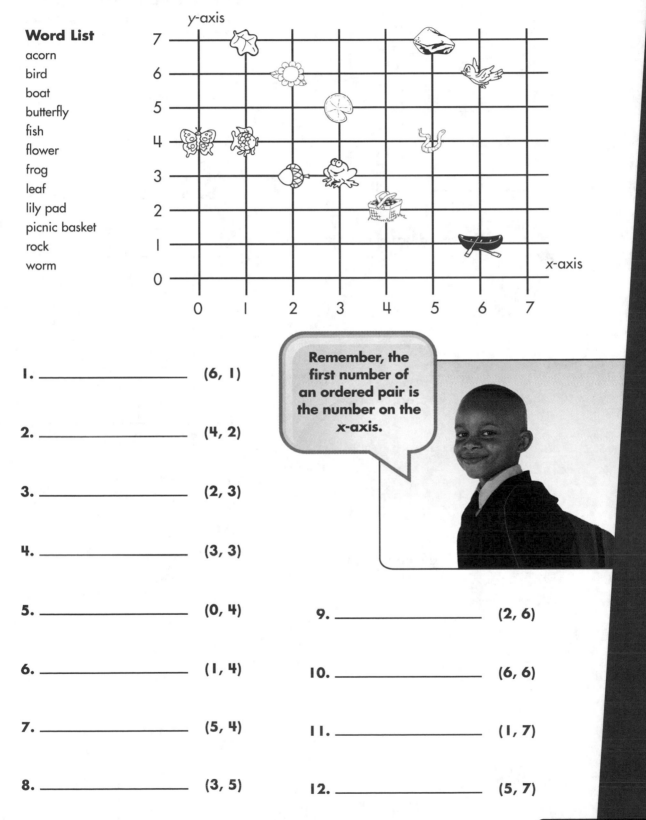

Word List

acorn
bird
boat
butterfly
fish
flower
frog
leaf
lily pad
picnic basket
rock
worm

Remember, the first number of an ordered pair is the number on the x-axis.

1. _____ (6, 1)

2. _____ (4, 2)

3. _____ (2, 3)

4. _____ (3, 3)

5. _____ (0, 4)

6. _____ (1, 4)

7. _____ (5, 4)

8. _____ (3, 5)

9. _____ (2, 6)

10. _____ (6, 6)

11. _____ (1, 7)

12. _____ (5, 7)

Using Coordinates

Directions: Use the graph below to answer the questions that follow.

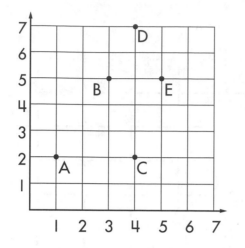

1. What are the coordinates of point A?

(A) (2, 1)

(B) (1, 2)

(C) (1, 1)

(D) (2, 2)

2. What are the coordinates of point B?

(F) (4, 2)

(G) (2, 4)

(H) (5, 3)

(J) (3, 5)

3. Which point has the coordinates (5, 5)?

(A) B

(B) E

(C) C

(D) D

4. If you were traveling from point C to point D, how many units would you need to travel on the y-axis?

(F) 2

(G) 5

(H) 7

(J) Not enough information

5. On the graph below, plot and label the following points:

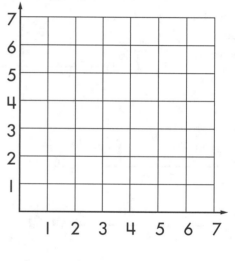

Point L (3, 3)

Point R (6, 2)

Point M (5, 7)

Point T (1, 4)

Name _____ Date _____

Using Coordinates

Directions: Follow the directions.

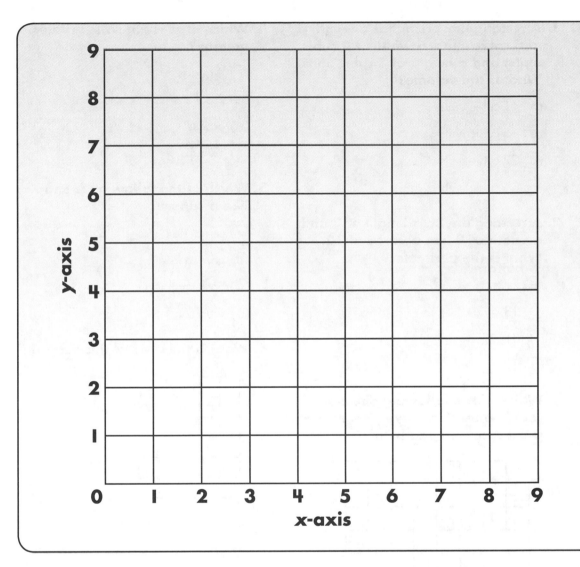

1. Draw a line from (2, 0) to (5, 9).

2. Draw a line from (5, 9) to (8, 0).

3. Draw a line from (8, 0) to (0, 5).

4. Draw a line from (0, 5) to (10, 5).

5. Draw a line from (10, 5) to (2, 0).

6. What shape have you drawn in the coordinate grid?

_____

Sample Test 8: Geometry

MATH
188

Directions: Read and work each problem. Find the correct answer. Fill in the circle.

1. **A rectangular prism has a length of 6 cubic units, a width of 2 cubic units, and a height of 3 cubic units. What is the volume?**

   (A) 11 cubic units

   (B) 15 cubic units

   (C) 22 cubic units

   (D) 36 cubic units

2. **A rectangle with a length of 3 and a width of 4 has an area of 12. What is the perimeter?**

   (F) 7

   (G) 14

   (H) 48

   (J) 12

3. **Which of the following directions could be used to move from zero to point A on the grid below?**

   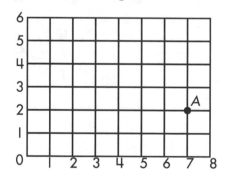

   (A) Go right 7 units and up 2 units.

   (B) Go right 6 units and up 1 unit.

   (C) Go right 8 units and up 2 units.

   (D) Go up 4 units and right 7 units.

4. **Which of these has the greatest volume?**

   (F) 4 quarts

   (G) 2 gallons

   (H) 8 pints

   (J) 17 cups

5. **Which of the following is shaped like a sphere?**

   (A) cereal box

   (B) garden hose

   (C) basketball

   (D) soup can

6. **What is the area of this shape?**

   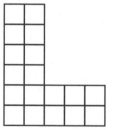

   (F) 16 square units

   (G) 20 square units

   (H) 22 square units

   (J) 18 square units

7. **A square has a perimeter of 20 inches. What is the area?**

   (A) 25 square inches

   (B) 10 square inches

   (C) 15 square inches

   (D) 40 square inches

GO

Sample Test 8: Geometry

Directions: Read each problem. Find the correct answer. Fill in the circle.

8. How many sides does an octagon have?

- (F) 5
- (G) 6
- (H) 7
- (J) 8

9. This is a(n) _____ triangle.

- (A) equilateral
- (B) isosceles
- (C) scalene
- (D) None of these

10. This quadrilateral is called a _____.

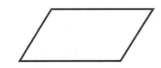

- (F) parallelogram
- (G) trapezoid
- (H) rhombus
- (J) rectangle

11. A quadrilateral with one set of parallel sides is a _____.

- (A) parallelogram
- (B) trapezoid
- (C) rhombus
- (D) rectangle

12. Which line segment is congruent to AB?

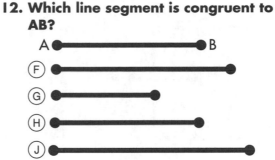

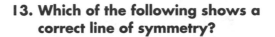

13. Which of the following shows a correct line of symmetry?

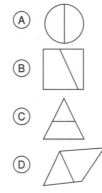

14. What is the perimeter of this figure?

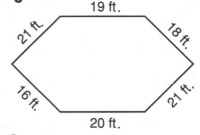

- (F) 95 feet
- (G) 380 feet
- (H) 115 feet
- (J) 420 feet

Sample Test 8: Geometry

Directions: Read each problem. Find the correct answer. Fill in the circle.

15. What kind of lines are shown here?

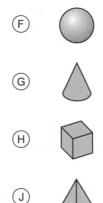

- (A) right
- (B) parallel
- (C) perpendicular
- (D) obtuse

16. Which of the figures below is a sphere?

- (F) ⬤
- (G) ▲
- (H) ◻
- (J) △

17. Which of the following statements is true?

- (A) A parallelogram has two sets of parallel sides.
- (B) A trapezoid has no parallel sides.
- (C) A rectangle has four sides of equal length.
- (D) A rhombus has no sides of equal length.

18. What is the perimeter of a triangular room if all the sides are 4.5 meters long?

- (F) 9 meters
- (G) 18 meters
- (H) 13.5 meters
- (J) 22.5 meters

19. The area of a rectangle is 943 square inches. The length of the rectangle is 41 inches. What is the width of the rectangle?

?

41 in.

- (A) 24 inches
- (B) 32 inches
- (C) 23 inches
- (D) 18 inches

20 Which word describes how the figure below was moved?

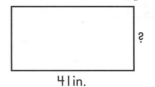

- (F) rotation
- (G) reflection
- (H) symmetry
- (J) None of these

21. Which is the area of this shape in square units?

- (A) 14
- (B) 12
- (C) 22
- (D) 20

GO

Sample Test 8: Geometry

Directions: Read each problem. Find the correct answer. Fill in the circle.

22. Which of the following is not a 2-D figure?

- (F) an oval
- (G) a rectangular prism
- (H) a trapezoid
- (J) a parallelogram

23. How many edges does a cube have?

- (A) 4
- (B) 6
- (C) 12
- (D) 8

24. A rectangle has a length of 36 and width of 20. What is the area?

- (F) 112
- (G) 720
- (H) 72
- (J) 56

25. Read the following description of a triangle. Then, choose the answer that best describes it.
All three angles measure less than 90°. Two of the sides have equal length.

- (A) an equilateral right triangle
- (B) an obtuse isosceles triangle
- (C) an acute scalene triangle
- (D) an acute isosceles triangle

26. Which word describes how the figure below was moved?

- (F) rotation
- (G) symmetry
- (H) replacement
- (J) reflection

27. Which 3-D shape has at least one face that is a circle?

- (A) pyramid
- (B) cone
- (C) cube
- (D) rectangular prism

28. Which of the following statements is not true?

- (F) An equilateral triangle has three sides that are the same length.
- (G) In a right triangle, one of the angles measures 180°.
- (H) In an obtuse triangle, one of the angles measures more than 90°.
- (J) None of the sides are the same length in a scalene triangle.

STOP

Measuring

Directions: Show which units would be best to measure these items by writing the letter of the unit next to each item. Each unit should be used only once.

1. _____ one apple   a. yards

2. _____ short distance races   b. ounces

3. _____ distance between cities   c. feet

4. _____ a jug of milk   d. miles

5. _____ size of a room   e. gallons

6. _____ liquid baby medicine   a. kiloliters

7. _____ height of a book   b. milligrams

8. _____ amount of water in a water tower c. milliliters

9. _____ towing capacity of a truck   d. kilograms

10. _____ amount of medicine in a pill   e. centimeters

11. _____ amount of time you sleep each night   a. degrees

12. _____ length of time you brush your teeth   b. tons

13. _____ how cold it is outside   c. minutes

14. _____ how much a truck weighs   d. hours

Measuring

Directions: Choose the best answer to each question below.

Example

Which unit would be best for measuring the length of a new pencil?

Ⓐ feet

Ⓑ meters

Ⓒ inches

Ⓓ liters

Answer: Ⓒ

---

1. Which of the following would you probably measure in feet?

Ⓐ length of a candle

Ⓑ distance between two cities

Ⓒ amount of juice left in a bottle

Ⓓ the length of a couch

2. What is the perimeter of the rectangle?

7 meters

4 meters

Ⓕ 22 meters

Ⓖ 18 meters

Ⓗ 11 meters

Ⓙ 3 meters

3. How many liters are in one kiloliter?

Ⓐ 10

Ⓑ 1

Ⓒ 100

Ⓓ 1,000

4. Which of these would you probably use to measure a person's waist?

Ⓕ meter stick

Ⓖ tape measure

Ⓗ yardstick

Ⓙ ruler

5. 3 yards is

Ⓐ 24 feet.

Ⓑ 32 feet.

Ⓒ 36 feet.

Ⓓ None of these

6. Leslie is making punch in a very large punch bowl. Orange juice comes in different-sized containers. Which size container should she buy in order to purchase the fewest number of containers?

Ⓕ a one-cup container

Ⓖ a one-gallon container

Ⓗ a one-pint container

Ⓙ a one-quart container

Pay close attention to the units used in each problem. If you misread, you may choose the wrong answer.

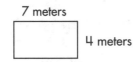

Measuring

194

Directions: Read and work each problem. Find the correct answer. Fill in the circle.

1. What is the length of this line to the nearest half centimeter?

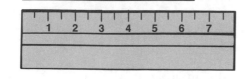

(A) 6 cm

(B) 3.5 cm

(C) 7.1 cm

(D) 6.5 cm

2. How many feet are there in one mile?

(F) 5,028 feet

(G) 5,280 feet

(H) 5,820 feet

(J) 8,520 feet

3. Renee measured her garden, and it is between 5 and 6 yards long. Which length below could be the length of Renee's garden?

(A) 101 feet

(B) 15 feet

(C) 15 feet 11 inches

(D) 18 feet 1 inch

4. You are mailing in your brother's college application today. It is a regular letter size. You must make sure you have enough postage. How much do you think it weighs?

(F) 1 pound

(G) 8 pounds

(H) 1 ounce

(J) 8 ounces

5. 5 kilograms is equal to

(A) 5,000 grams

(B) 500 grams

(C) 50 grams

(D) 5 dekagrams

6. If Nick has a water bottle that holds 2 gallons, which of the following would fill it?

(F) 4 cups

(G) 3 pints

(H) 8 quarts

(J) 1 liter

7. How many ounces are in 1 pound?

(A) 6 ounces

(B) 8 ounces

(C) 16 ounces

(D) 32 ounces

8. Cooper wants to find the weight of a box of cereal. What unit of measurement will he probably find on the side of the box?

(F) millimeters

(G) pounds

(H) hectoliters

(J) ounces

Measuring

Directions: Read each problem. Find the correct answer. Fill in the circle.

1. **If you wanted to measure the length of a football field, what unit would you most likely use?**

   (A) inches

   (B) centimeters

   (C) yards

   (D) miles

Make sure you fill in the answer circle completely.

2. **The load limit on a small bridge is 8 tons. What is the load limit in pounds?**

   (F) 16,000 pounds

   (G) 1,600 pounds

   (H) 160 pounds

   (J) 8,000 pounds

3. **Sanjana made a painting that measures 22 inches by 18 inches. Which of the following frames would be large enough for her to use?**

   (A) 22 in. by 16 in.

   (B) 26 in. by 12 in.

   (C) 20 in. by 20 in.

   (D) 24 in. by 20 in.

4. **Benjamin ordered a glass of lemonade with his lunch. Which of the following measurements shows how much lemonade he most likely got?**

   (F) 24 ounces

   (G) 8 ounces

   (H) 2 liters

   (J) 1 pound

5. **Kylie ran 5 miles on Tuesday. How many feet did she run?**

   (A) 500 feet

   (B) 10,000 feet

   (C) 26,400 feet

   (D) 41,250 feet

6. **Which of the following shows the correct order from largest to smallest?**

   (F) centimeter, millimeter, meter, kilometer

   (G) millimeter, centimeter, meter, kilometer

   (H) millimeter, centimeter, kilometer, meter

   (J) kilometer, meter, centimeter, millimeter

Name _____ Date _____

Comparing Units of Measurement

Directions: Fill in each blank with the equivalent measurement. Use the conversion charts below to help you find your answers.

1 foot = 12 inches
1 yard = 3 feet
1 mile = 5,280 feet

1   7 yards = _____ feet

4. 10 miles = _____ feet

2. 24 inches = _____ feet

5. 60 inches = _____ feet

3. 6 feet = _____ yard(s)

1 tablespoon = 3 teaspoons
1 cup = 16 tablespoons = 8 fluid ounces
1 pint = 2 cups
1 quart = 2 pints
1 gallon = 4 quarts

6. 8 gallons = _____ quarts

11. 24 quarts = _____ gallons

7. 28 quarts = _____ pints

12. 2 cups = _____ fluid ounces

8. 10 pints = _____ cups

13. 9 teaspoons = _____ tablespoons

9. 18 cups = _____ pints

14. 2 cups = _____ tablespoons

10. 4 tablespoons = _____ teaspoons

Comparing Units of Measurement

Directions: Fill in each blank with the equivalent measurement. Use the conversion charts below to help you find your answers.

> **1 pound (lb.) = 16 ounces (oz.)**
>
> **1 ton (t.) = 2,000 pounds (lb.)**

1. 2 lb. = _____ oz.

2. 160 oz. = _____ lb.

3. 15 lb. = _____ oz.

4. 4,000 lb. = _____ t.

5. 6 t. = _____ lb.

6. 64 oz. = _____ lb.

> **1 centimeter (cm) = 10 millimeters (mm)**
>
> **1 meter (m) = 100 centimeters (cm)**
>
> **1 kilometer (km) = 1,000 meters (m)**

7. 6 centimeters + 12 millimeters =

_____ millimeters

8. 29 kilometers = _____ meters

9. 12,000 meters = _____ kilometers

10. 276 centimeters = _____ meters +

_____ centimeters

11. 89 centimeters = _____
millimeters

12. 15 kilometers + 49 meters =

_____ meters

MATH
198

Comparing Units of Measurement

Directions: Read each problem. Find the correct answer. Fill in the circle.

1. Which of the following is not true?

(A) 6 meters = 600 centimeters

(B) 300 centimeters = 30 millimeters

(C) 4,500 meters = 4.5 kilometers

(D) 1,000 millimeters = 1 meter

2. Which of the following is not true?

(F) 1 kilometer > 1 mile

(G) 120 centimeters = 1 meter 20 centimeters

(H) 100 meters < 1,000 millimeters

(J) 1 centimeter < 1 inch

3. Which of the following is not true?

(A) 3 cups = 48 tablespoons

(B) 1 gallon = 8 pints

(C) $\frac{1}{2}$ cup = 8 tablespoons

(D) 2 pints > 1 quart

4. Which of the following is not true?

(F) 72 inches = 6 feet

(G) 18 feet > 2 yards

(H) 30 miles > 100,000 feet

(J) $\frac{1}{2}$ mile = 2,600 feet

5. Which of the following is not true?

(A) 2 tons = 3,000 pounds

(B) 5 pounds = 80 ounces

(C) $\frac{1}{4}$ pound = 4 ounces

(D) $\frac{1}{2}$ ton = 1,000 pounds

6. Which of the following is not true?

(F) Beverages are often measured in ounces.

(G) An ounce is less than a pound.

(H) There are 4 quarts in 1 gallon.

(J) There are 1,000 kilometers in a meter.

7. Which of the following is not true?

(A) A millimeter is smaller than an inch.

(B) The weight of a ship might be measured in tons.

(C) The length of a crayon might be measured in meters.

(D) The metric system is based on units of 10.

8. Which of the following is not true?

(F) There are more tablespoons than teaspoons in a cup.

(G) Milk is usually measured in gallons or quarts.

(H) There are 36 inches in one yard.

(J) A yard and a meter are similar in length.

Time and Temperature

Directions: Read each problem. Find the correct answer. Fill in the circle.

1. How did the temperature change between Saturday and Sunday? On Sunday, it was

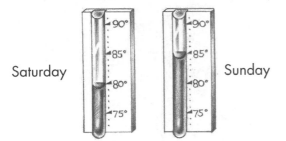

Saturday   Sunday

(A) 5 degrees cooler than Saturday.

(B) 10 degrees cooler than Saturday.

(C) 5 degrees warmer than Saturday.

(D) 10 degrees warmer than Saturday.

2. What time does this clock show?

(F) 8:52

(G) 9:52

(H) 10:52

(J) None of these

3. Which of the following times shows 25 minutes to eight o'clock?

(A) 8:25

(B) 7:40

(C) 6:35

(D) 7:35

4. Scott ran 1 mile in 7 minutes and 42 seconds at the start of the track season. By the end of the track season, Scott could run 1 mile in 6 minutes and 37 seconds. How much time did Scott cut off his running time?

(F) 1 minute, 3 seconds

(G) 1 minute, 9 seconds

(H) 5 seconds

(J) None of these

5. How many minutes are in a day?

(A) 84

(B) 1,400

(C) 240

(D) 1,440

6. What temperature will this thermometer show if the temperature rises 10°?

(F) 32°

(G) 35°

(H) 55°

(J) 43°

Think about your answer before you look at the choices. Then, choose the option that is closest to your answer.

Time and Temperature

Directions: Choose the best answer to each question below.

1. What temperature does this thermometer show?

Ⓐ 87°F

Ⓑ 82°F

Ⓒ 80°F

Ⓓ 78°F

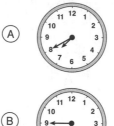

2. Rachelle started her homework at 3:00. She finished at 5:15. For how long did she work?

Ⓕ 3 hours

Ⓖ 2 hours

Ⓗ 140 minutes

Ⓙ 2 hours, 15 minutes

3. How many hours are in a week?

Ⓐ 84 hours

Ⓑ 168 hours

Ⓒ 60 hours

Ⓓ 336 hours

4. Toby left his house for school at 7:35 A.M. He arrived at school at 7:50 A.M. How many minutes did it take Toby to get to school?

Ⓕ 15 minutes

Ⓖ 20 minutes

Ⓗ 25 minutes

Ⓙ 10 minutes

5. It is 6:00 now and the movie starts in 40 minutes. What time will it be then?

Ⓐ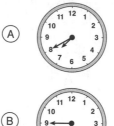

Ⓑ

Ⓒ

Ⓓ

6. The average daily temperature in June is 84°. In August, the average daily temperature is 91°. What is the difference in the two temperatures?

Ⓕ 12°

Ⓖ 9°

Ⓗ 8°

Ⓙ 7°

Name _____   Date _____

Time and Temperature

Directions: Use the calendar to answer the questions that follow.

1. The school fair starts the Tuesday after school ends. If school ends on Friday, June 9, on what date does the school fair begin?

(A) May 31

(B) June 6

(C) June 20

(D) June 13

2. Wyatt's birthday is on June 7. His little sister's birthday is 3 weeks later. What is the day and date?

(F) Wednesday, June 21

(G) Wednesday, June 28

(H) Wednesday, June 14

(J) Tuesday, June 28

3. On Monday, June 19, Mr. Takahashi's sister calls to say that she will be in town a week from Thursday. When will she be arriving?

(A) June 29

(B) June 22

(C) June 19

(D) June 25

Directions: Work each problem, and choose the best answer.

4. When Ryan's dad gets home at 6:20, Ryan tells him that Grandpa called half an hour ago. Which clock shows what time Grandpa called?

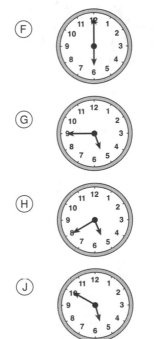

5. Louisa has an hour and a half to walk the dog, practice piano, and clean her room. How long can she spend on each activity?

(A) 25 minutes

(B) 20 minutes

(C) 30 minutes

(D) 40 minutes

6. Kelsey has the flu. On Saturday, her temperature was 102.4°. On Sunday, it was 1.3° higher. On Friday, it was 3° lower than it was on Sunday. What was her temperature on Friday?

(F) 99.4°

(G) 100.7°

(H) 103.7°

(J) 100.4°

Money

Directions: Read and work each problem. Find the correct answer. Fill in the circle.

1. **You have coins that total $0.71. What coins do you have?**

   Ⓐ 3 dimes, 1 nickel, 1 penny

   Ⓑ 1 quarter, 3 dimes, 1 penny

   Ⓒ 2 quarters, 1 dime, 1 nickel, 1 penny

   Ⓓ 2 quarters, 2 dimes, 1 penny

2. **Angela saved her allowance to buy a new pair of sneakers. She had $70.00. After buying the sneakers, how much money did she have left?**

   Ⓕ $9.25

   Ⓖ $8.75

   Ⓗ $7.65

   Ⓙ Not enough information

3. **Phong buys a new sweatshirt for $15.48. He pays with one $10, one $5, and one $1 bill. How much change will he get back?**

   Ⓐ $0.48

   Ⓑ $1.00

   Ⓒ $52

   Ⓓ $0.52

4. **Ms. Pawnee picked up some new art supplies for her students. Her total was $27.46. She paid with two $20 bills. What was her change?**

   Ⓕ $12.54

   Ⓖ $12.45

   Ⓗ 11.54

   Ⓙ $21.44

5. **Danny and Li decided to pitch in together for Justin's birthday present. They bought him a book by his favorite author and a new set of colored pencils. Which of the following is the most likely amount they spent?**

   Ⓐ $3

   Ⓑ $15

   Ⓒ $54

   Ⓓ $82

6. **Blake purchased two books that cost $6.95 each and one book that cost $11.95. He had a coupon for $2.00 off his purchase. What was his total before tax?**

   Ⓕ $25.85

   Ⓖ $23.85

   Ⓗ $25.58

   Ⓙ $23.65

Money

Directions: Read and work each problem. Find the correct answer. Mark the space for your choice.

1. **Lance has $5.00 in change. Which coins does he have?**

   Ⓐ 14 quarters, 10 dimes, 8 nickels, 5 pennies

   Ⓑ 20 quarters, 1 dime, no nickels or pennies

   Ⓒ 12 quarters, 12 dimes, 2 nickels, 10 pennies

   Ⓓ 16 quarters, 8 dimes, 1 nickel, 15 pennies

2. **Ruby took her laundry to the Laundromat. She put a $20 bill into the coin machine and received the same amount back in quarters. It costs $1.25 to wash each load of laundry, and it costs $1.50 to dry each load. How many loads of laundry can Ruby wash and dry, and how many quarters will she have left?**

   Ⓕ 6 loads with 5 quarters left

   Ⓖ 7 loads with 3 quarters left

   Ⓗ 7 loads with 4 quarters left

   Ⓙ 8 loads with no quarters left

3. **Ms. Patel buys a toothbrush for $2.45 and a tube of toothpaste for $3.99. She receives $0.06 in change. Which combination of bills and coins did she give to the cashier?**

   Ⓐ one $5 bill, two $1 bills, a quarter, and 2 dimes

   Ⓑ one $5 bill, one $1 bill, 2 quarters, and 2 dimes

   Ⓒ one $5 bill, one $1 bill, and 2 quarters

   Ⓓ one $5 bill, one $1 bill, and 4 dimes

4. **Ivan's bill at the restaurant was $12.15. He left a $2.50 tip, and he paid with a $20 bill. What was his change?**

   Ⓕ $7.85

   Ⓖ $6.35

   Ⓗ $5.33

   Ⓙ $5.35

5. **Sophie, Ian, and Molly have been collecting money for a charity. Sophie has two $5 bills, twelve $1 bills, and 15 quarters. Ian has one $5 bill, fourteen $1 bills, and 12 quarters. Molly has eighteen $1 bills and 11 quarters. How much money have they collected altogether?**

   Ⓐ $68.50

   Ⓑ $51.00

   Ⓒ $63.50

   Ⓓ $67.25

6. **Mr. Ruiz's bill at the diner was $11.22. He left a $2 tip, and he paid with a $20 bill. What was his change?**

   Ⓕ $6.98

   Ⓖ $6.78

   Ⓗ $5.98

   Ⓙ $6.08

MATH
204

Money

Directions: Read and work each problem. Find the correct answer. Fill in the circle.

1. Becca makes $5.00 an hour helping her mom file business papers. How many hours will she need to work to buy a camera that costs $62?

   Ⓐ 13

   Ⓑ 16

   Ⓒ 14

   Ⓓ 12

2. Which number sentence did you use to find the answer to question 1?

   Ⓕ $62 - 5 = \square$

   Ⓖ $62 \div 5 = \square$

   Ⓗ $62 + 5 = \square$

   Ⓙ $62 \times 5 = \square$

3. Cooper and Maya want to make dinner for their parents. They buy a loaf of bread, a box of spaghetti, a jar of tomato sauce, and a bag of lettuce. Which of the following is the most likely amount they spent?

   Ⓐ $48

   Ⓑ $4

   Ⓒ $26

   Ⓓ $12

4. Jenna has been saving part of her allowance to donate to an animal shelter at the end of the year. Her parents told her that for every dollar she donates, they'll donate $0.50. Jenna saved $60 for the animal shelter. What will Jenna's parents donate?

   Ⓕ $30

   Ⓖ $40

   Ⓗ $60

   Ⓙ $120

5. Calvin has a $5 bill, 3 quarters, and 2 dimes. Gabby has a $5 bill, 1 quarter, 3 dimes, 4 nickels, and 7 pennies. Kate has four $1 bills and 9 quarters. Who has the most money?

   Ⓐ Calvin

   Ⓑ Gabby

   Ⓒ Kate

   Ⓓ Calvin and Gabby have the same amount.

6. The Cavanaugh family went out to dinner to celebrate Henry's birthday. They spent $50 on dinner. Which amount shows the tip that they most likely left?

   Ⓕ $1

   Ⓖ $2

   Ⓗ $8

   Ⓙ $20

Name _____ Date _____

Estimating Measurement

Directions: Choose the best answer to each question below.

1. **Which measurement is about the same as the length of a baseball bat?**

   (A) 1 meter

   (B) 1 kilometer

   (C) 1 centimeter

   (D) 1 millimeter

2. **An apple weighs _____.**

   (F) a few milligrams

   (G) a few liters

   (H) a few pounds

   (J) a few ounces

3. **About how long might it take a person to run a kilometer?**

   (A) 1 hour

   (B) 12 minutes

   (C) 2 minutes

   (D) 3 hours

4. **How much does a car weigh?**

   (F) about 2,000 ounces

   (G) about 200 pounds

   (H) about 2 tons

   (J) about 2,000 grams

5. **There is a bottle of juice in the Gomez's refrigerator. Most of it is gone, but there is enough left for Ana's breakfast. About how much is left?**

   (A) 1 gallon

   (B) 32 ounces

   (C) 8 ounces

   (D) $\frac{1}{2}$ liter

6. **Samuel got home from school at 3:25. It took him 3 minutes to change his clothes, 6 minutes to make popcorn and pour a drink, and 18 minutes to write a few e-mails. About what time did he begin his homework?**

   (F) 3:30

   (G) 4:15

   (H) 3:45

   (J) 4:00

7. **Toby left his house for school at 7:33 A.M. He arrived at school at 7:50 A.M. About how many minutes did it take Toby to get to school?**

   (A) 15 minutes

   (B) 25 minutes

   (C) 30 minutes

   (D) 10 minutes

Sample Test 9: Measurement

Directions: Choose the best answer to each question below.

1. If Jerry walked 2 miles for charity, how many feet did he walk?

- (A) 20 feet
- (B) 6 feet
- (C) 3,520 feet
- (D) 10,560 feet

2. If it is 3:30 now, what time was it 20 minutes ago?

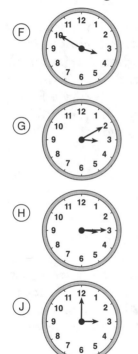

3. Zara wants to measure how much applesauce she made this fall. If she uses metric, which unit should she use?

- (A) gram
- (B) liter
- (C) kilogram
- (D) centimeter

4. A truck carries 6 tons of cargo. How many pounds is that?

- (F) 12,000 pounds
- (G) 1,200 pounds
- (H) 120 pounds
- (J) 12 pounds

5. Which of the following thermometers shows that it is 67°F?

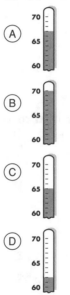

6. Darnell used 8 quarts of water when he washed his hands and face. How many pints of water did he use?

- (F) 8 pints
- (G) 16 pints
- (H) 24 pints
- (J) 32 pints

7. 4 minutes =

- (A) 120 seconds
- (B) 240 seconds
- (C) 360 seconds
- (D) 480 seconds

GO

Sample Test 9: Measurement

Directions: Choose the best answer to each question below.

8. Brayden wants to buy a science kit he saw in a catalog. It costs $65.00. Brayden earns $9 a week doing chores and helping out with yard work. How many weeks will he need to save to buy it?

(F) 9 weeks

(G) 7 weeks

(H) 8 weeks

(J) 6 weeks

9. 177 kilometers = _____ meters

(A) 177,000

(B) 17,700

(C) 1770

(D) 17.70

10. It took Cameron 8 hours and 47 minutes to read his book. How many minutes is this?

(F) 527 minutes

(G) 480 minutes

(H) 572 minutes

(J) 500 minutes

11. Which of these statements is not true?

(A) 1 yard = 36 inches

(B) 4 foot = 48 inches

(C) 1 pint = 4 cups

(D) 8 ounces = 1 cup

12. Mohammed brought all his change to the bank. He had 60 quarters, 20 dimes, 16 nickels, and 300 pennies. How much cash is his change worth?

(F) $20.00

(G) $20.80

(H) $18.20

(J) $16.00

13. You would most likely measure a caterpillar using _____.

(A) millimeters

(B) feet

(C) kilometers

(D) yards

14. Tonio left the house at 8:10. It took him 20 minutes to ride his bike to Liliana's house, 15 minutes to get to the library, and 25 minutes to get to the park. What time was it when he arrived at the park?

(F) 8:45

(G) 8:50

(H) 9:00

(J) 9:10

15. Which statement is not true?

(A) 3 yards > 38 inches

(B) 65 miles = 65 kilometers

(C) 120 seconds < 4 minutes

(D) 8 cups = 2 quarts

STOP

Probability

Directions: Roll a die 30 times. Record the results of your experiment below.

1. Predict how often you expect to roll each number.

_____

_____

_____

_____

2. Predict how often you expect to roll an even number.

_____

3. Predict how often you expect to roll an odd number.

_____

4. Number of times you rolled a 1:

_____

5. Number of times you rolled a 2:

_____

6. Number of times you rolled a 3:

_____

7. Number of times you rolled a 4:

_____

8. Number of times you rolled a 5:

_____

9. Number of times you rolled a 6:

_____

10. How do your actual results compare with the results you predicted?

_____

_____

_____

_____

_____

_____

_____

Probability

Directions: Look at the spinners. Mark the probability that the arrow will land on each of the following shapes or numbers.

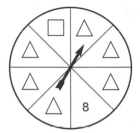

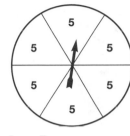

1. a number

- (A) certain
- (B) likely
- (C) unlikely
- (D) impossible

2. an 8

- (F) certain
- (G) likely
- (H) unlikely
- (J) impossible

3. a circle

- (A) certain
- (B) likely
- (C) unlikely
- (D) impossible

4. a shape

- (F) certain
- (G) likely
- (H) unlikely
- (J) impossible

5. a triangle

- (A) certain
- (B) likely
- (C) unlikely
- (D) impossible

6. a 5

- (F) certain
- (G) likely
- (H) unlikely
- (J) impossible

7. an odd number

- (A) certain
- (B) likely
- (C) unlikely
- (D) impossible

8. a triangle

- (F) certain
- (G) likely
- (H) unlikely
- (J) impossible

9. a 2

- (A) certain
- (B) likely
- (C) unlikely
- (D) impossible

Probability

MATH 210

Directions: Use the spinner to answer the questions that follow.

1. What is the probability that the spinner will land on Will?

Ⓐ $\frac{2}{6}$

Ⓑ $\frac{1}{6}$

Ⓒ $\frac{1}{3}$

Ⓓ $\frac{1}{4}$

2. What is the probability that the spinner will land on a boy?

Ⓕ 4 out of 6

Ⓖ 2 out of 6

Ⓗ 1 out of 2

Ⓙ 1 out of 6

3. How would you write your answer to number 2 as a fraction in simplest form?

Ⓐ $\frac{1}{6}$

Ⓑ $\frac{4}{6}$

Ⓒ $\frac{2}{3}$

Ⓓ $\frac{3}{4}$

4. Which of the following statements is not true?

Ⓕ The spinner is equally likely to land on Lena and Max.

Ⓖ The spinner is more likely to land on Jess than Will.

Ⓗ The spinner is more likely to land on a boy than a girl.

Ⓙ The spinner is certain not to land on a name that starts with *T*.

5. How likely is it that the spinner will land on a name that ends with *s*?

Ⓐ certain

Ⓑ likely

Ⓒ unlikely

Ⓓ impossible

6. What are the chances the spinner will land on Nicholas, Lena, or Max?

Ⓕ 1 out of 2

Ⓖ 3 out of 4

Ⓗ 1 out of 6

Ⓙ 2 out of 6

Remember to read the questions carefully. One small word (like *not*) can make all the difference!

Probability

Directions: Use the following information to answer the questions below. Mark the space for your choice.

A bag contains 7 red marbles, 3 white marbles, 3 yellow marbles, and 2 green marbles.

1. The probability of picking a blue marble is _____.

   (A) certain

   (B) likely

   (C) impossible

   (D) unlikely

2. Which color are you most likely to pull out?

   (F) red

   (G) white

   (H) green

   (J) yellow

3. What are your chances of pulling out a white or yellow marble?

   (A) 3 out of 15

   (B) 6 out of 15

   (C) 6 out of 6

   (D) 3 out of 12

4. What are your chances of pulling out a green marble?

   (F) 2 out of 6

   (G) 2 out of 2

   (H) 3 out of 15

   (J) 2 out of 15

5. A number cube is rolled. What is the probability of rolling a 6?

   (A) $\frac{1}{1}$

   (B) $\frac{1}{2}$

   (C) $\frac{1}{3}$

   (D) $\frac{1}{6}$

6. A number cube is rolled. What is the probability of rolling a 5 or a 6?

   (F) $\frac{1}{6}$

   (G) $\frac{5}{6}$

   (H) $\frac{2}{6}$

   (J) $\frac{1}{2}$

7. Which spinner would give you the best chance of landing on the number 2?

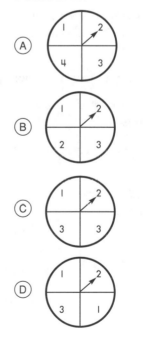

Name _____   Date _____

Probability

Directions: Read each problem. Find the correct answer. Fill in the circle.

1. **One letter is randomly chosen from the word *isosceles*. What are the chances the letter will be an *s*?**

   (A) $\frac{3}{9}$

   (B) $\frac{2}{3}$

   (C) $\frac{2}{9}$

   (D) $\frac{3}{3}$

2. **One letter is randomly chosen from the word *mathematics*. Which three letters each have a probability of 2 out of 11 of being chosen?**

   (F) m, a, e

   (G) a, t, s

   (H) m, a, t

   (J) m, e, c

3. **One letter is randomly chosen from the word *million*. Which statement is true?**

   (A) The letter *m* is most likely to be chosen.

   (B) The letter *i* and the letter *o* are equally likely to be chosen.

   (C) The letter *n* is more likely to be chosen than the letter *l*.

   (D) The letter *i* and the letter *l* are equally likely to be chosen.

4. **One letter is randomly chosen from the word *triangle*. Which statement is not true?**

   (F) The chances of choosing *g* are 1 out of 8.

   (G) The letter *a* is least likely to be chosen.

   (H) The chances of choosing an *r* or an *l* are 2 out of 8 or 1 out of 4.

   (J) Each letter is equally likely to be chosen.

5. **In which word below does *e* have the same probability of being chosen as it does in *perimeter*?**

   (A) minute

   (B) employees

   (C) feet

   (D) area

6. **One letter is randomly chosen from the word *symmetry*. Which statement is true?**

   (F) The letter *m* is more likely to be chosen than the letter *y*.

   (G) The letter *i* and the letter *y* are equally likely to be chosen.

   (H) There is a $\frac{1}{8}$ chance of choosing an *m*. There is a $\frac{1}{8}$ chance of choosing a *y*.

   (J) It is impossible that a *u* will be chosen.

Solving Word Problems

Directions: Read and work each problem. Find the correct answer. Fill in the circle.

Example

A store has 3,802 CDs on the shelves. The store receives 2 new cases of CDs. There are 320 CDs in each case. How many CDs does the store have now?

- (A) 640 CDs
- (B) 3,802 CDs
- (C) 4,442 CDs
- (D) 3,482 CDs

Answer: C

Reread a problem if you don't understand it. It may make more sense the second time around!

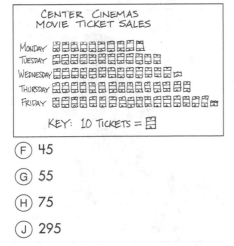

1. Grant went to get a frozen yogurt from the concession stand. He could choose vanilla, chocolate, or twist yogurt. He could have a cup, wafer cone, or sugar cone. How many possible combinations does Grant have?

- (A) 6
- (B) 3
- (C) 8
- (D) 9

2. How many more tickets were sold on Friday than on Tuesday?

```
CENTER CINEMAS
MOVIE TICKET SALES

MONDAY
TUESDAY
WEDNESDAY
THURSDAY
FRIDAY

KEY: 10 TICKETS =
```

- (F) 45
- (G) 55
- (H) 75
- (J) 295

3. If you wanted to compare the features of two different solid shapes, the best thing to use would be a

- (A) Venn diagram.
- (B) pie chart.
- (C) tally chart.
- (D) line graph.

4. Larry, Carey, and Harry went out for lunch. Each friend ordered a salad. The choices were egg, tuna, and chicken. Carey won't eat egg. Larry never orders tuna. Harry only likes chicken. Each friend ate something different. Who ordered tuna?

- (F) Larry
- (G) Carey
- (H) Harry
- (J) Not enough information

Solving Word Problems

Directions: Read and work each problem. Find the correct answer. Fill in the circle.

1. **A worker at Command Software makes $720 a week. You want to figure out how much he makes in an hour. What other piece of information do you need?**

   Ⓐ the number of weeks he works each year

   Ⓑ the number of vacation days he takes

   Ⓒ how much money he makes each day

   Ⓓ how many hours he works each week

2. **You have coins that total $1.23. What coins do you have?**

   Ⓕ 10 dimes, 1 nickel, 3 pennies

   Ⓖ 3 quarters, 3 dimes, 3 pennies

   Ⓗ 4 quarters, 1 dime, 2 nickels, 3 pennies

   Ⓙ 4 quarters, 3 dimes, 3 pennies

3. **A yard is surrounded by 400 feet of fence. It took Nora 8 days to paint the fence. Which number sentence can Nora use to figure out how much fence she painted in a day?**

   Ⓐ $400 \times 8 = \square$

   Ⓑ $400 \div 8 = \square$

   Ⓒ $400 - 8 = \square$

   Ⓓ $400 + 8 = \square$

4. **Five students want to find their average height in inches. Their heights are 54 inches, 56 inches, 52 inches, 57 inches, and 53 inches. How would you find the average height of the students?**

   Ⓕ Add the heights, and multiply by 5.

   Ⓖ Add the heights, and divide by 5.

   Ⓗ Add the heights, and divide by the number of inches in 1 foot.

   Ⓙ Multiply the heights, and divide by the number of inches in 1 foot.

5. **Mr. Cook was 25 years old when Nevaeh was born. How old will he be when Nevaeh has her 13th birthday?**

   Ⓐ 38 years old

   Ⓑ 12 years old

   Ⓒ 25 years old

   Ⓓ 13 years old

6. **Write a number sentence to verify your answer to question 5.**

   _____

   _____

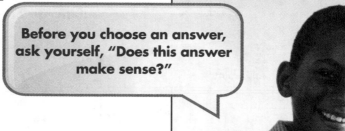

Before you choose an answer, ask yourself, "Does this answer make sense?"

Name _____ Date _____

Solving Word Problems

Directions: Read and work each problem. Find the correct answer. Fill in the circle.

1. **Giraffes and birds are drinking at a watering hole. There are 10 animals with a total of 30 legs. How many 2-legged birds are there? How many 4-legged giraffes are there?**

   (A) 5 birds, 5 giraffes

   (B) 4 birds, 3 giraffes

   (C) 2 birds, 5 giraffes

   (D) 6 birds, 1 giraffe

2. **The school basketball team scored a total of 1,148 points during 28 games in the season. What was the average number of points scored per game?**

   (F) 47

   (G) 1,120

   (H) 40

   (J) None of these

Directions: Use the graph below to answer the questions that follow.

Favorite Vacation Destination

beach	🕶 🕶 🕶 🕶
water park	🕶 🕶 🕶 🕶 🕶
amusement park	🕶 🕶 🕶 🕶 🕶 🕶

Key: 🕶 = 8 votes

3. **How many votes does one symbol stand for?**

   (A) 2

   (B) 5

   (C) 6

   (D) 8

4. **How many people answered this survey?**

   (F) $14\frac{1}{2}$

   (G) 72

   (H) 148

   (J) None of these

5. **How many more people would rather go to an amusement park than the beach?**

   (A) 10

   (B) 12

   (C) 20

   (D) 22

Solving Word Problems

Directions: Read and work each problem. Find the correct answer. Fill in the circle.

1. Hanna used $\frac{1}{8}$ of a stick of butter to make muffins. She then used $\frac{2}{3}$ of a cup of flour to make bread. How much butter did she use in the muffins and bread?

   (A) $\frac{1}{8}$ stick

   (B) 1.4 stick

   (C) $\frac{2}{3}$ stick

   (D) Not enough information

2. Sara has a piece of ribbon that is 60 inches long. She will use $\frac{2}{3}$ of the ribbon to make bows. If the answer to this problem is 20 inches, what is the question?

   (F) How much ribbon did she use?

   (G) How much ribbon is left over?

   (H) How much is $\frac{2}{3}$?

   (J) How many bows does she make?

3. There were 488 balloons decorating the gymnasium for a party. There were 97 students at the party. If each student brought home an equal number of balloons after the party, how many balloons were left over?

   (A) 3 balloons

   (B) 46 balloons

   (C) 12 balloons

   (D) None of these

4. If you burn 318 calories in 60 minutes of playing tennis, how many calories would you burn in 30 minutes?

   (F) 159 calories

   (G) 636 calories

   (H) 258 calories

   (J) 288 calories

5. There are 62 students on a class trip. They are taking a bus to the nature park. The ride to the park takes 25 minutes, and the ride home takes 30 minutes. Lunch at the park costs $3.25 per child. How much money do the students spend to get into the park?

   (A) $201.50

   (B) $50.00

   (C) $120.25

   (D) Not enough information

6. The school play sold out every night. The play ran for 3 nights, and 345 people attended each night. Tickets cost $4.25 each. How much money did the school play make?

   (F) $1,239.50

   (G) $1,466.25

   (H) $1,035.00

   (J) $4,398.75

Look for key words in each problem. They will help you figure out how to solve it.

Solving Word Problems

Directions: Use the information below to help you answer the questions that follow.

You have some stickers to share with your class. There are 25 students in your class. You want each student to get 7 stickers.

1. What operation will you use to figure out how many stickers you need?

- (A) addition
- (B) subtraction
- (C) multiplication
- (D) division

2. How many stickers do you need in all?

- (F) 200
- (G) 175
- (H) 1,500
- (J) 145

3. Two students are absent on the day you hand out the stickers. Write a number sentence to show how many stickers you will have left over.

_____

_____

4. Jill bought 5 books. Each book cost $3.95. Which number sentence shows how much she paid for all 5 books?

- (A) 5 + $3.95 = ☐
- (B) 5 × $3.95 = ☐
- (C) 5 − $3.95 = ☐
- (D) $3.95 + $3.95 = ☐

5. Caleb has 16 rocks. How many rocks would he have if he adds 7 additional rocks each minute for 5 minutes?

- (F) 50 rocks
- (G) 48 rocks
- (H) 51 rocks
- (J) Not enough information

6. Rocco bought tennis balls that cost $2.50 per can. What else do you need to know to find out how much money Rocco spent in all?

- (A) whether he played singles or doubles
- (B) how many cans of tennis balls he bought
- (C) whether he won his tennis match
- (D) how many cans of tennis balls the store had in stock

Solving Word Problems

Directions: Use the graph below to answer the questions that follow.

The fourth-grade students at Trenton Elementary were asked to do reports on one of the following five big cats: leopard, cheetah, panther, lion, or tiger.

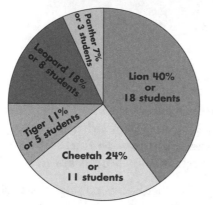

3. Which two cats combined get more than 50 percent of the vote?

(A) lion and cheetah

(B) panther and leopard

(C) panther and tiger

(D) lion and panther

4. What percent of the vote do the panther, leopard, and tiger make up together?

(F) 40%

(G) 25%

(H) 30%

(J) 36%

1. How many fourth graders are at Trenton Elementary?

(A) 100

(B) 45

(C) 47

(D) 50

2. Which of the following lists the cats from least to greatest favorite?

(F) lion, cheetah, leopard, tiger, panther

(G) tiger, panther, leopard, cheetah, lion

(H) panther, tiger, leopard, cheetah, lion

(J) leopard, lion, cheetah, tiger, panther

> **Carefully read the titles and labels on any charts or graphs. They can contain important information.**

Solving Word Problems

Directions: Read and work each problem. Find the correct answer. Fill in the circle.

1. The Southlake High School football team has scored a total of 162 points during 9 games so far this season. What was the average number of points scored per game?

   Ⓐ 15
   Ⓑ 81
   Ⓒ 18
   Ⓓ 19

2. Garth took $15.00 to the art supply store. He spent $12.76 on art supplies. He wants to buy one more item that costs $2.50. Does he have enough money?

   Ⓕ yes
   Ⓖ no

3. A dripping faucet leaks 3 gallons of water each day. If the faucet leaks for 20 days before it is fixed, and the price of water is $0.30 per gallon, how much did the leak cost?

   Ⓐ $18.00
   Ⓑ $1.80
   Ⓒ $10.50
   Ⓓ $24.50

4. Alicia wants to buy a toy that costs $1.39. She has the coins below. How much more does she need?

   Ⓕ $1.04
   Ⓖ 69¢
   Ⓗ 70¢
   Ⓙ $1.05

5. Which of the following sets of figures shows $\frac{1}{3}$ shaded?

   Ⓐ ①①①①①①①
   Ⓑ ①①①①①①
   Ⓒ ①①①①①①
   Ⓓ ①①①①①①

6. In the picture below, 1 book represents 5 books. How many books does this picture stand for?

   Ⓕ 25
   Ⓖ 45
   Ⓗ 40
   Ⓙ 30

Solving Word Problems

Directions: This is Chris's favorite sugar cookie recipe. Use it to answer the questions that follow.

Sugar Cookies

$\frac{1}{3}$ cup butter or margarine, softened

$\frac{1}{3}$ cup shortening

$\frac{3}{4}$ cup sugar

1 teaspoon baking powder

pinch salt

1 egg

1 teaspoon vanilla

2 cups all-purpose flour

Beat butter and shortening thoroughly. Add sugar, baking powder, and a pinch of salt. Mix until well combined. Beat in egg, vanilla, and flour.

Cover and chill for at least 1 hour. Split the dough in half, and roll one half at a time. Cut out with cookie cutters.

Bake at 325°F on an ungreased cookie sheet for about 7 to 8 minutes, until edges are firm and bottoms are lightly browned. Don't overcook.

Makes 36 cookies.

---

1   **If Chris bakes 36 cookies, how much flour does he need?**

(A) 1 cup

(B) $1\frac{1}{2}$ cups

(C) 2 cups

(D) 3 cups

2. **If Chris bakes 2 batches of cookies, how many cookies will he bake?**

(F) 66

(G) 72

(H) 76

(J) 84

3. **How much flour will he need to bake the 2 batches of cookies?**

(A) 2 cups

(B) $2\frac{1}{2}$ cups

(C) 3 cups

(D) 4 cups

4. **Chris needs to bake 3 batches of cookies for a party. How much butter or margarine will he use?**

(F) $\frac{1}{3}$ cup

(G) $\frac{2}{3}$ cup

(H) 1 cup

(J) 3 cups

Solving Word Problems

Directions: Describe how to solve each problem in the space provided.

1. A box of 20 tennis balls costs $35.80. What is the cost for each tennis ball?

2. A roller coaster holds a total of 184 people. If each car holds 8 people, how many cars are there?

3. Marcos has $47.82. He plans to spend $25 on presents. How much money will he have left?

4. If a machine can sort 120 pieces of mail a minute, how many pieces of mail can it sort in 30 seconds?

5. Mrs. Stassen made zucchini pie for dinner on Thursday. She and her daughter ate $\frac{1}{2}$ of the pie at dinner. They ate $\frac{1}{4}$ of the pie at lunch the next day. How much of the pie did they eat?

6. Rosa left dance class at 3:30 in the afternoon. She arrived home at 4:17. How long did it take her to get home?

Organizing and Displaying Data

Directions: The chart below shows a person's heart rate while jogging. Use the data to answer the questions on this page.

Data

Time	Heart Rate
0 min.	80
5 min.	120
10 min.	135
15 min.	148
20 min.	159
25 min.	150

3. At what time was the jogger's heart rate the highest?

_____

4. During which time interval did the jogger's heart rate increase the most?

_____

5. During which time interval did the jogger's heart rate increase the least?

_____

6. During which interval did the jogger's heart rate decrease?

_____

1. Use the data in the chart to complete this line graph.

Line Graph
Heart Rate While Jogging

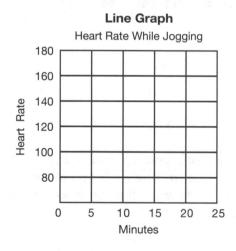

2. Use the data in the chart to complete this bar graph.

Bar Graph
Heart Rate While Jogging

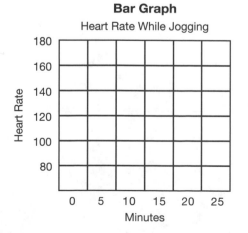

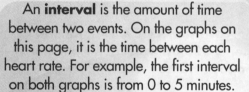

An **interval** is the amount of time between two events. On the graphs on this page, it is the time between each heart rate. For example, the first interval on both graphs is from 0 to 5 minutes.

Organizing and Displaying Data

Directions: The crossing guards at Howell Elementary are concerned that a large number of cars cross a street that they do not monitor. They are using a tally chart to help present their findings to the principal. Answer the following questions based on the tally chart below.

Number of Cars on Johnson Ave.
3:00 P.M. to 3:30 P.M.

Day	Tallies
Monday	卌 卌 卌 ||||
Tuesday	卌 卌 卌 |
Wednesday	卌 卌 卌 卌 ||
Thursday	卌 卌 ||||
Friday	卌 卌 卌 卌 ||||

One way to organize data is to use a **tally chart**. One mark is used for each number, and a slash is drawn through every 4 marks to represent 5.

1. What is the least number of cars that crossed Johnson Avenue in one day?

_____

2. What is the greatest number of cars that crossed Johnson Avenue in one day?

_____

3. Which day had the least number of cars?

_____

4. What is the total number of cars that crossed from Monday through Friday?

_____

5. The principal may allow an extra crossing guard for one day of the week. Which day should the crossing guards recommend?

_____

Organizing and Displaying Data

Directions: Choose the best answer to each question below.

1. Which of these questions could you answer using the information in the tally chart?

Brown	Black	Blond	Red
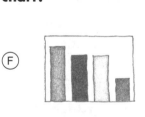			

(A) How often do the students get their hair cut?

(B) How many students dye their hair?

(C) Which students have long hair?

(D) How many more brown-haired students are there than blond-haired students?

2. Which graph below best represents the data on the tally chart?

(F)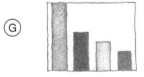

(G)

(H)

(J)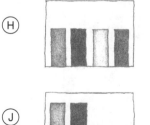

3. Which circle shows the fraction of the students on the tally chart that have black hair?

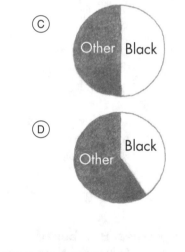

(A) Other / Black

(B) Black / Other

(C) Other / Black

(D) Other / Black

Look at each graph closely before choosing your answer.

Organizing and Displaying Data

Directions: The bar graph below shows the different kinds of sandwiches sold at a sandwich shop in a week. Use the graph to answer the questions that follow.

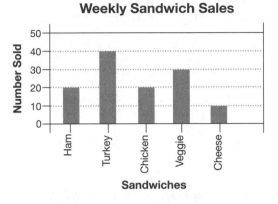

Weekly Sandwich Sales

1. How many ham sandwiches were sold during the week?

- (A) 30
- (B) 20
- (C) 10
- (D) 40

2. How many sandwiches were sold altogether?

- (F) 120
- (G) 12
- (H) 100
- (J) 40

3. Which of the following correctly shows the number of sandwiches sold in order from least to greatest?

- (A) turkey, veggie, ham, chicken, cheese
- (B) cheese, chicken, ham, veggie, turkey
- (C) chicken, cheese, ham, veggie, turkey
- (D) cheese, chicken, ham, turkey, veggie

4. Which two types of sandwiches sold equal amounts?

- (F) ham and chicken
- (G) chicken and cheese
- (H) veggie and turkey
- (J) ham and veggie

5. How many more of the most popular sandwiches were sold compared to the least popular?

- (A) 40
- (B) 20
- (C) 30
- (D) 10

6. What number sentence could you use to find the answer to question 5?

- (F) 40 + 10 =
- (G) 40 − 30 =
- (H) 30 + 10 =
- (J) 40 − 10 =

Organizing and Displaying Data

MATH 226

Directions: The table below shows the number of hurricanes and tropical storms during a period of 100 years. Use the table to answer the questions.

Month Formed	Tropical Storm	Hurricanes
January–April	4	1
May	14	3
June	57	23
July	68	35
August	221	114
September	311	179
October	188	84
November	42	22
December	6	3

1. Which two months had the greatest number of tropical storms?

(A) July and August

(B) September and October

(C) August and September

(D) August and October

2. In July, how many more tropical storms were there than hurricanes?

(F) 68

(G) 103

(H) 34

(J) 33

3. When are hurricanes least likely to happen?

(A) late summer

(B) fall

(C) winter/early spring

(D) late spring/early summer

4. Based on the table, which of the following statements is not true?

(F) All tropical storms turn into hurricanes.

(G) Hurricanes are unlikely in January.

(H) Most hurricanes occur in the summer and fall.

(J) There are more tropical storms than hurricanes.

5. Plot the hurricane data for June through October on the line graph below.

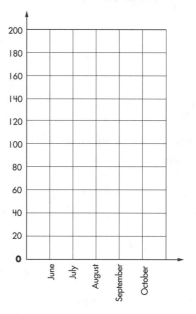

Organizing and Displaying Data

Directions: Use the chart to answer the questions that follow.

Conservation Efforts at Coe School			
Year	Pounds of Paper Recycled	Pounds of Cans Recycled	Number of Trees Planted
2009	550	475	120
2010	620	469	250
2011	685	390	320

1. Which sentence is true about paper recycling at Coe School?

(A) Students recycled more paper each year.

(B) Students recycled less paper each year.

(C) Students never recycled paper.

(D) Students recycled the same amount of paper each year.

2. Which conservation project did not show better results each year?

(F) recycling paper

(G) recycling cans

(H) planting trees

(J) They all showed better results each year.

3. How many more pounds of paper were recycled in 2011 than in 2009?

(A) 65 pounds

(B) 133 pounds

(C) 135 pounds

(D) 70 pounds

4. How many pounds of cans were recycled altogether?

(F) 1,855 pounds

(G) 1,433 pounds

(H) 690 pounds

(J) 1,334 pounds

5. If you had to predict how many pounds of paper were recycled in 2008, what would be the most likely answer?

(A) 497 pounds

(B) 644 pounds

(C) 202 pounds

(D) 768 pounds

6. If you had to predict how many pounds of paper would be recycled in 2012, what would be the most likely answer?

(F) 497 pounds

(G) 644 pounds

(H) 202 pounds

(J) 768 pounds

Name _____ Date _____

Sample Test 10: Applications

Directions: Read and work each problem. Find the correct answer. Fill in the circle.

Example

Jesse bought a pack of cards for $1.25 and a baseball for $8.39. He has $5.36 left over. How much money did he start with?

- Ⓐ $20.00
- Ⓑ $9.64
- Ⓒ $1.78
- Ⓓ $15.00

Answer: D

---

1. Aidan bought a slice of pizza and bottle of juice at the arcade. The pizza cost $4.50, and the juice cost $2.75. Aidan paid with a $10 bill. How much change did he receive?

- Ⓐ $5.50
- Ⓑ $3.00
- Ⓒ $2.75
- Ⓓ $7.25

2. If 1 pound of potatoes costs $2.60, and Miko needs to buy 8 pounds to make potato salad, what formula would she use to find the total cost?

- Ⓕ $2.60 + 8 = ☐
- Ⓖ 8 − $2.60 = ☐
- Ⓗ $2.60 × 8 = ☐
- Ⓙ 8 ÷ $2.60 = ☐

3. Terrance collected 468 seashells in 18 visits to the beach. On average, how many seashells did he collect during each visit?

- Ⓐ 29
- Ⓑ 26
- Ⓒ 32
- Ⓓ 23

Directions: Use the pie chart to answer the following questions.

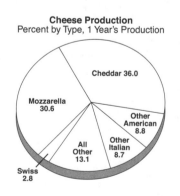

Cheese Production
Percent by Type, 1 Year's Production

Cheddar 36.0
Mozzarella 30.6
Other American 8.8
Other Italian 8.7
All Other 13.1
Swiss 2.8

4. Which cheese is made the least?

- Ⓕ other Italian
- Ⓖ mozzarella
- Ⓗ cheddar
- Ⓙ Swiss

5. Which two cheeses together make up 66.6% of the year's production?

- Ⓐ other American and other Italian
- Ⓑ cheddar and mozzarella
- Ⓒ mozzarella and Swiss
- Ⓓ cheddar and Swiss

6. What percent of cheese production is made up of cheeses other than cheddar and mozzarella?

- Ⓕ 33.4%
- Ⓖ 30%
- Ⓗ 66.6%
- Ⓙ 8.8%

GO

Sample Test 10: Applications

Directions: Study the graph. Use the information to answer the questions.

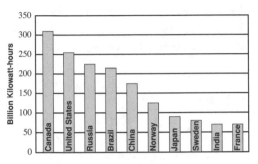

Top Countries Generating Hydroelectric Power

8. Which country produces more hydroelectricity than Brazil and less than the United States?

(F) Russia

(G) China

(H) Canada

(J) Brazil

7. Which country produces more hydroelectricity than the United States?

(A) Brazil

(B) China

(C) Canada

(D) India

9. Which two countries produce about the same amount of hydroelectricity?

(A) India and France

(B) Russia and Brazil

(C) Japan and Sweden

(D) Sweden and India

Directions: Read and work each problem. Find the correct answer. Fill in the circle.

10. A sailboat takes 124 passengers on a cruise on a lake. If the sailboat makes 53 tours a month, how many people ride on the boat each month?

(F) 5,789 people

(G) 5,499 people

(H) 6,845 people

(J) 6,572 people

11. A gas station sells an average of 847 gallons of gasoline per day. About how many gallons will it sell in a week?

(A) 4,235 gallons

(B) 5,929 gallons

(C) 5,299 gallons

(D) Not enough information

Sample Test 10: Applications

Directions: Read and work each problem. Find the correct answer. Fill in the circle.

12. A truck driver makes 23 trips each month. Each trip is 576 miles long. How many miles does the truck driver travel in a month?

- (F) 13,248 miles
- (G) 12,248 miles
- (H) 13,589 miles
- (J) 14,553 miles

13. A store manager ordered 4 cases of juice boxes. There are 6 boxes in each package and 12 packages in a case. How many juice boxes did he order altogether?

- (A) 24 boxes
- (B) 288 boxes
- (C) 48 boxes
- (D) Not enough information

Directions: Look at the spinner. Mark the probability that the arrow will land on each of the following shapes.

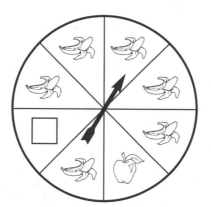

14. a fruit

- (F) certain
- (G) likely
- (H) unlikely
- (J) impossible

15. a star

- (A) certain
- (B) likely
- (C) unlikely
- (D) impossible

16. a triangle

- (F) certain
- (G) likely
- (H) unlikely
- (J) impossible

17. an apple

- (A) certain
- (B) likely
- (C) unlikely
- (D) impossible

18. a banana

- (F) certain
- (G) likely
- (H) unlikely
- (J) impossible

MATH 230

GO

Sample Test 10: Applications

Directions: Use the following information to answer the questions below. Mark the space for your choice.

A bag contains 6 red mittens, 4 blue mittens, 6 striped mittens, and 2 gray mittens.

19. What is the probability of pulling out a green mitten?

- (A) certain
- (B) likely
- (C) impossible
- (D) unlikely

20. Which of the following statements is not true?

- (F) It is unlikely that a gray mitten will be pulled out.
- (G) A blue mitten is more likely to be pulled out than a gray mitten.
- (H) There is an equal chance of pulling out a red or a striped mitten.
- (J) A blue mitten is more likely to be pulled out than a striped mitten.

21. What is the probability of pulling out a red or striped mitten?

- (A) certain
- (B) likely
- (C) impossible
- (D) unlikely

Directions: Read and work each problem. Find the correct answer. Fill in the circle.

22. You have coins that total $2.17. What coins do you have?

- (F) 6 quarters, 3 dimes, 7 nickels, and 2 pennies
- (G) 10 quarters, 3 dimes, 6 nickels, and 7 pennies
- (H) 20 dimes, 4 nickels, and 2 pennies
- (J) 4 quarters, 6 dimes, 18 nickels, and 7 pennies

23. Kareem bought 6 peaches. Each peach cost $0.65. Which number sentence shows how much he paid for all 6 peaches?

- (A) $6 \div \$0.65 = \square$
- (B) $6 \div \square = \$0.65$
- (C) $6 - \$0.65 = \square$
- (D) $6 \times \$0.65 = \square$

24. You toss a coin 4 times. On the fourth time, what is your probability of the coin coming up heads?

- (F) $\frac{1}{2}$
- (G) $\frac{4}{4}$
- (H) $\frac{2}{2}$
- (J) $\frac{3}{4}$

25. One letter is randomly chosen from the word *synonym*. What are the chances the letter will be a *y*?

- (A) $\frac{2}{7}$
- (B) $\frac{2}{2}$
- (C) $\frac{1}{7}$
- (D) $\frac{1}{4}$

STOP

Practice Test 3: Math
Part 1: Concepts

Directions: Read and work each problem. Show each fraction in its simplest form. Find the correct answer. Fill in the circle.

1. **Mark is selling fruit baskets for the school band. He sells 2 on the first day, 6 on the second day, and 10 on the third day. If this pattern continues, how many will he sell on the fourth day?**

   (A) 20

   (B) 18

   (C) 12

   (D) 14

2. **Which of these is a group of odd numbers?**

   (F) 17, 19, 25, 99

   (G) 5, 14, 23, 67

   (H) 13, 16, 19, 21

   (J) 6, 35, 48, 98

3. **What number makes this number sentence true?**
   $$\frac{\square}{2} = \frac{2}{4}$$

   (A) 0

   (B) 4

   (C) 1

   (D) 2

4. **How many tens are in 5,569,273?**

   (F) 5

   (G) 2

   (H) 3

   (J) 7

5. **What should replace the $\square$ in the number sentence below?**
   $$7 \;\square\; 6 = 42$$

   (A) +

   (B) −

   (C) ×

   (D) ÷

6. **A number rounded to the nearest ten is 350. When it is rounded to the nearest hundred, the number becomes 400. What is the number?**

   (F) 349

   (G) 359

   (H) 353

   (J) 345

7. **What number is missing from the sequence show below?**
   64, 55, 46, _____, 28, 19

   (A) 37

   (B) 36

   (C) 30

   (D) 34

8. **How many hundreds are in 2,674?**

   (F) 2

   (G) 6

   (H) 4

   (J) 7

Practice Test 3: Math
Part 1: Concepts

Directions: Read each problem. Find the correct answer. Fill in the circle.

9. What fraction of the shape below is shaded?

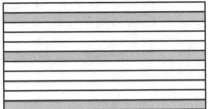

(A) $\frac{3}{10}$

(B) $\frac{3}{11}$

(C) $\frac{1}{3}$

(D) $\frac{2}{3}$

10. Which of these numerals has a 6 in the hundreds place?

(F) 11,610

(G) 10,006

(H) 6,313

(J) 16,452

11. Which numeral fits in this number sentence to make it true?
$24 - \square = 8$

(A) 16

(B) 3

(C) 12

(D) 14

12. Which of the following is the closest estimate for the equation?
$358 \times 2 = \square$

(F) 700

(G) 600

(H) 900

(J) 400

13. What is another way to write 45 thousands?

(A) 450,000

(B) 45,000

(C) 450

(D) 4,500

14. Which decimal below names the smallest number?

(F) 0.06

(G) 0.6

(H) 0.64

(J) 0.064

15. What is the correct sign to complete the equation below?
$\$426.10 \ \square \ \$416.19$

(A) =

(B) <

(C) >

(D) None of these

16. Which of these has a greater value than $\frac{1}{8}$?

(F) $\frac{1}{18}$

(G) $\frac{1}{16}$

(H) $\frac{1}{6}$

(J) $\frac{1}{32}$

Practice Test 3: Math
Part 1: Concepts

Directions: Read each problem. Find the correct answer. Fill in the circle.

GO

17. What is the value of the underlined digit?

9,<u>4</u>39

Ⓐ forty

Ⓑ four thousand

Ⓒ four hundred

Ⓓ four

18. The function table below shows input and output numbers. The rule used to change the numbers is shown. What number completes the table?

IN	OUT
3	13
4	—
5	17

Ⓕ 14

Ⓖ 16

Ⓗ 15

Ⓙ None of these

19. Which number in $1.62 would you look at to round it to the nearest dollar?

Ⓐ 1

Ⓑ 6

Ⓒ 2

Ⓓ None of these

20. The soccer team had $9\frac{1}{2}$ feet of submarine sandwich for their party. They ate 7 feet. Which equation below would you use to find out how much sandwich they had left?

Ⓕ $9\frac{1}{2} + 7 = \square$

Ⓖ $9\frac{1}{2} - 7 = \square$

Ⓗ $9\frac{1}{2} \times 7 = \square$

Ⓙ $9\frac{1}{2} \div 7 = \square$

21. Which shows the numbers ordered from greatest to least?

Ⓐ 5,693; 6,432; 43,534; 710,002

Ⓑ 14,632; 346; 123,152; 9,965

Ⓒ 711,002; 182,976; 6,234; 1,624

Ⓓ 643,342; 72,816; 143,524; 9,569

22. 0.59 =

Ⓕ $\frac{5}{9}$

Ⓖ $\frac{590}{100}$

Ⓗ $\frac{59}{100}$

Ⓙ $\frac{59}{10}$

23. Which of the following number facts does not belong to the same family or group as 35 ÷ 7 = 5?

Ⓐ 7 × 5 = 35

Ⓑ 35 ÷ 5 = 7

Ⓒ 5 × 7 = 35

Ⓓ 5 + 7 = 12

Practice Test 3: Math
Part 1: Concepts

Directions: Read each problem. Find the correct answer. Fill in the circle.

24. What is the numeral for three million, five hundred sixty-two thousand, forty-five?

Ⓕ 3,562,450

Ⓖ 3,562,045

Ⓗ 356,245

Ⓙ 3,526,045

25. What does the 6 in 12,613 mean?

Ⓐ 6

Ⓑ 60

Ⓒ 600

Ⓓ 6,000

26. Elliot is in line to see a play. There are 25 people in line, and he is in the middle. What is his place in line?

Ⓕ tenth

Ⓖ twelfth

Ⓗ thirteenth

Ⓙ fifteenth

27. The sum of two numbers is 21, and their product is 98. What are the 2 numbers?

Ⓐ 12 and 8

Ⓑ 14 and 7

Ⓒ 77 and 21

Ⓓ 7 and 9

28. What number makes this number sentence true?
□ + 64 = 86

Ⓕ 12

Ⓖ 22

Ⓗ 25

Ⓙ 32

29. What is the expanded numeral for 56,428?

Ⓐ 50,000 + 6,000 + 400 + 20 + 8

Ⓑ 56,000 + 6,400 + 20 + 8

Ⓒ 56,000 + 400 + 28

Ⓓ 50,000 + 6,000 + 400 + 28

30. Which number is greater than 425 and has a 1 in the tens place?

Ⓕ 519

Ⓖ 416

Ⓗ 318

Ⓙ 471

STOP

Name _____   Date _____

Practice Test 3: Math
Part 2: Computation

Directions: Choose the correct answer to each problem. Remember to reduce fraction answers to simplest form. Choose "None of these" if the correct answer is not given.

1. 132
   × 4

   (A) 528

   (B) 136

   (C) 478

   (D) None of these

2. $1\frac{2}{4} - \frac{3}{4} =$

   (F) $1\frac{5}{4}$

   (G) $\frac{3}{4}$

   (H) $\frac{2}{14}$

   (J) None of these

3. □ + 6 = 44

   (A) 38

   (B) 50

   (C) 264

   (D) None of these

4. 3)90

   (F) 3

   (G) 180

   (H) 30

   (J) None of these

5. 2 × 5 × 9 =

   (A) 16

   (B) 19

   (C) 91

   (D) None of these

6. 5)473

   (F) 94.3

   (G) 94

   (H) 94 R3

   (J) None of these

7. $\frac{3}{9}$
    $+ \frac{2}{9}$

   (A) $\frac{1}{9}$

   (B) $\frac{5}{9}$

   (C) $\frac{6}{9}$

   (D) None of these

8. 12 × □ = 144

   (F) 132

   (G) 1,728

   (H) 12

   (J) None of these

9. $0.12
    $4.69
   +$5.87

   (A) 10.68

   (B) $10.12

   (C) $10.68

   (D) None of these

10. 245
   +127

   (F) 372

   (G) 118

   (H) 3.72

   (J) None of these

Practice Test 3: Math
Part 2: Computation

Directions: Choose the correct answer to each problem. Remember to reduce fraction answers to simplest form. Choose "None of these" if the correct answer is not given.

11. $\frac{3}{8} + \frac{6}{8} =$

   (A) $\frac{3}{8}$

   (B) $1\frac{1}{8}$

   (C) $\frac{9}{8}$

   (D) None of these

12. 757
   −129

   (F) 6.28

   (G) 886

   (H) 628

   (J) None of these

13. 8,941 + 1,278 =

   (A) 9,219

   (B) 10,119

   (C) 10,219

   (D) None of these

14. $4\overline{)369}$

   (F) 92

   (G) 92 R1

   (H) 0.92

   (J) None of these

15. 46
   ×82

   (A) 3,772

   (B) 3,672

   (C) 128

   (D) None of these

16. 67 × 6 =

   (F) 402

   (G) 420

   (H) 73

   (J) None of these

17. $1\frac{5}{6}$
   $-\frac{6}{6}$

   (A) $2\frac{5}{6}$

   (B) $\frac{5}{6}$

   (C) $1\frac{11}{6}$

   (D) None of these

18. 77 − □ = 43

   (F) 120

   (G) 43

   (H) 34

   (J) None of these

19. $8\overline{)78}$

   (A) 86

   (B) 8

   (C) 9

   (D) None of these

20. $7.00
   −$2.48

   (F) $4.52

   (G) $9.48

   (H) 9.48

   (J) None of these

STOP

Practice Test 3: Math
Part 3: Geometry

Directions: Choose the best answer to each question below.

1. Which word describes the figure's movement?

- Ⓐ refraction
- Ⓑ reflection
- Ⓒ rotation
- Ⓓ symmetry

2. What type of triangle is this?

- Ⓕ obtuse
- Ⓖ right
- Ⓗ acute
- Ⓙ None of the above

3. Which of the following letters has a line of symmetry?

- Ⓐ **F**
- Ⓑ **R**
- Ⓒ **J**
- Ⓓ **H**

4. A quadrilateral with 2 sets of parallel sides and opposite side equal length is a _____.

- Ⓕ hexagon
- Ⓖ trapezoid
- Ⓗ cube
- Ⓙ parallelogram

5. A child's paper party hat is shaped like a _____.

- Ⓐ cylinder
- Ⓑ cone
- Ⓒ pyramid
- Ⓓ sphere

6. What type of triangle is this?

- Ⓕ scalene
- Ⓖ equilateral
- Ⓗ isosceles
- Ⓙ None of the above

7. How many faces does a sphere have?

- Ⓐ 0
- Ⓑ 1
- Ⓒ 2
- Ⓓ 4

Practice Test 3: Math
Part 3: Geometry

Directions: Read and work each problem. Find the correct answer. Fill in the circle.

8. Mrs. Joplin wants to get new linoleum for her kitchen. At the hardware store, the employee asks her the area of her kitchen. She tells him it measures 12 feet by 14 feet. What is its area?

(F) 25 square feet

(G) 52 square feet

(H) 172 square feet

(J) 168 square feet

9. What is the perimeter of Mrs. Joplin's kitchen?

(A) 25 feet

(B) 52 feet

(C) 172 feet

(D) 168 feet

10. A rectangular prism is 6 cubic units long, 4 cubic units wide, and has a volume of 72 cubic units. What is the height?

(F) 2 cubic units

(G) 3 cubic units

(H) 4 cubic units

(J) 5 cubic units

11. Which of these has the greatest volume?

(A) 8 quarts

(B) 8 gallons

(C) 8 pints

(D) 8 cups

12. On the graph below, plot and label the following points:

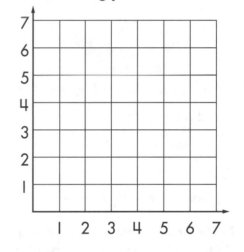

Point A (1, 3)
Point B (6, 5)
Point C (2, 7)
Point D (4, 1)

Practice Test 3: Math
Part 4: Measurement

Directions: Read and work each problem. Find the correct answer. Fill in the circle.

1. **What is the temperature in Celsius shown on this thermometer?**

   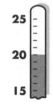

   25
   20
   15

   (A) 75°F

   (B) 20°C

   (C) 25°C

   (D) 70°F

2. **Which of the following is not true?**

   (F) 32 cups = 2 gallons

   (G) 4 quarts = 1 gallon

   (H) 3 yards = 1 foot

   (J) 1 centimeter = 10 millimeters

3. **Mona started her chores at 3:30 P.M. She needed to take out the garbage, wash the dishes, water the houseplants, feed the dog, and clean up her room. Mona finished her chores just as her dad came home at 5:20 P.M. How long did it take Mona to do her chores?**

   (A) 50 minutes

   (B) 2 hours

   (C) 1 hour and 50 minutes

   (D) None of these

4. **Which of the following would you use to measure the length of a boat?**

   (F) inches

   (G) meters

   (H) millimeters

   (J) kilometers

5. **If the temperature in the morning is 56°F, what will the temperature be when it rises 25°F this afternoon?**

   (A) 78°F

   (B) 76°F

   (C) 81°F

   (D) 85°F

6. **What is the value of 1 nickel, 2 dimes, 1 quarter, and 1 penny?**

   (F) $0.56

   (G) $0.50

   (H) $0.51

   (J) $0.57

7. **Which of these would be the best unit of measurement to measure a tree?**

   (A) kilometers

   (B) centimeters

   (C) meters

   (D) millimeters

GO ▶

Practice Test 3: Math
Part 4: Measurement

Directions: Read and work each problem. Find the correct answer. Fill in the circle.

8. **One tablespoon holds about 15 milliliters. About how many tablespoons of soup are in a 225–milliliter can?**

   Ⓕ 45 tablespoons

   Ⓖ 5 tablespoons

   Ⓗ 3,375 tablespoons

   Ⓙ 15 tablespoons

9. **Aaliyah went to school at 8:00 in the morning. She had soccer practice after school for $1\frac{1}{2}$ hours. What time did Aaliyah get home in the evening?**

   Ⓐ 5:30

   Ⓑ 9:30

   Ⓒ 4:00

   Ⓓ Not enough information

10. **About how much does this container probably hold?**

    Ⓕ 1 gallon

    Ⓖ 1 quart

    Ⓗ 2 pints

    Ⓙ 2 cups

11. **Tierra used 8 liters of water when she washed her hands and face. How many milliliters of water did she use?**

    Ⓐ 8,000 mL

    Ⓑ 80 mL

    Ⓒ 800 mL

    Ⓓ 80,000 mL

12. **Parker starts his school sale on the Sunday of the first full week in May. The sale lasts for 2 weeks and 3 days. On what day must Parker turn in his sales slip?**

SUN	MON	TUE	WED	THUR	FRI	SAT
			1	2	3	4
5	6	7	8	9	10	11
12	13	14	15	16	17	18
19	20	21	22	23	24	25
26	27	28	29	30	31	

    Ⓕ Monday

    Ⓖ Tuesday

    Ⓗ Wednesday

    Ⓙ Thursday

STOP

Practice Test 3: Math
Part 5: Applications

Directions: Read and work each problem. Find the correct answer. Fill in the circle.

1. **Emilio rolled a number cube. What are the chances he will roll an even number?**

   (A) 2 out of 2

   (B) 3 out of 6

   (C) 2 out of 6

   (D) 1 out of 6

2. **Mr. Sykes left the nature center at 2:37. He got home at 3:05. How long did it take him to get home?**

   (F) 28 minutes

   (G) 40 minutes

   (H) 38 minutes

   (J) 22 minutes

3. **One letter is randomly chosen from the word *school*. Which statement is not true?**

   (A) The letter *o* is most likely to be chosen.

   (B) The letter *c* and the letter *h* are equally likely to be chosen.

   (C) The letter *s* is more likely to be chosen than the letter *l*.

   (D) The letter *s* and the letter *h* are equally likely to be chosen.

4. **Nate wants to buy a notebook that costs $2.25. He has 3 quarters, 8 dimes, 4 nickels, and 6 pennies. How much more money does he need?**

   (F) $0.40

   (G) $0.48

   (H) $0.64

   (J) $0.44

5. **Katya is getting her little sister ready for picture day. She can choose a pink bow, a green bow, or a flowered bow for Kyra's hair. She can also choose a striped dress, a green dress, or a polka-dot dress. How many possible combinations are there?**

   (A) 3

   (B) 9

   (C) 5

   (D) 6

6. **If each 🙂 stands for 3 people, how would you show 12 people?**

   (J) None of these

Practice Test 3: Math
Part 5: Applications

Directions: Read and work each problem. Find the correct answer. Fill in the circle.

7. A chicken pot pie was cut into 8 slices. For dinner, the Wilsons ate $\frac{3}{8}$ of the pie. For lunch, the Wilsons ate $\frac{1}{4}$ of the pie. How much of the pie did they eat altogether?

(A) $\frac{5}{8}$

(B) $\frac{2}{8}$

(C) $\frac{4}{12}$

(D) $\frac{1}{3}$

8. Which of the following directions could be used to move from zero to point Y on the graph below?

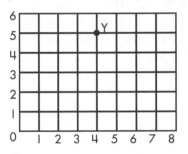

(F) Go over 4 units and up 1 unit.

(G) Go over 3 units and up 5 units.

(H) Go over 5 units and up 4 units.

(J) Go over 4 units and up 5 units.

9. Luke helps take care of the plants at a nursery. He makes $7.00 an hour. If you want to know how much Luke makes in a week, what other piece of information do you need?

(A) the number of hours he works each day

(B) the number of days he works each week

(C) the number of hours he works in a week

(D) the number of weeks in a year

10. Dbenge and his sister combine their money to buy a new game. Dbenge has $7.48, and his sister has $8.31. How much money do they have in all?

(F) $0.83

(G) $15.79

(H) $16.89

(J) Not enough information

11. Owen scored 1,832 points on a video game. Lily's score was twice as much as Owen's. Brooklyn scored 234 points less than Lily. What was Brooklyn's score?

(A) 3,320 points

(B) 3,664 points

(C) 3,430 points

(D) 468 points

12. There are 21 fish in every square yard of water in a lake. If the lake is 812 square yards, how many fish are in the lake?

(F) 17,052

(G) 23,708

(H) 29,987

(J) 14,879

GO

Name _____   Date _____

Practice Test 3: Math
Part 5: Applications

Directions: Read and work each problem. Find the correct answer. Fill in the circle.

13. Bryson has a piece of wood that is 40 inches long. He will use $\frac{1}{4}$ of the wood for a birdhouse he is making. If the answer to the problem is 30 inches, what is the question?

(A) What is $\frac{1}{4}$ of 40?

(B) How big will the birdhouse be?

(C) How much wood did Bryson use?

(D) How much wood is left?

14. A machine makes 188 parts per hour. At that rate, how many parts can be made in 8 hours?

(F) 1,504 parts

(G) $23\frac{1}{2}$ parts

(H) 180 parts

(J) 196 parts

Directions: Use the graph below to answer the questions that follow.

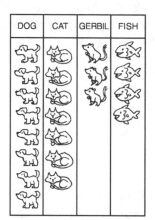

15. What is the least favorite pet in Ms. Sheely's class?

(A) dog

(B) cat

(C) gerbil

(D) fish

16. Which list correctly shows the popularity of pets in order from most to least?

(F) gerbil, fish, cat, dog

(G) dog, cat, fish, gerbil

(H) dog, cat, gerbil, fish

(J) cat, dog, fish, gerbil

17. If each cat on the graph represented 5 cats, how many students chose cats as their favorite pet?

(A) 35

(B) 30

(C) 7

(D) 42

18. Which spinner would give you the best chance of landing on gray?

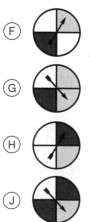

(F)

(G)

(H)

(J)

GO

Practice Test 3: Math
Part 5: Applications

Directions: Use the graph below to answer the questions that follow.

Favorite Flavors of Ice Cream

KEY — 4th Graders, 5th Graders

19. The y-axis shows _____.

- (A) 4th and 5th graders
- (B) favorite flavors
- (C) number of students
- (D) number of ice-cream flavors

20. What is the most popular ice cream flavor overall?

- (F) vanilla
- (G) chocolate
- (H) mint
- (J) vanilla and chocolate

21. How many fourth graders took part in this survey?

- (A) 20
- (B) 30
- (C) 40
- (D) 50

22. The two grade levels didn't always agree about flavor preference. On which two flavors did their answers differ the most?

- (F) vanilla and chocolate
- (G) vanilla and mint
- (H) chocolate and mint
- (J) Not enough information

Directions: Use the graph below to answer the questions that follow.

Grade Level	Number of Students
Kindergarten	✶✶✶✶✶✶✶✶✶
1st Grade	✶✶✶✶✶✶✶✶✶✶✶✶
2nd Grade	✶✶✶✶✶✶✶
3rd Grade	✶✶✶✶✶✶✶✶
4th Grade	✶✶✶✶✶✶✶✶✶✶✶✶✶
5th Grade	✶✶✶✶✶✶✶

Number of Students at Highview School

Key: ✶ = 5 students

23. How many students attend Highview School all together?

- (A) 285
- (B) 275
- (C) 750
- (D) 290

24. How many more students are in fourth grade than in fifth grade?

- (F) 10
- (G) 20
- (H) 30
- (J) 25

25. If no students leave Highview School and no new students enroll, how many third graders will there be next year?

- (A) 45
- (B) 30
- (C) 40
- (D) 35

Practice Test 3: Math
Part 5: Applications

Directions: Solve each problem. Fill in the circle for the correct answer.

Use the information in the box to answer the questions that follow.

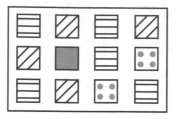

26. The tiles above are in a bag. If you randomly chose one without looking, which type would you most likely choose?

F ▧
G ▤
H ▦
J ⬚

27. Which spinner would give you the best chance of landing on the number 2?

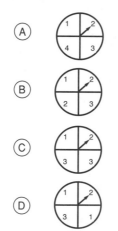

Ⓐ

Ⓑ

Ⓒ

Ⓓ

28. One letter is randomly chosen from the word *accident*. What are the chances the letter will be a *c*?

Ⓕ $\frac{2}{8}$

Ⓖ $\frac{1}{2}$

Ⓗ $\frac{1}{8}$

Ⓙ $\frac{3}{8}$

29. A bookshelf contains 7 science fiction books, 6 nonfiction books, 3 adventures, 4 fairy tales, and 5 mysteries. If you pull a book randomly from the shelf, what is the probability that it will be a mystery?

Ⓐ $\frac{1}{25}$

Ⓑ $\frac{5}{25}$

Ⓒ $\frac{1}{10}$

Ⓓ $\frac{5}{20}$

30. One letter is randomly chosen from the word *encyclopedia*. Which statement is true?

Ⓕ The letter *c* is most likely to be chosen.

Ⓖ The letter *n* and the letter *e* are equally likely to be chosen.

Ⓗ The letter *c* and the letter *y* are equally likely to be chosen.

Ⓙ The letter *e* is more likely to be chosen than the letter *o*.

page 9
1. C
2. F
3. C
4. G
5. D
6. F
7. A
8. H

page 10
1. B
2. H
3. A
4. H
5. A
6. F
7. B

page 11
1. D
2. J
3. B
4. G
5. C
6. F
7. A
8. F
9. A

page 12
1. B
2. G
3. C
4. F
5. A
6. J
7. C

page 13
1. D
2. H
3. C
4. F
5. D

page 14
1. B
2. J
3. A
4. H
5. D
6. G
7. B

8. H

page 15
1. B
2. H
3. D
4. H
5. D
6. G

page 16
1. D
2. G
3. A
4. J
5. C
6. G

page 17
1. B
2. F
3. D
4. G
5. A
6. G

page 18
1. B
2. J
3. A
4. J
5. C
6. H
7. D
8. F

page 19
1. A
2. J
3. B
4. H
5. C
6. H
7. A
8. J

page 20
9. A
10. F
11. C
12. F
13. C
14. F
15. D
16. F

17. B
18. G

page 21
19. B
20. J
21. D
22. H
23. D
24. J
25. B

page 22
26. H
27. A
28. J
29. B
30. F
31. C
32. J

page 23
1. D
2. F

page 24
1. B
2. J
3. B
4. H

page 25
1. D
2. H

page 26
1. C
2. J
3. B
4. H

page 27
1. B
2. G
3. D
4. H
5. A
6. H

page 28
1. A
2. J
3. C
4. G
5. D
6. F

page 29
1. B
2. G

page 30
1. C
2. F
3. D
4. H

page 31
1. D
2. F

page 32
1. C
2. J
3. A
4. Answers will vary.
Possible answer:
Chloe was stuck in a
tree.

page 33
1. A
2. F
3. D

page 34
1. B
2. H
3. D
4. G

page 35
1. A
2. H

page 36
1. B
2. H
3. D
4. Answers will vary.
Possible answers:
after they started
going down the hill
so fast, twist, a loop,
fast turns, everyone
screamed in delight

page 37
1. A
2. G
3. C

page 39
1. B

2. H
3. C
4. J
5. A
6. H

page 41

1. A
2. H
3. D
4. H
5. A
6. G

page 42

1. Answers will vary. Possible answer: The narrator likes the family tradition and feels good about making other kids happy.
2. Maggie hugged her stuffed animal and smiled.
3. It is not like a traditional birthday.
4. Answers will vary. Possible answer: Yes, because the narrator seems to enjoy the happiness the tradition brings to others.

page 43
1. C
2. F

page 44
1. D
2. G
3. D

page 46
1. Answers will vary. Students should mention the origin of the telegraph.
2. Answers will vary. Students should cite details from the selection, such as Morse's inspiration

on the ship and the stages of the development of his invention.
3. C
4. H
5. B
6. G

page 48
1. B
2. F
3. C
4. F
5. C
6. G

page 50
1. C
2. J
3. B
4. J
5. D
6. F

page 51
1. C
2. Answers will vary. Possible answer: The passage gives details about Jacqueline Cochran's life, including her early years, her dreams, and her achievements.

page 52
1. D
2. Answers will vary. Possible answer: It is about an animal. It teaches a lesson and has a moral.
3. G
4. Answers will vary. Possible answer: It is written in short lines. It has rhythm and rhyme.

page 53
1. C
2. J

3. A

page 54
4. J
5. C
6. F

page 56
7. B
8. F
9. A
10. J
11. D
12. J

page 57
1. A
2. J
3. C
4. F
5. B
6. F
7. D
8. G

page 58
9. A
10. G
11. C
12. F
13. B
14. H
15. A
16. J
17. D

page 59
18. J
19. B
20. J
21. C
22. H
23. C
24. F
25. A

page 60
26. H
27. B
28. F
29. C
30. G
31. A
32. J
33. C

page 61
1. C
2. H
3. B

page 63
4. H
5. A
6. G
7. D
8. H
9. A

page 64
10. J
11. C
12. G

page 65
13. C
14. G
15. C

page 66
16. H
17. D
18. Answers will vary. Possible answer: Europeans may not have had to make as many preparations for winter because food and other goods were more available in stores or markets. They probably did not rely on the forest as much either.

page 68
19. J
20. B
21. H
22. B
23. F
24. C

page 69
1. D
2. H
3. D
4. H
5. B
6. G

page 70
1. B
2. J
3. C
4. J
5. C
6. G
7. A
8. H
9. D

page 71
1. A
2. F
3. B
4. G
5. D

page 72
1. D
2. F
3. D
4. G
5. A
6. H
7. D
8. G

page 73
1. A
2. J
3. D
4. H
5. A
6. G

page 74
1. Tyson began singing "The Star-Spangled Banner."
2. Vikram read an article about Canadian geese in a magazine.
3. We sold school supplies to help raise money for the Red Cross.
4. "I'm really glad you are here," Abby said.
5. Will you tell Dr. Singh I called?
6. Riley will be the champion of West Jefferson Little League.
7. "I suggest you go to the library to do research," said Mom.
8. Has Amina been reading *James and the Giant Peach* all afternoon?

page 75
1. D
2. H
3. D
4. G
5. B
6. F
7. A

page 76
1. C
2. F
3. C
4. G
5. A
6. J
7. B
8. J
9. A
10. G

page 77
1. B
2. H
3. A
4. F
5. C
6. F
7. C
8. J
9. A

page 78
1. D
2. G
3. C
4. F
5. B
6. F
7. D

page 79
8. H
9. B
10. J
11. B
12. G
13. A
14. G
15. D

page 80
16. H
17. C
18. J
19. B
20. G
21. C
22. J
23. C

page 81
24. J
25. D
26. F
27. B
28. J
29. A
30. H
31. B
32. F
33. A

page 82
1. B
2. J
3. D
4. J
5. C
6. G

page 83
1. B
2. J
3. B
4. G
5. A
6. F
7. B
8. H
9. A
10. G

page 84
1. D
2. F
3. C
4. G

page 85
1. A
2. G
3. A
4. G
5. C
6. F
7. B
8. G

page 86
1. C
2. H
3. B
4. J
5. C

page 87
1. C
2. G
3. B
4. J

page 88
1. S
2. F
3. S
4. F
5. F
6. S
7. S
8. S
9. F
10. S
11. and
12. but
13. or
14. but
15. and

page 89
1. A
2. F
3. B
4. J
5. C
6. F
7. C

page 90
1. B
2. G

page 91
1. D
2. J
3. D
4. F

page 92
1. B
2. G
3. B

page 93
1. A
2. F
3. C
4. G

page 94
1. B
2. G
3. A
4. F
5. C

page 95
1. C
2. H
3. A
4. H
5. A
6. G

page 96
1. B
2. F
3. B
4. F
5. D

page 97
1. D
2. F
3. D
4. H

page 98
1. C
2. F
3. C
4. G
5. B
6. G
7. B

page 99
8. H
9. D

10. G
11. C
12. F

page 100
13. C
14. J
15. B

page 101
16. J
17. A
18. J
19. C

page 102
20. G
21. B
22. F
23. D

page 103
1. C
2. F
3. Answers will vary. Possible answer: It would give me a plan to follow and help me organize my information in a logical order. It would make it easier for me to write my drafts.

page 104
Answers will vary, but students should include details and feelings.

page 105
1. a snowstorm
2. the night
3. mice
4. ice
5. kite
6. Answers will vary. Possible answer: cold; ice
7. Answers will vary. Possible answer: sister
8. Answers will vary. Possible answer:

warm; a blanket
9. Answers will vary. Possible answer: beautiful painting
10. Answers will vary. Possible answer: a smile that sparkled

page 106
1. Their car has broken down in the middle of the desert.
2. Answers will vary.
3. Answers will vary. Students should list sights, sounds, and feelings that someone in this situation might experience.
4. Answers will vary.

page 107
1. Answers will vary.
2. Answers will vary. Students should give clear reasons why others might enjoy their choice.
3. Answers will vary. Students should cite parts of the book or movie that support their answers to question 2.
4. Answers will vary. Students should write a short persuasive essay. They should include their reasons and cite examples from the book or movie.

page 108
Answers will vary, but students' paragraphs should explain an activity using a logical order of directions and sufficient detail.

page 109

1. Answers will vary but should include descriptive words and at least two similes.
2. Answers will vary but should include several time-order words.

page 110
Answers will vary but should be clearly written and include details, descriptions, and feelings.

page 111
1. B
2. G
3. A
4. J
5. B
6. G
7. A
8. H

page 112
9. D
10. H
11. A
12. G
13. C
14. J
15. B
16. F

page 113
17. B
18. F
19. C
20. H

page 114
21. D
22. H
23. C
24. J
25. B
26. H
27. A
28. J
29. B

page 115

30. G
31. C
32. F
33. A
34. G
35. C
36. G
37. B
38. H
39. D

page 116
1. A
2. H
3. A
4. F
5. D
6. G
7. B

page 117
8. H
9. D
10. G
11. B
12. J

page 118
13. C
14. F
15. D

page 119
16. F
17. B
18. G
19. D

page 120
20. G
21. C
22. H
23. D
24. F

page 121
25. C
26. G
27. D
28. G
29. D
30. H
31. B

page 122
1. Answers will

vary, but students should state their position clearly and use examples and reasons to support their arguments.
2. Answers will vary, but students should use details and descriptive words.

page 123
1. C
2. J
3. C
4. F
5. B

page 124
1. C
2. J
3. B
4. F
5. C
6. H
7. D
8. H

page 125
1. A
2. H
3. B
4. H
5. D
6. F
7. B
8. F

page 126
1. D
2. H
3. B
4. H
5. A
6. G
7. B
8. D

page 127
1. C
2. G
3. D
4. H
5. A

6. F

page 128
1. C
2. G
3. C
4. H
5. A
6. G
7. C
8. G

page 129
1. B
2. G
3. A
4. G
5. D
6. F
7. C
8. G

page 130
1. B
2. J
3. D
4. G
5. C

page 131
1. C
2. F
3. B
4. J
5. B
6. F
7. B
8. J

page 132
1. D
2. F
3. C
4. G
5. A
6. J
7. D

page 133
1. 23; 88; 50 divide by 2
2. 63; 3; 45 add 6
3. 61; 125; 98 subtract 5

4. 44; 88; 8 multiply by 4

page 134
1. A
2. J
3. C
4. G
5. A

page 135
1. B
2. J
3. A
4. H
5. D
6. G

page 136
1. D
2. F
3. A
4. H

page 137
1. D
2. J
3. B
4. F
5. A
6. G
7. A
8. F

page 138
1. C
2. J
3. B
4. F
5. C
6. G
7. A

page 139
1. D
2. H
3. C
4. G
5. C
6. J

page 140
1. D
2. G
3. A
4. J

5. B
6. J
7. D
8. G

page 141
1. C
2. H
3. D
4. G
5. D

page 142
1. C
2. J
3. D
4. F
5. B
6. F
7. B
8. H

page 143
1. 7, 9; +2
2. 60, 40, 30; –10
3. 29, 36, 43; +7
4. 27, 24, 21, 18; –3
5. 70, 55, 40, 25; –15
6. 37, 28, 19, 10; –9
7. 41, 49, 57, 65; +8
8. 90, 72, 66, 60; –6
9. 77, 55, 33, 22; –11
10. 48, 60, 72, 84; +12

page 144
1. variable: n (or any other letter)
sentence: $3 + n = 9$
solution: $n = 6$
2. variable: p (or any other letter)
sentence: $4 + p = 13$
solution: $p = 9$
3. variable: b (or any other letter)
sentence: $314 \times \$500 = b$

solution: $b = \$157,000$
4. variable: k (or any other letter)
sentence: $7 - 5 = k$
solution: $k = 2$

page 145
1. C
2. A
3. C
4. A
5. C
6. C
7. C
8. A
9. A
10. C

page 146
1. $225 + 15$
2. $6 + (8 + 20)$ or $(6 + 20) + 8$
3. $9 + 3$
4. $(37 \times 59) \times 3$ or $(37 \times 3) \times 59$
5. $1 \times (2 \times 18)$ or $(1 \times 18) \times 2$
6. 56×17
7. 3×4
8. $5 + 6 + 8$ or $8 + 6 + 5$ or $6 + 5 + 8$ or $6 + 8 + 5$
9. $(7 \times 4) \times 3$ or $4 \times (7 \times 3)$
10. $(4 \times 3) \times 7$ or $(3 \times 4) \times 7$ or $7 \times (3 \times 4)$
11. $13 + 26$
12. $(11 \times 4) \times 2$

page 147
1. A
2. J
3. D
4. G
5. D
6. F

page 148
7. C
8. J
9. D
10. F

11. A
12. G
13. A
14. F

page 149
1. D
2. G
3. B
4. F
5. B
6. F
7. A
8. H

page 150
1. 481
2. 786
3. 691
4. 884
5. 185
6. 190
7. 126
8. 173

page 151
1. B
2. H
3. A
4. J
5. A
6. H
7. B
8. H

page 152
1. 69
2. 16
3. 19
4. 27
5. 184
6. 264
7. 187
8. 565
9. 313
10. 170

page 153
1. C
2. G
3. D
4. F
5. B
6. H

7. D
8. F

page 154
1. B
2. F
3. D
4. H
5. C
6. F
7. B
8. G

page 155
1. B
2. H
3. B
4. H
5. A
6. H
7. C

page 156
1. A
2. F
3. B
4. J
5. C
6. G
7. A
8. G
9. B
10. H

page 157
1. A
2. G
3. B
4. F
5. B
6. H
7. C
8. H

page 158
1. D
2. H
3. B
4. F
5. B
6. F
7. B
8. H

page 159

1. A
2. F
3. D
4. F
5. C
6. G
7. C
8. J

page 160
1. A
2. J
3. B
4. J
5. C
6. G
7. D
8. F

page 161
1. C
2. G
3. D
4. H
5. A
6. H
7. A
8. G

page 162
1. B
2. F
3. D
4. F
5. B
6. H
7. D
8. F

page 163
1. B
2. G
3. D
4. F
5. C
6. 21, 27, 30, 20, 24, 36; G

page 164
1. A
2. H
3. 42, 48, 66, 18, 45, 54, 72; A
4. G

5. B
6. H
7. D
8. H

page 165
1. 4 × 7; 2 × 2
2. 6 × 3; 2 × 3
3. 9 × 6; 3 × 3; 2 × 3
4. 6 × 6; 2 × 3; 2 × 3
5. 1, 2, 3, 5, 7, 11, 13, 17, 19, 23, 29

page 166
1. A
2. H
3. B
4. H
5. C
6. H
7. B
8. F
9. A

page 167
10. F
11. B
12. J
13. A
14. J
15. C
16. H
17. D
18. G
19. B

page 168
1. C
2. J
3. C
4. J

page 169
1. C
2. G
3. A
4. H
5. A
6. G

page 170
1. rotation
2. rotation

3. reflection
4. reflection
5. rotation
6. reflection

page 171
1. parallelogram
2. rectangle
3. trapezoid
4. square
5. parallelogram
6. quadrilateral
7. parallelogram
8. rectangle
9. trapezoid

page 172
1. B
2. F
3. C
4. F
5. B
6. H

page 173
1. B
2. J
3. D
4. J
5. D
6. G

page 174
1. B
2. J
3. C
4. J
5. A
6. G

page 175
Drawings will vary.

page 176
1. A
2. J
3. C
4. F
5. C

page 177
1. D
2. G
3. B
4. G
5. D

6. F

page 178
1, 6, 6, 0
0, 12, 8, 0
8, 5, 0, 0

Possible answers:
1. cube
2. rectangular prism
3. pyramid
4. cylinder

page 179
Drawings will vary.
Possible answers:
1. the trash can
2. a globe
3. a filing cabinet
4. a party hat
5. a tent
6. a building block

page 180
1. B
2. H
3. B
4. J
5. C
6. G
7. A
8. G

page 181
1. B
2. F
3. D
4. H
5. A
6. G
7. B
8. H

page 182
1. C
2. F
3. B
4. F
5. B

page 183
1. height = 4
length = 4
width = 1
16 cubic units

2. height = 2
length = 3
width = 4
24 cubic units

3. height = 3
length = 3
width = 2
18 cubic units

4. height = 3
length = 2
width = 2
12 cubic units

5. height = 2
length = 5
width = 2
20 cubic units

page 184
1. C
2. F
3. D
4. G
5. D
6. G
7. A
8. F

page 185
1. boat
2. picnic basket
3. acorn
4. frog
5. butterfly
6. fish
7. worm
8. lily pad
9. flower
10. bird
11. leaf
12. rock

page 186
1. B
2. J
3. B
4. G

5.

page 187

6. star

page 188
1. D
2. G
3. A
4. G
5. C
6. J
7. A

page 189
8. J
9. B
10. F
11. B
12. H
13. A
14. H

page 190
15. C
16. F
17. A
18. H
19. C
20. G
21. A

page 191
22. G
23. C
24. G
25. D

26. F
27. B
28. G

page 192
1. b
2. a
3. d
4. e
5. c
6. c
7. e
8. a
9. d
10. b
11. d
12. c
13. a
14. b

page 193
1. D
2. F
3. D
4. G
5. D
6. G

page 194
1. D
2. G
3. C
4. H
5. A
6. H
7. C
8. J

page 195
1. C
2. F
3. D
4. G
5. C
6. J

page 196
1. 21
2. 2
3. 2
4. 52,800
5. 5
6. 32
7. 56
8. 20

9. 9
10. 12
11. 6
12. 16
13. 3
14. 32

page 197
1. 32
2. 10
3. 240
4. 2
5. 12,000
6. 4
7. 72
8. 29,000
9. 12
10. 2; 76
11. 890
12. 15,049

page 198
1. B
2. H
3. D
4. J
5. A
6. J
7. C
8. F

page 199
1. C
2. F
3. D
4. J
5. D
6. G

page 200
1. B
2. J
3. B
4. F
5. C
6. J

page 201
1. D
2. G
3. A
4. J
5. C
6. G

page 202
1. D
2. J
3. D
4. F
5. B
6. G

page 203
1. D
2. G
3. C
4. J
5. A
6. G

page 204
1. A
2. G
3. D
4. F
5. C
6. H

page 205
1. A
2. J
3. B
4. H
5. C
6. J
7. A

page 206
1. D
2. G
3. B
4. F
5. A
6. G
7. B

page 207
8. H
9. A
10. F
11. C
12. G
13. A
14. J
15. B

page 208
1. Answers will vary.
Possible answer:

5 times for each number
2. Answers will vary. Possible answer: 15 times
3. Answers will vary. Possible answer: 15 times
4. Answers will vary.
5. Answers will vary.
6. Answers will vary.
7. Answers will vary.
8. Answers will vary.
9. Answers will vary.
10. Students should compare their results to the expected results.

page 209
1. C
2. H
3. D
4. G
5. B
6. F
7. A
8. J
9. D

page 210
1. B
2. F
3. C
4. G
5. B
6. F

page 211
1. C
2. F
3. B
4. J
5. D
6. H
7. B

page 212
1. A
2. H
3. D
4. G
5. B
6. J

page 213
1. D
2. G
3. A
4. G

page 214
1. D
2. H
3. B
4. G
5. A
6. $25 + 13 = \square$

page 215
1. A
2. J
3. D
4. J
5. C

page 216
1. D
2. G
3. A
4. F
5. D
6. J

page 217
1. C
2. G
3. $175 - 14$
4. B
5. H
6. B

page 218
1. B
2. H
3. A
4. J

page 219
1. C
2. G
3. A
4. G
5. D
6. H

page 220
1. C
2. G
3. D
4. H

page 221
Answers may vary.
Possible answers:
1. Divide $35.80 by 20.
2. Divide 184 by 8.
3. Subtract $25 from $47.82.
4. Divide 120 by 2.
5. Add $\frac{1}{2}$ and $\frac{1}{4}$.
6. Add 30 and 17.

page 222

1.

Line Graph
Heart Rate While Jogging

2.

Bar Graph
Heart Rate While Jogging

3. 20 minutes
4. from 0 to 5 minutes
5. from 15 to 20 minutes
6. from 20 to 25 minutes

page 223
1. 14
2. 29
3. Thursday
4. 100
5. Friday

page 224
1. D
2. G
3. A

page 225
1. B
2. F
3. B
4. F

5. C
6. J

page 226
1. C
2. J
3. C
4. F
5.

page 227
1. A
2. G
3. C
4. J
5. A
6. J

page 228
1. C
2. H
3. B
4. J
5. B
6. F

page 229
7. C
8. F
9. A
10. J
11. B

page 230
12. F
13. B
14. G
15. D
16. J
17. C
18. G

page 231

19. C
20. J
21. B
22. F
23. D
24. F
25. A

page 232
1. D
2. F
3. C
4. J
5. C
6. H
7. A
8. G

page 233
9. B
10. F
11. A
12. F
13. B
14. F
15. C
16. H

page 234
17. C
18. H
19. B
20. G
21. C
22. H
23. D

page 235
24. G
25. C
26. H
27. B
28. G
29. A
30. F

page 236
1. A
2. G
3. A
4. H
5. D
6. H
7. B

8. H
9. C
10. F

page 237
11. B
12. H
13. C
14. G
15. A
16. F
17. B
18. H
19. D
20. F

page 238
1. C
2. G
3. D
4. J
5. B
6. F
7. A

page 239
8. J
9. B
10. G
11. B
12.

page 240
1. B
2. H
3. C
4. G
5. C
6. H
7. C

page 241
8. J
9. D
10. F
11. A

12. H

page 242
1. B
2. F
3. C
4. J
5. B
6. G

page 243
7. A
8. J
9. C
10. G
11. C
12. F

page 244
13. D
14. F
15. C
16. G
17. A
18. G

page 245
19. C
20. J
21. D
22. G
23. B
24. J
25. D

page 246
26. F
27. B
28. F
29. B
30. J